New Ways for Managing
Global Financial Risks

New Ways for Managing
Global Financial Risks

The Next Generation

Michael Hyman

John Wiley & Sons, Ltd

Other Wiley Editorial Offices

John Wiley & Sons Inc., 111 River Street, Hoboken, NJ 07030, USA

Jossey-Bass, 989 Market Street, San Francisco, CA 94103-1741, USA

Wiley-VCH Verlag GmbH, Boschstr. 12, D-69469 Weinheim, Germany

John Wiley & Sons Australia Ltd, 42 McDougall Street, Milton, Queensland 4064, Australia

John Wiley & Sons (Asia) Pte Ltd, 2 Clementi Loop #02-01, Jin Xing Distripark, Singapore 129809

John Wiley & Sons Canada Ltd, 22 Worcester Road, Etobicoke, Ontario, Canada M9W 1L1

Wiley also publishes its books in a variety of electronic formats. Some content that appears
in print may not be available in electronic books.

Library of Congress Cataloguing-in-Publication Data

Hyman, Michael H.
   New ways for managing global financial risks, the next generation / Michael Hyman.
     p. cm.
   Includes bibliographical references and index.
   ISBN 13 978-0-470-01288-8 (cloth)
   ISBN 10 0-470-01288-9 (cloth)
   1. Financial futures.   2. Risk management.   3. Globalization—Economic aspects.   I. Title.
   HG6024.3.H96   2006
   658.15′5—dc22

                                                2005020015

British Library Cataloguing in Publication Data

A catalogue record for this book is available from the British Library

ISBN 13 978-0-470-01288-8 (HB)
ISBN 10 0-470-01288-9 (HB)

Typeset in 10/12pt Times by TechBooks, New Delhi, India
Printed and bound in Great Britain by Antony Rowe Ltd, Chippenham, Wiltshire
This book is printed on acid-free paper responsibly manufactured from sustainable forestry
in which at least two trees are planted for each one used for paper production.

For Carolyn

Contents

Acknowledgements

I have so many people to thank, particularly those who stood by me, offered advice, ideas and, most importantly, support when the going got really rough: Al and Pat Gribben, Peter and Shellie Maconie, Professor Roger Nagel, Keith Krenz, Guy Coughlan, Arthur Bass, Bobby Mbom, Nick Golden, Karl Hennessy, Harvey Shapiro, Professor Jim Cash, Professor Clayton Christensen, Professor Ben Shapiro, Morley Speed, George Stuart-Clarke, Nick Adams, Hugh Holloway, Kathleen O'Donovan, Alan Parker, Professor Eli Talmor, Professor Paul Embrechts, Keith Bradley, my parents-in-law, Neville and Valerie Velkes and, most importantly, my wife, Carolyn and children, Aidan, Erin and Benjamin. Thank you for standing by me.

Acknowledgements

Introduction

Once upon a time I was a global fixed-income money manager, investing in government bond markets worldwide. Being a global bond money manager was my core professional competence. But to get to a country's bond market that I thought made good investment sense, I had to incur foreign exchange risks. I never thought that currency risk was an asset class, but a means to an end, my end being the government bond markets. The last thing I ever wanted for my client was to see great bond investment performance wiped out by the associated currency risks. I used all the available derivative instruments to manage currency risks in many and various ways – forward foreign exchange agreements, futures and swaps to lay off risk, options to mitigate or play with risk – all at considerable expense. Sometimes they did hedge the global financial risks, but often they failed to perform in the way I had hoped.

I recognized that the management of global risks would become a growth area in the financial services industry and that the existing practice of using derivative instruments was in need of improvement. With the globalization of business around the world, more and more companies are doing business with each other, but as a result they are also incurring greater global financial risks. Corporates have currency transaction and translation risks, and if they are manufacturers they have hard commodity price risks. Insurance companies are in the business of selling insurance products, but at the same time they have assets, capital reserves and premiums received that must be invested in such a way as to ensure that they meet all of their liabilities to their policyholders. Non-life companies must invest their assets in a different way than life insurance companies because the liability of life insurance is a long-term risk, although non-life policies have long-term risks as well. Investing these assets, even with the most knowledgeable actuaries employed by the insurance companies, is not a core competency for many insurance companies. Traditionally, insurance companies have been allowed to buy and hold their investment portfolio without marking-to-market their investment values but accounting them at book or value. However, insurance company regulations have been changing throughout the world, forcing insurance companies to mark-to-market their investment portfolios. The new risk-based capital reserving is causing many insurance companies to rethink the way they manage their investment portfolios. Pension fund schemes are also finding themselves in a peculiar position, with huge deficits between the assets that pensioners and corporate sponsors set aside for their pensioners' retirement. The way pension funds invest their assets and manage the relative risk between assets and liabilities must change. The investment management aspects of pension fund schemes will have to dramatically change to ensure that assets meet pensioner liabilities into the future. Most of these risks are not core to any business, whether manufacturing or financial services.

I have seen enough financial catastrophes; some were due to mismanaging the hedging of global financial risks or the misuse of derivative instruments, causing large-scale financial losses, intended or unintended. New models for managing capital market price volatility were being introduced, such as value-at-risk, which focused investors' and risk managers' minds on the actual capital market risks that any single institution is underwriting on any given day. But one of my main preoccupations was the damage that derivative instruments could do in the wrong hands: they are strictly for the use of professionals, the risk managers in the financial sector, and not for those whose risks they are designed to limit! Furthermore, global financial risks were being concentrated in the hands of fewer and fewer banking institutions.

While I was thinking about all of this I heard a speech by Alan Greenspan, Chairman of the Federal Reserve Board in the United States, on 14 April 2000. He talked about the need for the private sector to come up with new ways for bundling and unbundling global financial risks and the need to invent a new business process in which global financial risks can be transferred in a more cost-effective, hedge-efficient, transparent and counterparty-diversified manner. It was like a call to arms, and it sent me on a journey that still continues in early 2005, the product of which is the subject of this book. The Greenspan speech was my mandate to create something new and innovative that would allow non-professionals to bundle up their non-core global financial risks into a single hedging instrument, and to develop a new business process which would allow those bundled risks to be transferred to the professional risk-taking institutions in a more cost-efficient, hedge-effective and transparent manner.

THE JOURNEY

The journey to develop new and innovative ideas for managing global financial risks has been long and arduous – never did I expect it to take more than four years. The original business plan took nearly a year to develop with the help of Professor Roger Nagel, a professor at Lehigh University. We spent hundreds of hours together talking through the many ideas that I had running through my mind about the new financial solution needed by the market. He helped to organize my thoughts, and opened doors for us to talk to many people in industry. Professor Nagel, who became a good friend during our work together, was a computer scientist; he introduced me to many senior executives at IBM, because we knew that the solutions for the next generation of risk management instrument would require technology to deliver them through the Internet, as would the development of the reverse auction technical platform that would be needed. At this point we were looking at an enormous and daunting start-up project.

In July 2000, I telephoned an old friend, Guy Coughlan, head of asset–liability advisory and risk management at JP Morgan, whom I knew from my money management days. He introduced me to value-at-risk (VaR) modelling and installed the RiskMetrics VaR software systems for my money management firm in 1995, before JP Morgan spun off RiskMetrics into the premier risk management software company it is today.

As the business plan was finalized in May 2001, Professor Nagel introduced me to Keith Krenz, the CEO and founder of a supply chain software company, who was looking for a new venture to get involved in. Keith joined me to help roll out the business plan from June 2001. As the dot.bomb stock market sell-off of Internet technology stocks gained ground in mid-2000, we were not very concerned because our view was that Internet technology was a means to an end, not the end itself. I never invested in any Internet-related stocks throughout the late 1990s.

Keith and I visited many financial institutions and were introduced to the Chase investment bank through colleagues in London, where we met Nick John. Nick led a team in the US which would introduce and steer third party companies through the Chase banking organization as we developed a business relationship with them. We were looking for a test bed in which to offer our concept transaction to risk-limiter client institutions such as corporates, insurance companies or pension funds. And on the other side of the transaction we sought risk-taking institutions to bid for the client risks through a reverse, or Dutch, auction.

When starting a new company there comes a point in time when someone has to take a leap of faith and be their first customer. That first customer will be keen on innovation, willing to try something new, and has to believe in the company. Our first customer was Nick John. He gave us the opportunity to launch our first client transaction through Chase Investor Services, the global custodian bank.

We were due to try a pilot transaction in October 2001. *Risk* magazine was hosting a conference at Windows on the World at the top of the World Trade Center a few weeks before, on 11 September. The conference was on the technology that the financial services industry would need to develop in the years to come. I was registered to be there, as was Nick John.

As I gathered my belongings from my desk in Allentown, Pennsylvania, at 8:30 a.m., to head for the bus to New York City, I saw the first plane hit the north tower of the World Trade Center. The world changed for all of us that day. Later I was shocked and deeply saddened to learn that Nick John was among those who had perished.

The Enron and WorldCom debacles soon followed; the global economy and financial environment were as bad as I had ever known. Many described those years as the greatest economic slump since the great depression that started in 1929 with the stock market crash. Could the events of recent times – the 2000 dot-com stock market sell-off, the attacks of 11 September 2001, the Enron and WorldCom debacles and the war on terrorism – lead to another great depression? I felt that my new solutions were needed more than ever, and that the new and forthcoming regulatory regime meant that now was the right time to introduce them, but I wondered who in the world would back an innovative new financial company at this time.

In the aftermath of 11 September, Enron, WorldCom, Tyco and the associated financial disruption to the global economy and system, in late 2002 we gave up looking for financial backing and concentrated on looking for our first client. During 2002, the global economy came to a screeching halt as economic growth of the 1990s turned into an economic recession, with some commentators talking about a 1930s style depression. The reader may recall that in the United States the largest 1000 companies had to recertify their annual reports and accounts in an effort to flush out any other WorldCom, Enron and Tyco financial irregularities. No one was talking about new business developments, and the telecoms industry collapsed as the Internet industry as a whole fell from grace.

I travelled to London regularly to see how the City was recovering from what I described as 'the perfect storm' of the past three years. But finally in spring 2003, I felt that the London market was in business again and slowly returning to normal. I moved back to London in July 2003 to start the company. Sadly, Keith had to remain in Pennsylvania. We had started the company in the United States but scrapped it when I returned to London and incorporated Global Financial Risk Solutions in December 2003.

THE ART OF SOLUTION SELLING

When selling a solution, one must understand not only the buyer's needs, issues and concerns but also the buyer's problem. The problem may be obvious to an outsider, but the client may not be able to see the wood for the trees. Like a physician, the seller must listen to the problem as the client sees it, ask lots of questions, produce a diagnosis and prescribe an appropriate treatment.

The same is true for an institutional money manager and a financial engineer, listening to the client's problem with their non-core global financial risks and how they impact the client company. Listening is the key. As the reader will learn from this book, the way in which the large global banks offer solutions is through their massive sales forces. Global banks want to sell their financial solutions and instruments to clients who know what they want to do – these services are not designed for non-professionals. In stark contrast to global capital market professional traders, many client risk-limiters – chief financial officers, treasurers, pension fund trustees and managers – do not really have a working understanding of the management of the global financial risks for which they are responsible. They have had their university grounding in derivative instruments but do not really understand their characteristics and the way in which they behave in relation to the underlying cash risks.

I want the reader to feel comfortable in admitting that they are not professionally qualified to understand the management of global financial risks – there is nothing to be embarrassed about, the global capital markets are a very specialized place and only the most professionally qualified and astute succeed. There is a new and innovative way to manage global financial risks and I hope that this book provides you with the information and capability to explore these new solutions.

WHAT'S IN THIS BOOK?

The book begins with a discussion of the present and traditional capital markets pipeline, the way in which client institutions manage their global financial risk through their relationship banking institutions. Chapter 1 discusses the way in which global banking institutions sell financial products from cash assets and instruments to derivative instruments. It shows how they align their products with their clients, the consolidation taking place within the industry and their ability to underwrite global financial risks, today and into the future. It is important to appreciate that modern banking institutions have increased their proprietary trading operations, trading in the global capital markets for their own benefit and in conflict with their many institutional clients. Finally, Chapter 1 discusses how the changes being introduced by the new Basel II capital accord will affect banks and their clients.

Chapter 2 begins by discussing the many problems that non-core global financial risks cause for different kinds of businesses. It reviews the way in which many corporates are being impacted by their non-core global financial risks and the financial cost of those risks. It then looks at the problems faced by insurance companies and the way they manage their assets in investment strategies in an attempt to meet their insured liabilities. Finally, it discusses how pension funds try to manage the relationship between their assets and their ability to meet the pension liabilities.

Chapter 3 begins a discussion on the typical and traditional ways in which global financial risks are managed by corporates, insurance companies and pension funds – the status quo. This chapter discusses the many solutions that each industry sector uses to try to limit the impact of non-core global financial risks. An examination of the use of derivatives highlights the many moving parts of these instruments and why they so often go wrong: hedge deviation, correlation deviation, time decay on options and other issues are discussed. The last part of this chapter introduces the new corporate governance laws, the new accounting rules for hedging global financial risks, the new insurance regulations and Basel II risk-based regulatory capital rule introductions, which have a wide ranging impact on everyone trying to manage global financial risks.

New banking regulations, called Basel II, are going to be implemented, which I will talk about later in the book; these new regulations were moving towards a more risk-based capital requirement for banking institutions, and I felt that the new regulations would ultimately affect the way banks would do business with their institutional customers. However, due to the Enron, Tyco and WorldCom corporate scandals in 2001 and 2002, new corporate governance laws were introduced, requiring the introduction of generational new accounting standards for derivatives, coupled with new insurance company regulations moving towards a risk-based capital solvency system. All of these are helpful to developing an innovative new instrument that fits the new regulatory regime now in place. Introducing innovation at such a time is a bit frustrating, but it is needed more today than ever before.

Chapter 4 introduces the notion that the global capital markets are more volatile and unpredictable than general market theory leads us to believe and begins to discuss the variety of attributes and characteristics that the client risk-limiters want in the next-generation risk management instrument. These include set and forget budget assurance, cost efficiency for hedging global financial risks, hedge efficiency, bundling many financial risks into one instrument, market pricing versus traditional proprietary bank pricing for financial risks, more counterparty bidders for pricing the risks and, finally and perhaps most importantly, they want an easy-to-use and simple-to-understand instrument.

Chapter 5 lifts the lid on the next generation instrument, its characteristics and how it can be applied to many global financial risk problems faced by corporates, insurance companies and pension funds.

Chapters 6 and 7 conclude the book by introducing case studies on the new ways to manage global financial risks using the next generation instrument, and providing a summary of the key points made in the book.

I hope that the reader will gain a much better understanding of the way in which global banks and the global capital markets operate, of the shortcomings of derivative instruments, and of the management of global financial risks, and I hope that the solutions presented in this book will be of value.

1
The Traditional Capital Market Pipeline

The revolutionary idea that defines the boundary between modern times and the past is the mastery of risk: the notion that the future is more than a whim of the gods and that men and women are not passive before nature.

Peter L. Bernstein[1]

Global businesses bring global problems: distribution, marketing, quality control and – not least – finance.

This first chapter is about the fundamental problems that have arisen with the way the capital markets pipeline operates. For the purposes of this book, the phrase *capital markets pipeline* refers to the way in which global financial risk solutions are created, priced, distributed and underwritten between the risk-limiting counterparties such as corporates, insurance companies and pension fund investors or the institutional investment management firms acting on their behalf, and the risk-taking investment and commercial banking institutions, the global financial risk underwriters.

This book is about new ways of managing global financial risks, but before we talk about the new and innovative method, process and solutions, we must review the present system of risk mitigation in the global financial markets. The new method, process and solutions have been created because of the present traditional capital markets pipeline.

The traditional capital markets pipeline allows risk-limiter institutional clients to ask their relationship banks for risk-mitigation products such as futures and options contracts, swaps and forward foreign exchange agreements. A relationship bank is where an institutional client has an ongoing formal connection with the bank for lending facilities and credit lines for other banking services along with lines to their global capital markets teams who service the client for their risk mitigation needs and transactions. The salesperson at the relationship bank will suggest an off-the-shelf product or the client will seek a specific solution. The relationship bank will price the solution through the bank's proprietary traders based upon their valuation, credit and counterparty risk models. The client will have a credit line agreement with the relationship bank, enabling the latter to sell a given amount of a product to the former. If the risk-mitigation solution is not an over-the-counter product it can be resold to any other banking institution; otherwise the over-the-counter product must be sold back or settled with the originating relationship bank. There are six problems with the traditional capital markets pipeline, and we will review each of these in this chapter.

Corporations, insurance companies and pension funds have financial needs which include borrowing money, financial transactions, making investments and hedging the unforeseen price volatility on their non-core global financial risks. For example, corporations have currency risks and interest rate risks when they borrow money; manufacturers may have to purchase hard commodities; insurance companies have investments in equity and bond portfolios used as reserves to meet their insurance liabilities; and pension funds have investments similar to

---

[1] Peter L. Bernstein (1996) *Against the Gods*. New York: John Wiley & Sons, Inc., p. 1.

those of insurance companies, perhaps riskier as they use their assets to meet future pension fund liabilities. Insurance companies and pension funds may also have large foreign currency exposures as part of their business or as part of their overseas investments.

All three industry sectors are exposed to unforeseen price volatility arising from non-core global financial risk, which they must do their best to try to manage. To do so they must borrow money or transact in the currency market as part of their core business. This would seem to require management to have a dual focus on selling their core product and on running a foreign exchange operation. It is unrealistic to expect them to be able to do this with the necessary competence.

The job of managing global financial risk is not easy; it requires a great deal of hard work, patience and talent. This is why corporations use their commercial bank and investment banking relationships to seek solutions for managing or hedging their global financial risks. The institutional client relies upon the banking institution for the best solution, the best available price as well as the underwriting capacity for handling their global financial risks.

THE STATE OF THE GLOBAL BANKING SYSTEM – THE PROBLEMS

We begin our journey with an exploration of the reasons why the pipeline from the client risk-limiter (the manufacturing or service corporation, insurance group or pension fund) to the commercial banking and investment banking risk-taker is not working efficiently or effectively. It does not provide the solutions, pricing and underwriting capacity required by clients seeking to limit risk. Most large banking institutions seek to do business with institutional clients who know what they want to do versus those who do not know how to go about managing their global financial risks. The discussion throughout this book will be focused on the method, process and solutions that are offered to institutional risk-limiters and the way the commercial and investment banks provide and process those instruments and solutions. We will discuss six key problems with the old bank pipeline system which moves the global financial risks from the institutional client risk-limiter to the bank risk-takers.

Traditional banking industry organization

The first problem has to do with the *traditional organization of the banking industry*. The way in which global financial risk passes from the client risk-limiter to a risk-taking bank is what we will term *the traditional pipeline*.

There are two types of financial institution: the commercial banks and the investment banks. Most commercial banks rely upon fee revenue for their profits, whilst the investment banks rely on a combination of fee revenue and trading revenue. Trading revenue is derived from the buying and selling of equities, bonds, currencies and commodities, along with other hybrid products, and realizing a capital gain from that activity. Fee revenue is derived from selling a product or a service to the client and generating a percentage fee from the transaction. Banking institutions which rely upon fee revenue will obviously want their clients to take as many of their products and services as they can, generating as much fee revenue as possible.

But there is a growing problem with both of these types of banking institution. Those relying on fee revenue are bundling more and more products and services together in an attempt to hang on to their clients. In so doing they are seeing rapidly diminishing marginal returns from each component of the bundle, even to the point of losing money on some products and services in an effort to profit from others. Many commercial banks are now looking at each client, and at the individual products and services being offered to them, and deciding that, if a client were to move one of the profitable products or services to another banking institution and the profitability of the relationship were compromised, they would cut off that client from the other bundled products and services being offered to them. Therefore, the client must accept the entire bundle of products and services offered by the commercial bank or seek a new bank.

The profit margin on bundling of product and services for their clients is going to fall further:

> Sir John Bond, chairman of HSBC, warned . . . of a global price war in the banking sector as the world's biggest banks use their growing surplus capital to undercut their rivals.[2]

As a result, banks which rely upon fee revenue as their sole or majority revenue source may find themselves seeking other banking operations for revenue sourcing.

As for the investment banks, which rely upon trading the global financial markets for their profits, these institutions are in competition with institutional money managers. They have investment or market positions that they want or do not want and will tell their client anything to either unload or accumulate those market positions. But what about the corporate, insurance company or pension fund client that is not professionally equipped or does not have the acumen to go head-to-head with the professional bank trader? They lose time and time again. Investment banks have a dual conflict, they are traditionally proprietary traders, competing with many of their clients as well as trying to generate fees, falling into the same trap as commercial banks. Therein lies the first problem of our old pipeline system.

This pressure is exacerbated by the simple fact that non-core global financial risks are often being managed by salaried employees and not professional risk-takers. In the opinion of one Fortune 50 executive: 'It is not reasonable to expect that my salaried employees can consistently outperform professional risk-takers whose livelihood depends on their market performance. Therefore, I cannot afford the equivalent of gaming to impact the core performance of my business which so many have worked so hard to achieve.' There are many stories of companies suffering significant losses as a result of their inexperience in these areas.

Product alignment

The second problem has to do with *product alignment* and the way banks behave towards their customers. A client risk-limiter has a problem which they need their commercial or investment bank to solve; the solution is provided by the relevant product department or silo of the bank. If the client's problem is related to currency risk, the currency sales and trading team will offer them a solution; the same is true for fixed income, equity and hard commodity. Unfortunately, however, the solution that each silo provides is an off-the-shelf standard product. If they were a shoe shop, they would offer, say, sizes 6, 7 and 8 in black or white. If a client wants size $6^{1}/_{2}$ in red, they do not have it and cannot order it – but they will try not to let the client leave the shop without a new pair of shoes!

Another problem lies in the way commercial and investment banks reward their sales forces. Banks' financial incentives programmes for product salespeople pay them to sell fast and furiously, in volume. Therefore, if the client's problem cannot be matched with a solution that a bank has on its shelf, the salespeople give up and move on to the next client. The salespeople's incentives force them to sell a product, earn their commission and move on to the next client, not caring about historic sales, but always focusing on where their next commission is coming from. Salespeople do not listen to their clients' problems; they are always selling, selling, selling.

---

[2] 'HSBC chairman warns price war looms for world's banks', *Financial Times*, 3 August 2004, p. 1.

For example, one insurance company went to six banking institutions seeking a solution to a regulatory capital problem. They were offered one or two inappropriate off-the-shelf products, and so their problem remained unsolved. A solution does exist for this insurance company, but it requires a bespoke product, and none of their bankers took the time to listen to and think about the insurance company's problem.

Another corporate client thought they had an emerging market currency problem and were sold a currency swap solution. In fact their problem was not a currency problem but an inflation-linked hedging problem. They were sold a very expensive currency swap . The company knew it was the wrong product but bought it because they had no other solution. Their bankers were not aware of their problem – they did not listen. Otherwise they would have created a solution tailored to the client's needs, because such a solution does exist.

Bank consolidations

The third problem with the old pipeline has to do with *bank consolidations*. These are having an enormous effect on bank behaviour, both externally and internally. Bank industry consolidation affects the way they treat and work with their institutional clients, as well as the way managers themselves behave.

Bank consolidation is necessary throughout the world and will continue. It creates greater pools of liquidity in which to raise capital generally and in various parts of the world, such as Europe. The introduction of the euro has helped integrate Europe, but within the context of the financial markets' integration, because exchange rate risks were eliminated, domestic government bond markets had to be integrated, bank lending would now be in a single currency, the euro, rather than in the individual domestic currencies. Bank consolidation with the ability to create large pools of liquidity was needed to ensure the success of European financial integration.

According to industry analysts there are four economic forces driving bank consolidations. The first is economies of scale: the ability to generate more profit per client as a merged company. The second is economies of scope, which Simon Kwan, Vice President, Financial Research at the Global Association of Risk Professionals, describes as a situation where the joint costs of producing two complementary outputs are less than the combined costs of producing the two outputs separately.[3] The third economic force Kwan describes is the potential for risk diversification. Geographic expansion would provide diversification benefits to a banking organization, not only reducing its portfolio risk on the asset side, but also lowering its funding risk on the liability side, as it spreads funding activities over larger geographic areas. The fourth economic force involves the personal management incentives that are offered by a merger or acquisition, creating a larger and more profitable banking institution.

One significant issue arising from bank consolidations was voiced to me by institutional clients of a major European bank going through a very difficult merger; they complained that both banking institution management teams were focused on the bank merger deal and most importantly on their ability to personally survive the bank consolidation process. The survival process trickles down to every individual throughout both banks, which causes enormous personal anxiety. This ultimately impacts the institutional client. Many senior and middle executives discover fairly quickly who is winning and losing in the internal corporate struggle,

---

[3] Simon Kwan, 'Industry Risk – Mega banks Pose System Risks' Global Association Of Risk Professionals, *Risk News*, 18 June 2004.

Table 1.1 Largest banks by market capitalization, July 2004

Company	Market capitalization ($ billions)
Citigroup	243
JP Morgan Chase & Co (Bank One)	132
Bank of America	170
HSBC Holdings	163
Royal Bank of Scotland	95
Wells Fargo	86
UBS	86
Wachovia	61
Barclays	57
Mitsubishi Tokyo Financial Group	57

curricula vitae are quickly updated, interviews arranged, departures are swift and numerous – and ultimately it is the clients who pays.

Another issue that drives bank consolidations is institutional client needs for greater amounts and differing structures of capital for mergers and acquisitions and other business activities. One of the reasons why investment banks were bought up by large commercial banks was that the former have the professional acumen to advise their corporate clients on the best strategy for a merger or acquisition, but often the company that seeks a merger or acquisition will require vast funding to take over the target company. Their funding needs include both short-term and long-term structures of capital; investment banks do not have the deep pools of liquidity or capital that the commercial banks have, with their funding capabilities and balance sheets. There is an enormous difference in size between the megabanks and the rest. The top five banks in each silo category, such as mergers and acquisitions, bond issuance, IPOs, equity trading, etc., capture, on average, 80% of that silo's market share. Thus, a bank that is not one of the top five will struggle to compete with the major megabanks. Table 1.1 lists the largest banks by market capitalization,[4] while Table 1.2 shows the top ten in terms of assets.[5]

The largest companies in the world will have no choice but to migrate to the largest banking institutions that are able to look after their total banking needs. The middle-tier banks and mid-capitalized companies will be left wanting. Two excellent examples of banks being left out in the cold are Credit Suisse First Boston (CSFB) and Deutsche Bank, whose management strategies have been extensively reported in the press. CSFB has seen its co-Chief Executive, John Mack, depart from the bank because he was unable to realize his ambition to make it one of the top five investment banks in mergers and acquisitions by merging with a large US bank. According to the *Financial Times*:

> Sources close to CSFB said, 'He [Mr Mack] believed this industry is consolidating and you don't want to be a fast follower. John's view is that we have to take the business to the next step . . .'Mr Mack thought consolidation was the best course for the bank to take to compete with the growing giants such as Citigroup and JP Morgan.[6]

The Board at CSFB disagreed, wanting the bank to remain independent, and Mr Mack resigned.

Deutsche Bank considered joining forces with Citigroup, becoming the European arm of what would have been the largest financial services organization in the world. The *Wall Street*

---

[4] From *The Banker*, 2 July 2004. I have combined the figures for the merged JP Morgan and Bank One.
[5] Ibid.
[6] 'Gentlemanly words as co-chief bows out,' *Financial Times*, 25 June 2004, p. 29.

Table 1.2   The largest banks by assets, June 2004

Company	Total assets ($ billions)
Mizuho Financial Group	1285
Citigroup	1264
UBS	1120
Credit Agricole Group	1105
Deutsche Bank	1104
HSBC Group	1034
BNP Paribas	986
Mitsubishi Tokyo Financial Group	974
Sumitomo Mitsui Financial Group	950
Royal Bank of Scotland	806

Journal reported that 'Deutsche wasn't big enough to compete with US titans such as Citigroup and the pending combination of JP Morgan Chase & Co and Bank One Corp.'[7] In early February 2004, Chief Executive Josef Ackerman 'thought he had a solution for the future of Germany's biggest banks: join forces with Citigroup Inc.' Unfortunately, Mr Ackerman argued his point 'to key members of the bank's supervisory board. But the board members balked at the prospect of Germany's only heavyweight international bank falling into foreign hands.'

Many European banks are facing similar problems to those of CSFB and Deutsche Bank, as the large US titans with huge capital and earnings are able to use their massive size advantage to place big bets in the global capital markets, use their large capital base to push into new markets and package more products and services into more competitive bundles for their institutional and retail clients. Recall Sir John Bond's observations, quoted earlier, concerning pressures from competition on profit margins from bundling products and services for all banking institutions.

The barriers to entry into the top five firms are all about capital, being able to capture market share, as well as an enormous IT financial commitment. A director of one of the major US investment banks told me that if an established banking institution is not in the top five for any single product or service silo and does not have the ability to invest billions of dollars in IT infrastructure, a newcomer does not have a chance. These established major banking institutions are investing billions of dollars in IT, and it is difficult for any newcomer to compete with budgets of that size.

A good example of the way in which technology costs and commitment have fragmented the banking industry is the consolidation of custody banking into a few major institutions. If one were to choose a custody bank, the only names that come to mind are Bank of New York, Northern Trust, State Street and JP Morgan. Interestingly, JP Morgan sold off its custody business to Bank of New York because they chose not to financially compete in this specific banking sector – but as a result of their merger with Chase, they are right back in as one of the leaders. The costs of maintaining and competing for custody banking business run into billions of dollars, and high trading volumes are required to generate low profit margins.

According to the *Wall Street Journal*,

Tight margins and high operating costs are forcing an increasing number of banks to effectively exit the foreign-exchange business. Rather than making markets in currencies themselves, these

---

[7] 'Deutsche Bank's Dilemma: Fight or Join U.S. Titans?' *Wall Street Journal*, 16 June 2004, p. 1.

banks are turning to bigger institutions, and distributing their prices and products. The practice, known as white labelling or liquidity outsourcing, isn't new; both UBS AG, of Switzerland, and Germany's Deutsche Bank AG have been offering the service for the past two years.[8]

So the megabanks are gaining and controlling more and more of the market share and liquidity of foreign exchange transactions, a process that will continue and expand into other mainstream product and service categories. More and more banks that are unable to vault into and maintain themselves in the top five will have to seek ways to be competitive and strive to find their own little niche.

A Standard & Poor's research paper[9] suggests that 'there is the beginning of a new trend afoot. In more concentrated markets, it would be natural to see more bundled products offered to clients'. The paper concludes that 'The consolidation has been most pronounced in wholesale banking, as formerly 12 to 15 money centre banks have consolidated into three independent banks. Such consolidation had resulted in large single-name exposures due to the dearth of banks downstream in the food chain to which to distribute the loans. Concentrations exacerbate the losses during credit down cycles like the one just ended. Having "got religion," these three large banks have modulated their businesses increasingly toward a model of pure intermediation – in other words, the investment banking model. Investment banking is, however, redefined to include syndicated lending. These three banks dominate syndicated lending, accounting for about 44% of volume of loans arranged. However, they have collectively reduced their balance sheet holdings of such loans by about $125 billion over the past two years – equivalent to at least several large banks' total loan portfolios. . . . At the same time, the big three banks have garnered an increasing share of the debt underwriting market and even of equity and advisory business, which has brought them into head-to-head competition with the investment banks.'

Bank consolidation is creating deeper pools of liquidity at some banking institutions; however, as seen from the numbers in the previous paragraph, there is diminishing liquidity in the overall liquidity pool.

However, there is a need for supermarket banking institutions with deep liquidity pools for medium or smaller companies as well. When I founded a money management firm, GH Asset Management Ltd, in London, one area of particular concern to me had to do with operational risks for the firm. Operational risks refer to anything that can go wrong with the operation of the money management firm, such as settlements errors, inputting the wrong number into a computer, and transferring monies between banks. One of my fundamental rules was to keep the number of moving parts of any transaction to a minimum; the more moving parts in a transaction, the more things that could go wrong and cost my firm enormous sums of money. For example, suppose I were to buy an overseas bond with one bank, buy and/or sell the foreign exchange needed to purchase the overseas bond with another bank and settle all of these transactions under one roof with my custodian banker – here there are too many inputs into my computer systems, too many instructions to various banks to wire monies from one place to another; in short, too many moving parts. As I mentioned earlier, my custodian bankers were JP Morgan; they could provide custody services and foreign exchange services, as well as bond dealing services. As there was little price competition between the major banks, I would effect my foreign exchange transaction with JP Morgan and if the JP Morgan bond dealers were price-competitive, I would purchase my bonds from them as well, reducing the enormity of my perceived operational risks. So there is a need for supermarket banking institutions and

---

[8] 'More banks are asking rivals to handle currency trading,' *Wall Street Journal*, 28 July 2004.
[9] Tanya Azarchs, 'The dark side of bank consolidation,' Standard & Poor's Rating Direct Report, 27 May 2004.

they have a role to play with clients of all kinds, which also makes my argument for entrants all the more difficult.

This problem brings us back to a point made earlier in this chapter. Tanya Azarchs concludes that the three large banks that formed from a dozen or so money centre banks are bundling more products and services together, driving the price of the bundled products and services downwards, which contributes to the pressure on investment banking fees, which, in turn, drives those who cannot compete with the large titan commercial banks into more proprietary trading. Proprietary trading creates an environment where greater risk-taking takes place, using regulatory capital to trade the global capital market versus reserving for fee-generating services. A bank is using its capital reserves to trade with investment and commercial banks' capital to generate its profits in addition to or instead of generating fee revenues, all of which hinders the institutional client relationship, because proprietary trading creates a conflict of interest between the bank and its client, and an increasing problem for the old capital market pipeline.

In conclusion on the third problem with the old banking system pipeline, the Federal Reserve Chairman, Alan Greenspan, gave the following testimony on the subject of bank consolidation and the state of the banking system before the US Senate Committee on Banking, Housing and Urban Affairs on 20 April 2004:

> Legislation designed to deregulate US banking markets, technology, and other factors have contributed to significant structural change in the banking industry and to a decline of 40 percent in the number of banking organizations since the mid-1980s, when industry consolidation began. Consolidation activity has slowed sharply in the past five years, but recent uptick in merger announcements, including a couple of very large transactions, may signal a return to a more rapid pace of bank merger activity. Since 1995, the ten largest US banking organizations have increased their share of domestic banking assets from 29 percent to 46 percent at year-end 2003. Yet, over the past decade, roughly 90 percent of bank mergers have involved a target with less than $1 billion in assets, and three-quarters have involved an acquiree with assets of less than $250 million.

Greenspan concludes by suggesting that

> this ongoing consolidation of the US banking industry has not, in my judgement, harmed overall competitiveness of our banking and financial markets.

I do not agree with Mr Greenspan's conclusions. I argue that bank consolidation is generating less product development, more off-the-shelf products and services, more pigeon-holing of clients by banks, less interest in providing the right solution for clients, and fewer bank counterparties for corporates, insurance companies and pension fund clients. There is less ability to seek out price competitiveness on products and services for global financial risk mitigation, as well as less of the financial underwriting capacity that is required by these institutional clients for risk mitigation. Finally, as most commercial or merchant banks cannot compete with the megabanks, they must turn to proprietary trading activities to generate profits, creating a conflict of client interests.

Global financial risk-underwriting capacity

The fourth problem with the old banking system pipeline concerns its ability to provide cost-efficient *underwriting capacity* for its clients' global financial risks. The present capacity in the global pipeline – the amount of capital (regulatory capital) that can be deployed for underwriting or buying the cash or derivative instruments that clients want to enable them to mitigate their institutional global financial risks – is cause for concern.

The value of derivative instruments depends on an underlying asset, which may be a currency price, a specific bond or equity, an index or a specific hard commodity. They come in various flavours. Futures contracts allow the purchaser to buy or sell an asset at a future date in time. Options contracts give the holder the right to buy or sell an asset at a specified price until a specified expiry date. Swap contracts are over-the-counter agreements to exchange a series of cash flows according to the prespecified terms of an interest rate, an exchange rate, an equity, a commodity price or any other index. They have limitations and are difficult to use, price and manage.

The number of banks within the banking system that want to buy or underwrite cash and derivative instruments is actually diminishing under the traditional bank pipeline system. In an article in *Risk* magazine in 2003, the US Office of the Comptroller of the Currency showed that seven banks in the US accounted for almost 96% of the total notional amount of derivatives in the commercial banking system: JP Morgan Chase, Bank One, Bank of America, Citibank, Wachovia Bank, HSBC and Wells Fargo.[10] JP Morgan Chase, for example, had $30.7 trillion (notional) of derivatives exposures, with only $622 billion in total assets. In second place, Bank of America had $13 trillion of total derivatives exposures with total assets of $574 billion. Citibank was in third place with $10.1 trillion in derivatives exposures and total assets of $515 billion. In a speech in Chicago reported in the same article, Alan Greenspan highlights his concerns about the impact that the decline in the number of major derivatives dealers will have for market liquidity and for the concentration of counterparty risk. He states that

> In each case, a single dealer seems to account for more than two thirds... when concentration reaches these kinds of levels, market participants need to consider the implications of exit by one or more leading dealers. Such an event could adversely affect the liquidity of types of derivatives that market participants rely upon for managing the risks of their core business functions.'[11]

A later article in the same magazine asks: 'What would happen if one of the world's largest investment banks pulled out of derivatives?[12] Need I say more? The ability to underwrite cash and derivative instruments and to provide the necessary financial liquidity to underwrite derivative instruments will be more and more difficult. Although Greenspan is in favour of further bank consolidation, he is concerned about the concentration of liquidity for derivative instruments and foreign exchange in fewer institutional hands. It is very easy to articulate the problem, to complain about the system, but what is the solution for a corporate, insurance company or pension fund, and who can provide it?

In addition, commercial bank credit lines rise and fall with the fortunes of the economy and their client company, and this does not provide the client company with the ability to manage their non-core global financial risks effectively. Businesses seek hedging instruments and the pricing of those instruments from their commercial and investment banking relationships, which may number from two to six institutions, depending upon the size of the client. In fact, as the business and economic cycle rises and falls, the demand for credit by the client risk-limiters will rise and fall as well. Competition within the banking industry is intense, and every bank wants to do business with the most creditworthy companies, although, as I pointed out earlier, there is a role for a megabank for medium and smaller companies. According to the *Financial Times*, corporate loan demand is tumbling and, what is of greater concern, so is the cost of borrowing for corporate borrowers: for A-rated firms the cost is a mere 22 basis points (0.22%) over the cost of money for the banks, and BBB firms pay only 56 basis

---

[10] 'Seven US banks have lion's share of derivatives,' *Risk*, July 2003.
[11] Ibid.
[12] 'The ultimate stress test: modelling the next liquidity crisis', *Risk*, November 2003.

points, down from 64 basis points in 1996.[13] Banking institutions are making less money from syndicated loans, from fewer customers and at a falling profit margin. The problem of diminishing marginal returns raises the issue for banks of finding alternative ways to generate profits – one of which is proprietary trading on the global capital markets.

The capacity that banks can provide for their client companies is limited at the best of times and, as Basel II comes into force in the coming years (see later in this chapter), they will be required to specify their client company risks as the banks' regulatory capital requirements. The specificity of those client risks will increase the regulatory capital required to be held by banks and will reduce the capacity for risk underwriting rather than creating a deeper pool of liquidity.

Derivative instruments themselves do not provide the effective hedging coverage one might expect; there are hedge deviations, correlation deviations and of course time value decay with options strategies that frustrate us all. There is counterparty risk when using over-the-counter products and pricing derivative instruments have become more commoditized or standardized, meaning fewer counterparties, less price competition and reduced capacity for the risk-taking underwriter. In Chapters 2 and 3 I will discuss the use of derivative instruments in greater detail.

When I first started researching this subject, I spent time with a Fortune 50 company in the United States, whose senior executives would complain that they did not have the necessary counterparty diversification to underwrite the entire amount of their currency risks; they accepted whatever price they were offered by the six banks with which they did business. They said they were desperate for counterparty diversification to enable them to increase their ability to mitigate their global financial risks, which included currencies and hard commodities. They wanted more banking institutions for the purposes of selling off more of their global financial risks, and they wanted greater price competition from their risks. They were able to hedge no more than 25–30% of their total currency risk exposures at any given time for this very reason. One would think that a major Fortune 50 manufacturer would not have to tolerate such a problem, but unfortunately the banking counterparties that this company used were the very largest, and it would have been very difficult to increase this company's ability to find greater amounts of underwriting capacity and price competition from the present banking pipeline. This problem is costing this company an unknown but large sum of money every year; they spend an enormous amount of money on hedge deviation using the traditional instruments, along with the unhedged sums facing the daily onslaught and price volatility of the global financial markets.

Proprietary trading

The fifth problem facing the old global banking system pipeline has to do with the fact that more and more traditional commercial banks are operating like investment banks and hedge funds, seeking to use *proprietary trading* and their own capital to trade the global financial markets. These banks are making an effort to achieve substantial total returns on investment. This bank activity causes greater conflicts of interest with their institutional clients because the banks are relying upon their proprietary trading as the means for generating profits, either in conjunction with, or instead of, the fees that are generated by their client products and services. As trading positions become more fundamental to the profitability of the bank, they will start to act in their own best interests rather than those of their clients and/or to use their client relationships as a mechanism to lay off their own proprietary trading positions. When times get difficult and the market environment is causing trading losses, desperate people do desperate things to

---

[13] 'Corporate Loan Demand Tumbles,' *Financial Times*, 21 June 2004.

get out of a bad market position; the bank will tell the client whatever is necessary to get the client to buy the bad market position from the bank. This is happening more and more, most recently in the Internet technology bubble of the late 1990s; when banks offered initial public offerings (IPOs) on behalf of new high-technology, Internet-related companies that wanted to raise new capital from the stock market, they issued new stock to their own clients, telling all sorts of stories to get them to buy the stock, when in fact the company had no revenue and no future hope for achieving profitability. But the hype of the Internet technology sector kept feeding the demand for these new stocks. The investment banks received enormous fees in the form of capital gains on the stock as the price rose dramatically.

Much has recently been made of the potential harm that banks may inflict upon themselves as they insist upon using their own trading activities to generate the high profits that shareholders have come to expect. These activities will not help the institutional client risk-limiter to find the right solution to mitigate their global financial risks.

A recent article in *The Economist* sums up the problem:

> The reason is simple: the size of banks' bets is rising rapidly. This is because returns have fallen as fast as markets have risen. Yields on corporate debt of all types, for example, have fallen dramatically, and commissions for all sorts of businesses have also dropped. So banks are having to bet more of their own money to continue generating huge profits. But the amount that they have put on the table in recent months has become worryingly large.[14]

The Economist is worried that 'big banks are in danger of turning into little more than hedge funds.'[15] It considers that 'Germany's biggest bank [Deutsche Bank] will soon be not much of a bank, unless it changes course.'[16] According to an article in the *Financial Times*, the proprietary trading operations of Citigroup in London accumulated losses of almost £1 billion in the wake of the 1998 Russian financial crisis. The parent company, Citigroup, had to inject $2 billion in order to maintain Salomon's capital position.[17]

According to the *Financial News* (27 September 2004) 'Morgan Stanley took a hit of as much as $1bn (€820m) in its proprietary trading business in the third quarter [of 2004], after it significantly increased its trading risk and big positions on interest rates, currencies, and commodities back-fired... The amount of risk taken on by Morgan Stanley, measured by Value at Risk, or VaR, a benchmark for the maximum risk a firm will take on, has increased almost 50% since a year ago, rising to $79m from $54m last year.... Most banks, including UBS, Deutsche Bank, SG and Credit Suisse First Boston have been increasing their trading risk.... The increase in risk has been accompanied by a number of big trading hits. Earlier this year, Deutsche Bank significantly cut its multi-billion dollar US convertible bond trading portfolio after suffering losses of $300m to $400m. Goldman Sachs took a $600m hit in equities in the second quarter.'

The stories are numerous, and proprietary trading is becoming a greater concern to many. It constitutes a clear conflict of interest between the banking institutions and their institutional clients.

One of the ways to monitor bank risk-taking is through the value-at-risk (VaR) model which 'determine[s] the amount of capital that banks must set aside against their trading positions, and purport[s] to show how many millions of dollars a bank might lose should the markets turn against it.' A full definition of VaR can be found in many places.[18] Value-at-risk is a

---

[14] 'Banks – the coming storm,' *The Economist*, 21 February 2004, p. 83.
[15] 'Trading wars,' *The Economist*, 28 August 2004, p. 13.
[16] 'Deutsche Bank: A giant hedge fund,' *The Economist*, 28 August 2004, p. 65.
[17] 'Capital markets arm of Citigroup in UK has accumulated losses of £960 million', *Financial Times*, 16 August 2004, p. 1.
[18] See, for example, 'VaR: Ready to Explode?', *Risk*, July 2004.

statistical technique that measures the probabilistic bound of market losses over a given period of time (the holding period) expressed in terms of a specific degree of certainty (the confidence interval). VaR is the worst-case loss expected over the holding period within the probability set out by the confidence interval. Larger losses are possible, but with a low probability. For example, a portfolio whose VaR is $20 million over a one-day holding period, with a 95% confidence interval, would have a 5% chance of suffering an overnight loss of greater than $20 million.

According to *The Economist* article cited earlier, 'markets have indeed become less volatile – volatility has halved at least in many markets in the past year and a half. Equity markets are now less volatile than they have been for almost a decade.'[19] The article continues: 'if markets are half as volatile, banks' positions can be twice as large for that same amount of capital.' In other words, if volatility is down, then VaR is lower for the same amount of capital at risk. The conclusion that one can draw is that banks are probably putting substantially more capital at risk.

The article in *Risk* magazine shows that most of the major banks have seen their VaR rise dramatically over the past year, emphasizing greater reliance on trading revenues for their profits. Table 1.3 shows how VaR has risen since 2002.[20] The table is a general representation of banks' trading positions and the market risks they are carrying. Each bank has its own unique market risk positions and one bank's market position may be radically different from another's. It is evident that there is trouble coming, with difficulties for the old bank system pipeline and for client risk-limiters that want to lay off or mitigate global financial risks. The client's relationship bank may have accumulated an enormous position in the risk that the client itself would like to mitigate, but because the bank has a similar position, the bank's price and underwriting capacity for their client risk may be greatly affected by their own market positions and risks.

The Securities and Exchange Commission (SEC) is introducing new rules aimed at bringing the broker-dealer institutions into line with the new capital requirements being established by the Basel Committee on Banking Supervision for internationally active banking institutions. According to *Risk* magazine,

> the [SEC's] greatest fear stems from a belief that highly geared proprietary trading activities that largely appear to have paid off last year ... may lead to some significant trading losses in 2004'.[21]

Many banks argue, however, that their large rise in capitalization in 2003 reflects their ability to take capital market risks, which is true when one looks at the statistics; market capitalization has risen more than the VaR amounts.

In a *Financial Times* article, cited earlier, Sir John Bond was quoted as warning 'that common risk management techniques raised the threat of sharp swings in capital markets, as financial institutions were taking similar investment decisions to one another, and many were highly geared. The risk of market disruption rises as financial institutions use increasingly similar technology to manage risk.'[22] There are a number of issues in Sir John's remarks, and we will return to them when I discuss market pricing versus traditional bank pricing for global financial risks in a later chapter. First of all, this comment stresses my point about the commoditization of pricing: banks will add a premium when pricing risks for which they have no appetite.

---

[19] 'Banks – the coming storm,' *The Economist*, 21 February 2004, p. 83.
[20] 'VaR: Ready to Explode?', *Risk*, July 2004.
[21] 'VaR: Ready to Explode?,' *Risk*, July 2004..
[22] 'HSBC chairman warns price war looms for world's banks', *Financial Times*, 3 August 2004, p. 1.

Table 1.3   Major banks' value-at-risk

Financial institution	2003 ($ million) VaR	2002 ($ million) VaR	Change in VaR (%)
UBS	104.7	70.7	48.0
JP Morgan Chase	103.2	64.6	59.8
Goldman Sachs	89.2	58.1	53.7
Citigroup	83.0	83.0	0.0
Deutsche Bank	75.4	34.5	118.2
Commerzbank	74.5	46.0	61.9
Morgan Stanley	58.0	53.0	9.4
Barclays	52.1	46.9	11.3
Merrill Lynch	50.0	32.9	51.9
Credit Suisse	46.9	41.4	13.4
Dresdner Bank	38.1	26.9	42.0
HSBC	31.9	22.6	41.1
West LB	30.9	25.6	20.7
Lehman Brothers	30.7	29.5	4.3
Societé Generale	30.1	27.3	10.6
ING	28.8	21.7	32.5
BNP Paribas	27.4	28.8	−5.0
Bank One	27.0	14.0	92.9
Bear Stearns	21.7	25.6	−15.5
Royal Bank of Scotland	18.6	19.1	−2.3
Wachovia	17.1	18.5	−7.7
Banca Intesa	13.1	10.5	24.6
HBOS	10.8	12.7	−14.4
Abbey	9.4	11.2	−16.1
Lloyds TSB Group	2.5	2.3	10.9
Average	43.0	33.1	25.8

Additionally, if a volatile event were to suddenly occur, banks would be moving in one direction: where does that leave the rest of us? Finally, taken together with his comments quoted earlier, Sir John is suggesting that diminishing marginal returns on the fee revenue side of bank operations are causing the global banks to take on greater amounts of proprietary trading risks for their source of revenue.

The *Financial Times* reported in September 2004 that

> Bosses of leading investment banks were ... warned of their personal responsibility for managing risks surrounding conflicts of interest and complex finance deals. ... Hector Sants, managing director of wholesale and institutional markets at the FSA, wrote to the bosses 'to remind you of your responsibility to implement appropriate processes and procedures for effective risk management of conflicts of interest and risks arising from financing transactions. Where your business profile gives rise to these risks, you should expect increasing scrutiny and challenge about current and developing practices from our supervisors in the coming months.'[23]

The point of highlighting this problem with the old bank pipeline is that corporations, insurance companies and pension fund risk-limiter customers will find it more difficult to find the appropriate solution, price and required capacity for underwriting their global financial risks because their relationship banks will have a growing conflict of interest between their capital market trading and the needs of their clients.

---

[23] 'FSA issues stern warning to bank bosses over conflicts of interest,' *Financial Times*, 25 September 2004, p. 2.

Basel II

The sixth problem affecting the old banking system pipeline is the *Basel II capital accord*. On 26 June 2004, the world's top central bankers put their seal of approval on the International Convergence of Capital Measurement and Capital Standards, more commonly known as Basel II, the new capital-adequacy framework for banks, intended to come into force in 2007. Basel II will have a significant impact on the way risk is transferred from the client risk-limiter to the banking system risk-takers. It offers a new set of standards for establishing minimum capital requirements for banking organizations. It was prepared by the Basel Committee on Banking Supervision, at the Bank of International Settlements (BIS), working with a group of central banks and bank supervisory authorities in the G-10 countries (The G-10 comprises 11 nations: the US, Japan, Germany, the UK, Italy, France, Canada, Sweden, Belgium, The Netherlands and Switzerland), which developed the original Basel capital accord standards in 1988.

According to the Global Association for Risk Professionals,[24] banks are required to maintain at least a minimum level of capital as a foundation for their future growth, but also, more importantly, to cushion against unexpected losses. The 1988 Basel capital accord originally defined the minimum requirement, dividing bank exposures into broad classes of borrowers. Regardless of the potential creditworthiness and risk of each borrower, all are subject to the same capital requirement. This capital requirement served its purpose but led to what is termed *moral hazard*, where banks could lend to any company and only be required to set aside the minimum capital requirement, whether that company were rated AAA or B.

The new Basel II capital accords differ and will have an impact on the way banks' client relationships develop over the longer term. The new framework is more reflective of the underlying risks in banking and provides stronger incentives for improved risk management. The new accord improves the capital framework's sensitivity to the risks that banks actually face. In a nutshell, the greater the risk, the greater the amount of regulatory capital that will need to be set aside. The accord introduces a new capital charge against operational risks which can occur internally within each banking system; banks will have to spend more money on IT investment to be able to manage their operational risks better.

The goal of the new Basel II capital accord is to promote the adequate capitalization of banks and to encourage improvements in risk management, thereby strengthening the stability of the financial system. There are three pillars to the agreement. Pillar 1 revises the 1988 accord's guidelines by aligning the minimum capital requirements more closely to each bank's actual risk of economic loss. Pillar 2 recognizes the necessity of exercising effective supervisory review of banks' internal assessments of their overall risks to ensure that bank management is exercising sound judgement and has set aside adequate capital for these risks. Pillar 3 leverages the ability of market discipline to motivate management by enhancing the degree of transparency in banks' public reporting.

There are problems; implementing these new practices will impose a huge burden, both in terms of management focus until they come into effect and ultimately in financial terms. Furthermore, once the new standards are in place, banks will have to adjust the regulatory capital that they set aside for each of their institutional clients, so they are bound to look even more carefully at the cost of doing business with these clients. Earlier in this chapter I discussed the problem of falling profit margins when banks bundle their products and services into one institutional client; from 2007, there will be an additional capital charge if those clients are less creditworthy than the minimum charges in effect today.

---

[24] *Basel II for Dummies*, Global Association for Risk Professionals, 28 June 2004.

In an article on the impact of Basel II on Japanese banks, JP Morgan concluded that the new accord would have a negative impact on Japan.

> We [JP Morgan] believe that banks [in Japan] are unlikely to extend the duration of their bond portfolios, as they did in 2003, but are likely to increase their hedge ratios for new fixed rate loans, including housing loans for individuals. [25]

One small change in a bank's asset profile due to regulatory changes causes a domino effect through one's economy, affecting, in this case, many large banks around the world.

A recent study conducted by FT Research and published in *The Banker* examined how banks are approaching the implementation of Basel II.[26] The key findings are as follows:

- European banks are further ahead than their US and Asian counterparts.
- Most banks expect significant organizational and corporate governance changes to result from a combination of Basel II and other initiatives (e.g., Sarbanes–Oxley).
- Basel II is expected to significantly affect the competitive landscape, with increased competition in retail lending, and shake-outs in corporate lending, specialized lending and emerging markets.
- Banks see substantial benefit from a more economically rational allocation of capital and more robust risk-based pricing as a result of Basel II.
- Planned spending on Basel II seems lower than documented in previous studies as banks seek to ensure maximum reuse of existing systems and look to adopt more centralized solutions where new systems are required.
- While IT infrastructure and resources are the major costs, many programmes in the US and Asia appear to lack sufficient IT involvement.
- Over 75% of European, North American and Australian banks are targeting an Internal Ratings Based (IRB) solution for credit risk by 2007, with a similar figure targeting IRB-advanced by 2010. The new IRB approach allows banks to use internal bank credit models in which those calculations are used to determine the final capital reserve calculation.
- Short-term ambitions for operational risk are more modest – less than half of the banks surveyed are targeting Advanced Measurement Approach (AMA) by 2007, although this rises to 70% by 2010. The AMA allows banks to use their own method for assessing their exposure to operational risk. Operational risk is defined as the risk of losses resulting from inadequate or failed internal processes, people and systems, or external events.
- Significant work remains to be done to satisfy the requirements of Pillars 2 and 3, with commensurate changes to capital management and investor communication strategies.

Basel II has a long way to go before it is implemented in 2007. Many banking institutions are preparing for its introduction. It will have an impact on banking relationships, although this does not seem to worry many corporate executives.

According to the *Financial Times*, daily currency turnover averaged about $1.9 trillion in autumn 2004.[27] If we assume a 200 business day year, then annual turnover is about $380 trillion. The top ten banks by foreign exchange transactions are shown in Table 1.4.[28] These top ten banking institutions manage, on average, 63.99% of all foreign exchange turnover, or $153.576 trillion per year. The top ten banks in Table 1.4 have a total of $866 billion of

---

[25] 'Impact of new BIS standards on Japanese banks' in *Japan Markets Outlook and Strategy*, JP Morgan Securities Asia, 28 July 2004.

[26] 'Reality check on Basel II', *The Banker*, 1 July 2004.

[27] 'World foreign exchange trading soars to peak of $1,900bn a day,' *Financial Times*, 29 September 2004, p. 1.

[28] Ibid.

Table 1.4   The largest banks by foreign exchange transactions

Bank	Proportion of overall volume (%)	Market capitalization ($ billion)	Total assets ($ billion)
UBS	12.36	86	1120
Deutsche Bank	12.18	46	1014
Citigroup	9.37	243	1264
JP Morgan[a]	5.76	132	770
HSBC Holdings	4.89	163	1034
Goldman Sachs[b]	4.54	21	403
Barclays	4.08	57	791
CSFB	3.79	42	777
RBS	3.51	95	806
Merrill Lynch[c]	3.49	27	494

[a] Market capitalization and total assets do not include Bank One.
[b] Market capitalization and total assets are from Goldman Sachs Report & Accounts 2003.
[c] Market capitalization and total assets are from Merrill Lynch Report & Accounts 2003.

market capitalization, along with $8.473 trillion in total assets. If you live anywhere near London, England, you will be familiar with a motorway called the M25. Near the Chertsey exit, the motorway goes from four lanes into three, lanes and then back to four lanes. As the four lanes merge into three the traffic slows dramatically; it takes ages to pass through the Chertsey exit before picking up speed. This is exactly what is happening with the foreign exchange markets: on average, $1.9 trillion tries to flow every day through a pipeline constituted by only ten major banking institutions, with no more than $866 billion in market capitalization – this particular motorway probably needs to be widened to eight lanes just to cope with existing capacity, let alone future growth. And we have neglected to consider here the derivative instrument volumes introduced earlier in this chapter: 96% of all the total notional amount of derivatives flows through six banking institutions, $53.8 trillion through three banks. There is, and will continue to be, a problem with the old banking pipeline, and there has to be a better way that allows the risk-limiters to manage their risks efficiently, cost-effectively, and in a more transparent, counterparty-diversified manner. We will discuss such a solution in a later chapter.

CONCLUSION

Let us review what we have learned about the traditional capital market pipeline. Banking institutions are either trading-revenue driven or fee-revenue driven, although more and more banks are starting up or increasing their proprietary trading operations. The way these banking institutions align their product offerings to their institutional clients is through product silos, currency, commodity, equity and fixed-income, along with the standard exchange-traded products and over-the-counter products, although these will differ from bank to bank. Bank consolidation is causing difficulties for some, particularly if you are employed by, or a client of, the acquired bank. Bank consolidation is creating large pools of liquidity for the top five global banking institutions, to enable them to provide the complete financial package for the very largest companies in the world. Additionally, these larger banks are purchasing regional and local banks to develop and build their asset base, as well as to be able to distribute retail product. But what about the other 995 banking institutions in the top 1000? They offer the same products and services as the top five but do not have the capital base to compete with them directly. It is up to them to find their niche.

However, we have learned that the banking industry is underwriting less risk as a whole than in preconsolidation days. The move toward proprietary trading by many banking institutions is gathering pace, losses are occurring, warnings have been issued by industry leaders and regulators. Soon the new Basel II capital accords will have a significant impact on the banking industry; although risk-based regulatory capital is the correct way to move forward, the impact on the banks and their client relationships may be significant.

The six problems outlined in this chapter represent a hindrance for corporates, insurance companies and pension funds in solving their global financial risk management problems. The banking counterparties do not appear interested in offering them relevant, tailor-made solutions or sufficient underwriting capacity. Against this background, I will discuss in the next chapter the various major global financial risks that risk-limiter institutions must deal with every day.

2
The Problem – Wake Up Management

The word 'risk' derives from the early Italian risicare, which means 'to dare.' In this sense, risk is a choice rather than a fate. The actions we dare to take, which depend on how free we are to make choices, are what the story of risk is all about. And that story helps define what it means to be a human being.

Peter L. Bernstein[1]

In this chapter I will outline and discuss the various non-core global financial risks and the problems that corporate, insurance company and pension fund decision-makers are facing. Many of their problems today are a function of the way they were created and managed in the past – legacy global financial risks solved with traditional instruments in the same way year after year.

The chapter is divided into four main sections. The first is an introduction to the many global financial risks faced by corporates, insurance companies and pension funds. The second discusses corporate issues and problems; the third, insurance companies; and the fourth is concerned with pension funds. In this chapter I focus on the problem, not the solution. Discussion of the solution comes later in the book.

INTRODUCTION

The sources of unforeseen price volatility that affect any core business arise from currency price volatility from overseas profit transactions or translations, the purchase of hard commodities by manufacturing companies, bond and equity price volatility affecting insurance company capital reserves and solvency ratios, and equity and bond price volatility affecting asset and liability management for pension funds.

Corporate managers, insurance company executives and pension fund trustees face enormous difficulties in managing the non-core global financial risks affecting their day-to-day business, and the global financial system does not offer any easy solutions. The impact of these global financial risks on profitability is enormous, unpredictable and uncontrollable, often making the difference between profit and loss. Company managers do not have the professional grounding and understanding of capital market professionals when it comes to grappling with these risks.

The simple fact, however, is that non-core global financial risks are being managed by salaried employees and not professional risk-takers. A Fortune 50 executive said: 'It is not reasonable to expect that my salaried employees can consistently outperform professional risk-takers whose livelihood depends on their market performance. Therefore, I cannot afford the equivalent of gaming to impact the core performance of my business which so many have worked so hard to achieve.'

There are a number of non-core global financial risks which will affect any company. Most general risk is *market risk*. According to Mary Pat McCarthy and Timothy Flynn,

---

[1] Peter L. Bernstein (1996) *Against the Gods*. New York: John Wiley & Sons, Inc., p. 8.

> Market risks, which include interest rates, foreign exchange rates, commodity risks, and equity prices, inject uncertainty into one's business and impact a company's ability to project future costs and returns.[2]

A more 'official' definition is as follows:

> Market risk is the risk of fluctuations in portfolio values because of movements in the level or volatility of market prices.[3]

Currency, equity, bond and commodity prices are in constant flux. Changes can occur independently or they can be correlated to each other in some way. The dynamic interrelationships between the various risks can be breathtaking at times, and as a global bond trader for more than twenty years, I can testify that it is a full-time job to watch over all of these risks.

There are two types of currency risk that affect corporates, insurance companies and, to a lesser extent, pension funds. The first, *translation exposure*, is caused by converting foreign-currency denominated earnings and assets into a corporation's base currency. The economic cost of this exposure is slight, ignoring the cosmetic effect on financial consolidation. However, the impact on reported earnings and earnings per share may influence investor perception of the corporation's share value. There is no actual cash flow impact. Translation exposure can also be termed *accounting exposure*.

The second currency risk is *transaction exposure*; it arises from everyday trading activity and has a cash flow impact which affects the amount of base-currency receivables and payables. Transaction exposures are physically converted into cash flows in the base currency of the corporation. As a result, there is a direct impact on the base-currency profit and loss account – unlike translation exposure, which only impacts the consolidated financial statements. Transaction exposure, therefore, is also termed *operating exposure*.

In addition to the non-core global financial risks discussed above, insurance companies must reserve funds for their insurance product liabilities, both short- and long-term. These reserves take the form of equity and/or bond investments in the global capital markets. If they fall in value, the insurance company may not have sufficient funds to meet its insurance liabilities and may have to raise money to do so. Insurance companies are in the business of selling insurance policies and products; they may not necessarily have the core competence to manage their investment portfolios or to determine the appropriate mix of assets their reserve portfolios should contain. Indeed, both insurance companies and pension funds have actuaries who determine the needed return-on-investment on their reserve portfolio investments, but the way in which those investments are to be managed is quite another matter. We will discuss this point in a later chapter; suffice it to say here that actuarial assumptions may be swamped by extreme and dramatic global capital market price volatility – extreme price-volatile events occur far too often in global capital markets.

The same is true for pension funds, which invest in assets such as equities, bonds and property, as well as in venture capital, to ensure that they meet their pensioners' liabilities in the long term. However, if their investment portfolio is adversely affected by falling prices, the corporate sponsor may have to raise additional monies for their pension fund to meet these liabilities.

Although I only managed global bonds, I had to be completely aware of what was happening in the equity and commodity markets. For example, if equity prices fall, expected equity

---

[2] Mary Pat McCarthy and Timothy Flynn (2004) *Risk from the CEO and Board Perspective*. McGraw-Hill, p. 113.
[3] Philippe Jorion (2003) *Financial Risk Manager's Handbook*, 2nd edn, Chichester: John Wiley & Sons, Ltd, p. 265.

dividend yields rise; these yields may offer better value than bond yields, and therefore in-vestors will shift funds from the bond market to the equity market. The act of shifting funds from equities to bonds will cause bond prices to fall and, all things remaining equal, equity prices to rise. If commodity prices are rising, they may cause inflationary pressures, because food companies, for example, will have to purchase commodities to make their product and, if possible, pass the additional cost on to their consumers. As I have already said, managing non-core global financial risks is a full-time job to be managed by capital market professionals, not salaried staff at the company who have never worked in the global capital markets.

Consider the following comment from the International Monetary Fund (IMF):

> Between 1990 and 1998, assets managed by mature market institutional investors more than doubled to over $30 trillion, about equal to world gross domestic product (GDP). Amid widespread capital account liberalization and increased reliance on securities markets, these investable funds became increasingly responsive to changing opportunities and risks in a widening set of regions and countries. Because global investment portfolios are large, proportionally small portfolio adjust-ments can be associated with large and volatile swings in capital flows. ... [Portfolio] adjustments sometimes had a significant impact on financial conditions in the recipient countries, both when they flowed in and when they flowed out. This underscores the powerful impact that portfolio rebalancing by global investors can have on the volume, pricing, and direction of international capital flows and on conditions in both domestic and international markets.[4]

Managing currency, bond, equity and commodity price risks is difficult and time consuming at the best of times, the more so if one is not a capital market professional. A great deal of time and thought must go into it, ensuring that the appropriate hedge instrument is used.

Many banks, investment firms and companies use the value-at-risk (VaR) concept to model potential financial price volatility and aggregate losses that could arise from a portfolio of currencies and other financial assets. We discussed VaR briefly in Chapter 1, but it is worth citing a general definition of it:

> the maximum loss over a target horizon such that there is a low, prespecified probability that the actual loss will be larger.[5]

One way of managing one's potential capital markets and measuring VaR is the RiskMetrics system originally designed by JP Morgan and spun off as a separate company. However, it should be borne in mind that the price volatility that the RiskMetrics model uses is historic price movements, as opposed to the implied volatility used by other models. In the original RiskMetrics technical document (1996), JP Morgan issued a strong health warning about using VaR: 'We remind our reader that no amount of sophisticated analysis will replace experience and professional judgement in managing risks. "RiskMetrics" is nothing more than a high quality tool for the professional risk manager involved in the financial markets and is not a guarantee of specific results.'

Changes in accounting standards and regulations will be discussed in the next chapter; suffice it to say at this point the global corporate environment has changed, and the way in which non-core business risks (whether they be global financial risks or something else) are managed and the way in which derivative instruments are used has had a major impact on corporate behaviour.

---

[4] 'International Capital Markets,' IMF, August 2001.
[5] Philippe Jorion (2003), *Financial Risk Manager's Handbook*, 2nd edn, Chichester: John Wiley & Sons, Ltd, p. 264.

THE CORPORATE PROBLEM

According to another Fortune 50 senior executive: 'Today my team and I are forced to waste large amounts of time focusing on factors out of our control, such as foreign exchange rates and/or commodity prices, rather than spending that time on factors we can control. The result is lost opportunities to reduce costs we can control and increase sales via product, quality and service factors we do control. I can't quickly quantify the value of these lost opportunities, but it is significant.'

In a recent misadventure, 'A Chinese state-owned company incurred one of the biggest derivatives losses in years by repeatedly doubling down on a chronically losing bet against rising oil prices over the past year,' according to the *Wall Street Journal* (3 December 2004).[6] 'The overseas arm of China's main jet-fuel supplier, revealed this week that it has racked up about $550 million in trading losses.'

'The Singapore Exchange scrambled yesterday [1 December 2004] to limit damage from the biggest scandal to hit it since rogue British trader Nick Leeson felled Barings bank, ordering an inquiry into $550m (£288m) derivatives loss by a Chinese company' according to the *Financial Times*.[7]

The FT's report went on to say that 'China Aviation Oil, one of Singapore's top China-related listings, sought court protection after running up the loss trading oil derivatives. The loss amounted to more than CAO's market value. One question is whether the Chinese parent knew of the losses when it sold a 15% stake in CAO to institutional investors in late October [2004], ...'

A further *Financial Times* article on the subject points out that 'The regularity with which derivatives-related disasters occur raises the question of whether they are inherently dangerous. . . . But the regularity with which unauthorised trading scandals emerge shows not every bank or trading house adopts such strict standards.'

Over the past fifteen years there have been a large number of headline-making derivative loss events:[8]

- *1989* – Hammersmith and Fulham Council in London is ruled to have acted beyond its legal powers by engaging in interest rate swap and options contracts totalling more than £6 billion. The market is closed to local authorities and both the council and the banks take losses.
- *1994* – Metallgesellschaft, a German industrial company, almost collapses after losses in oil futures contracts. Speculative trading leads to DM2.3bn (then $1.35bn) loss.
- *1994* – Procter & Gamble, the US consumer products group, loses US $157 million on interest rate swap transactions. The problem trades used highly complex formulae that were inconsistent with the company's internal policies.
- *1994* – Orange County, California, takes a leveraged bet on interest rates. Losses of $1.5 billion are made on structured notes that look safe because they appear to carry a US government guarantee, while in reality they are high-risk.
- *1995* – Nick Leeson, a trader in Barings' Singapore office, runs up a loss of £791 million through unauthorized derivatives trading.
- *1996* – Sumitomo Corp trader Yasuo Hamanaka makes a $1.76 billion loss on unauthorized copper futures trading.

---

[6] 'How a Singapore Fuel Company lost $550 million in Oil Trading,' *Wall Street Journal*, 3 December 2004.
[7] 'Singapore hit by new $550m trading scandal,' *Financial Times*, 2 December 2004. pp. 1 and 26.
[8] 'Singapore hit by new $550m trading scandal,' *Financial Times*, 2 December 2004, p. 26.

- *1998* – The hedge fund Long-Term Capital Management faces collapse after losing $550 million in one day when counterparties demand more collateral to cover widening spreads. The New York Federal Reserve heads a bank bail-out.
- *2002* – Allied Irish Bank's John Rusnak, a trader at its US subsidiary, Allfirst, runs up foreign exchange losses of $691m.
- *2004* – National Australian Bank loses A$600 million on unauthorized foreign exchange options dealing.

The derivative loss events detailed above occurred either by over-leveraging or misunderstanding the derivative marketplace. In the Procter & Gamble incident, for example, the company was mis-sold derivative instruments by Bankers Trust, but the fact that the company bought the derivatives, relying upon Bankers Trust, indicates a lack of understanding by Procter & Gamble about the derivatives, along with the models used to price and manage the derivative positions.

In the case of Metallgesellschaft, a case study by John Digenan, Dan Felson, Robert Kelly and Ann Wiemert[9] outlines the problem that the company faced, the deal and why it went wrong.

CASE STUDY: METALLGESELLSCHAFT AG

In December, 1993, Metallgesellschaft AG revealed publicly that its "Energy Group" was responsible for losses of approximately $1.5 billion, due mainly to cash-flow problems resulting from large oil forward contracts it had written. In a lucid discussion of this infamous derivatives debacle, Digenan, Felson, Kelly and Wiemert explore the trading strategies employed by the conglomerate, how proper supervision could have averted disaster and how similar financial crises may be avoided in the future.

Background

Metallgesellschaft AG, or MG, is a German conglomerate, owned largely by Deutsche Bank AG, the Dresdner Bank AG, Daimler-Benz, Allianz, and the Kuwait Investment Authority. MG, a traditional metal company, has evolved in the last four years into a provider of risk management services. It has several subsidiaries in its 'Energy Group', with MG Refining and Marketing Inc. (MGRM) in charge of refining and marketing petroleum products in the U.S. In December, 1993, it was revealed publicly that the 'Energy Group' was responsible for losses of approximately $1.5 billion. MGRM's expanded venture into the derivatives world began in 1991 with the hiring of Mr Arthur Benson from Louis Dreyfus Energy. It was Benson's strategy that eventually contributed to the massive cash flow crisis that MG experienced.

The Deals

MGRM committed to sell, at prices fixed in 1992, certain amounts of petroleum every month for up to 10 years. These contracts initially proved to be very successful since they guaranteed a price over the current spot. In some cases the profit margin was around $5 per barrel. By September of 1993, MGRM had sold forward contracts amounting to the equivalent of 160 million barrels. What was so unique about these deals was that the vast

---

[9] http://www.stuart.iit.edu/fmtreview/fmtrev3.htm

majority of these contracts contained an 'option' clause which enabled the counterparties to terminate the contracts early if the front-month New York Mercantile Exchange (NYMEX) futures contract was greater than the fixed price at which MGRM was selling the oil product. If the buyer exercised this option, MGRM would be required to pay in cash one-half of the difference between the futures price and the fixed prices times the total volume remaining to be delivered on the contract. This option would be attractive to a customer if they were in financial distress or simply no longer needed the oil. The sell-back option was not always an option, because MGRM sometimes amended its contracts to terminate automatically if the front-month futures price rose above a specified 'exit price'.

The MGRM Strategy

MGRM provided its customers with a method that enabled the customer to shift or eliminate some of their oil price risk. The petroleum market is an environment plagued with large fluctuations in the price of oil-related products. MGRM believed their financial resources gave them the ability to wholesale and manage risk transference in the most efficient manner. In fact, MGRM's promotional literature boasts about this efficiency at risk management as a key objective to continued growth in acquiring additional business. MGRM's hedge strategy to manage spot price risk was to use the front-end month futures contracts on the NYMEX. MGRM employed a 'stack' hedging strategy. It placed the entire hedge in shortdated delivery months, rather than spreading this amount over many, longer-dated, delivery months, because the call options mentioned above were tied to the front-month futures contract at the NYMEX. Studies have demonstrated the effectiveness of using stacked hedging. MGRM's strategy was sound from an economic standpoint.

The futures contracts MGRM used to hedge were the unleaded gasoline and the No. 2 heating oil. MGRM also held an amount of West Texas Intermediate sweet crude contracts. MGRM went long in the futures and entered into OTC energy swap agreements to receive floating and pay fixed energy prices. According to the NYMEX, MGRM held the futures position equivalent of 55 million barrels of gasoline and heating oil. By deduction, their swap positions may have accounted for as much as 110 million barrels to completely hedge their forward contracts. The swap positions introduced credit risk for MGRM.

What Went Wrong?

The assumption of economies of scale was mistaken. MGRM attributed to such a great percentage of the total open interest on the NYMEX that liquidation of their position was problematic. Without adequate funding in case of immediate margin calls, this seemingly sound strategy becomes reckless. MGRM's forward supply contracts left them in a vulnerable position to rising oil prices. Therefore, MGRM decided to hedge away the risk of rising prices as described. However, it was the decline in the price of oil that ultimately led MGRM to financial distress.

Another problem MGRM encountered was the timing of cash flows required to maintain the hedge. Over the entire life of the hedge, these cash flows would have balanced out. MG's problem was a lack of necessary funds needed to maintain their position. Given the fact that this risk management strategy played a key role in acquiring business pursuant to their corporate objectives, management should have obtained an understanding of the strategy. Did MG's Supervisory Board really know what was going on?

Once again, the misunderstanding of derivative instruments, their use and management caused this problem to happen. Understanding the liquidity of the futures or options markets is essential; tracking open interest, the outstanding number of contracts at the close of the day, is an important aspect of exchange-traded derivative instruments. When open interest rises or falls, it indicates the way traders are positioning themselves, and available liquidity.

The Enron and WorldCom disasters of 2001 and 2002 have taught us that desperate people do desperate things in an attempt to achieve their stated or projected corporate objectives, particularly those of a financial nature. These unfortunate incidents have led to calls for greater transparency of accounting standards and reporting, and less leveraging (the use of derivatives or borrowed money) to achieve corporate or investment objectives. Corporate governance has now been legislated through the Sarbanes–Oxley Act; as a result, managements have to spend more time focused on the way they manage their finances and hedge their global financial risks.

Some companies do not believe that profit translation is at risk from foreign exchange price volatility; it is pure profit which does not need to be hedged, as discussed in the introduction to this chapter. Other companies have a majority of their revenues coming from overseas to be reported in their home country; they forecast earnings-per-share and profit, therefore dividend expectations are a function of the overseas earnings-per-share at risk from currency translation risks. If the home reporting currency moves adversely by 1% over the fiscal year, profits will be affected by 1%, and therefore the company must find that 1% profit margin somewhere to meet its dividend projections. Otherwise, the company must hedge its profit translation from the beginning of the fiscal year to ensure that it meets its dividend payments. If it hedges 100% of its expected overseas profit and only achieves 80% of its projections, it has over-hedged and has a mismatched currency hedge exposure and could be held accountable for speculating on its overseas currency profit translations. It isn't easy, is it?

If a company invests its home source currency in a new office or factory in a foreign country, it may want to hedge the value of its investment, particularly if the foreign country has higher inflation. Hedging the purchasing value of one's investment involves more than merely selling a forward foreign exchange agreement. If a company has to purchase hard commodities or components – denominated in US dollars, say – that are to be used in its home country's manufacturing process, the company must sell the home source currency to purchase US dollars, and it may want to hedge this currency risk. This is known as transaction risk and was defined in the introduction to this chapter.

A financial engineering MSc student whom I was teaching at CASS Business School, Timur Sibgatullin, introduced me to Gary Klopfenstein and Alex Koh's discussion of the debate between transaction and translation currency risks, which is worth quoting at length:

> The management of translation risk has been a subject of heated debate over the years. The basic issue is whether the use of hedging techniques, which incur real cash cost in order to protect an accounting figure, is a waste of time and money. Viewpoints on this issue differ widely depending on the circumstances of the corporation and the nature of its investors. The management of translation risk is essentially unique to the circumstances of the corporation.
>
> For example, a corporation which is viewed as a U.S. stock but with 90 percent of its profits and 80 percent of its assets arising from outside the United States and funded mainly by U.S. currency borrowings will vigorously defend translation hedging.
>
> This is because any adverse currency movements will impact both its balance sheet and earnings. We can contrast this with another corporation which is well-diversified globally, has foreign assets matched by foreign liabilities and is characterized by significant currency earnings and expense. Such a corporation may not want to carry out any translation hedging at all on the basis that the assets and liabilities are approximately matched, and the wide spread at currency flow will even

out any balance-sheet and earnings translation gains and losses over time. The costs of hedging may also be prohibitive in view of the significant foreign-currency asset base and currency spread of cash flows.

The decision to hedge translation risk or not depends on whether management performance is judged or focused on the managing of cash flow or earnings per share. A focus on earnings implies that translation risk management is likely to be practiced. However, the treasury departments of major multinationals have in the past five to ten years focused on managing cash flows and away from translation hedging.

... Therefore, the decision for translation risk hedging must be carefully considered with all the facts at hand as there is no hard and fast rule on this issue.

There is little economic cost arising from this exposure, apart from an 'optical' accounting effect on financial consolidation. However, the impact on reported earnings and earnings per share may influence investors' perception of the corporation's share value. There is no actual cash-flow impact.[10]

A company wanting to hedge its many currency risks will not have the depth of liquidity, the instrumentation or the capacity to hedge its exposures in every market where it has a risk, particularly the less-developed markets. Because of the lack of liquidity and capacity of the currency hedging instruments available, many companies will have to use a proxy market, such as the US dollar, euro, sterling, yen or other developed capital market, to find the required liquidity, capacity and instruments. The *Financial Times* cited a report by the Conference Board, a US-based research group, according to which 'Businesses are frequently managing foreign exchange risk by concentrating exposure in a handful of "universal" currencies such as the dollar and the euro ... But globalisation of those currencies can create separate economic problems for their home economies.'[11] How adequate the use of a proxy is will be reflected by its correlation with the actual currency being hedged. If a company is euro-denominated, it may use US dollars to hedge against certain Latin American or Asian currencies because some of these currencies are fixed or linked to the value of the US dollar. This is not a perfect hedge but it does enable a degree of currency price volatility protection.

In the same article, the *Financial Times* also said: 'At the suggestion of Paul Volcker, former chairman of the Federal Reserve, the board surveyed chief executives and chief financial officers globally about how they dealt with exchange rate volatility and whether currency swings created economic inefficiencies in investment allocation. The survey's key finding was [that] exchange rate risk is becoming more important to business, but that it is still not a dominant factor in decision-making. What the survey did show, however, was concentration in the number of currencies used.'

In a later article, the *Financial Times* points out that:

Companies terrified of seeing their balance sheets dented by adverse currency movements may be contributing to the dollar's two-year demise.

Transactional hedging, used by corporates to protect against swings in the value of overseas earnings and import costs, has long been a feature of the currency market. But now translational hedging – used to protect the value of overseas assets and liabilities – has grown in importance as corporates react to the extreme currency volatility of 2003.

And a growing number of companies are also protecting themselves for up to two years, eschewing the one-year forwards that were once *de rigueur* in the marketplace. 'We have seen the impact of the weakening of the US dollar on customer behaviour,' said Yogesh Shetty, head of commercial forex at Travelex. 'Companies are not only hedging their future payments, they are

---

[10] Gary Klopfenstein and Alex Koh (1997) *Foreign Exchange: Managing Global Currency Risk – The Definitive Handbook for Corporations and Financial Institutions.* Glenlake.

[11] 'Powerhouse currencies make waves in their homelands,' 'Market Insight', *Financial Times,* 24 June 2004, p. 48.

also hedging their balance sheets. Whilst management is focused on profits and ultimately bonuses, their shareholders are just as concerned about the net asset value of the company. Companies that have assets or even liabilities overseas are hedging their value.'

Travelex's own research suggests that corporate treasury departments' growing enthusiasm for balance-sheet hedging has been responsible for a 25 percent rise in the use of yearly forwards so far this year.

This trend is most noticeable for European companies with US assets, which will have declined in value in euro or sterling terms as the trade-weighted dollar has fallen 21.7 percent since early 2002. . . . The long-term benefits of transactional hedging are less clear, however. If a corporate has no intention of selling assets held overseas, hedging their value every year will incur an annual cost without delivering any tangible benefit over a long-term cycle.[12]

Interestingly, the government of Brazil has long been a currency hedge supplier of last resort to Brazilian private companies; the government has consistently been raising US dollars in the capital markets, using US dollar-linked debt and foreign exchange swaps to ensure that Brazilian private companies have sufficient US dollar liquidity to enable them to hedge their overseas activities. The alternative for the Brazilian government is to allow their private companies to raise their own US dollars and US dollar currency hedging instruments for themselves. Of course, the Brazilians pay an enormous price for this currency liquidity programme: when the Brazilian real moves adversely against the US dollar, Brazil's US dollar debt repayments move with it. The point of this example is that every country handles differently the issue of providing a deep liquid capital market for its private companies, insurance companies and pension funds for their overseas business and risk management activities.

Many companies may not hedge their currency translation risks but will hedge their transaction risks. However, they may want to hedge their translations if their overseas earnings form part or all of the company's dividend payments. What about the movements in inflation? What does one do when transacting in a high-inflation emerging market that has a currency board? If, after a year, the currency board is not holding together, what happens when it becomes a floating rate currency regime? What if there are no deep liquidity pools available to currency hedgers in that country: does one use a proxy currency to achieve the necessary risk management objectives? And which global bank will offer you the necessary products and services to support your risk management activities? It isn't easy, although if ignored or not handled correctly the consequences are financially enormous, as you will discover later in this chapter. A colleague told me that the stock market never credits a company for good risk management but they will punish that company for poor risk management practices.

There is no question in my mind that the Enron and WorldCom corporate disasters in 2001 and 2002 were a watershed for the way companies must manage their financial affairs. Although this book is not about corporate governance and the Enron and WorldCom debacles were related to fraud, the focus on the way companies manage their non-core global financial risks has changed for the better.

In the aftermath of Enron and WorldCom, the transparency in corporate reporting changed significantly. The days of keeping financial problems hidden within one's profit and loss or balance sheet statements are gone. On the contrary, corporate risk management and behaviour is all over our newspapers and professional journals. One such publication is *Risk* magazine, which, after Enron and WorldCom, started to publish corporate risk disclosures each month. Its disclosures represent a wide array of types of risk and the outcome from risk management activities.

---

[12] 'Vicious circle of hedging continues to weigh on dollar,' 'Market Insight', *Financial Times*, 29 July 2004, p. 42.

Table 2.1 gives a number of examples, taken from three *Risk* magazine articles.[13] Reading through the lists published in *Risk*, a number of similarities and differences become evident. There are companies affected by single currency devaluations, companies affected by home or source currency problems, those with both commodity and currency risks, currency risks affecting the balance sheet, some that have achieved a positive translation effect, those which are writing down the values of derivatives used to hedge their financial risks because of the change in accounting standards, and, perhaps the worst category of all, companies who have had a hedge deviation between their underlying cash financial risk and the way the derivative instrument correlated with the cash market. Table 2.1 presents a number of examples of disclosure statements from three *Risk* magazine articles.[14] One interesting aspect of the examples is the way each company reports its non-core global financial risks, some with detail and others merely describing the problem.

In connection with disclosures such as these I performed a few calculations on a few companies' data to show how large an effect non-core global financial risks have on both profits and sales.

Alliance Unichem's group reported overseas earnings of 43%, even though 53% is denominated in euros. According to its Report and Accounts (2003), changes in cumulative translation effects cost the company £56.6 million and (in 2002) £59.6 million, representing a cost on operating cash flow of 17.56% in 2003 and 29.71% in 2002.

According to AstraZeneca's Report and Accounts (2003), exchange movements on the cash flow from operating activities fluctuated from $-\$47.0$ million (2001) to \$75.0 million (2002) and \$82 million (2003), with foreign exchange adjustments as a percentage of shareholders funds representing -5.35% (2001), $+11.54\%$ (2002) and $+12.77\%$ (2003).

BOC Group, according to its Annual Report and Accounts (2003), hedged currency risks that arise from (i) the translation of the opening net assets of overseas operations, (ii) the retranslation of retained earnings of overseas operations from average to closing rates of exchange, and (iii) the translation or conversion of foreign exchange borrowings taken to hedge overseas assets. The company used currency swaps and forward foreign exchange agreements denominated in US dollars, Australian dollars, Japanese yen, South African rand and sterling. Changes in total translation affected the company by $-£62.5$ million in 2001, $-£136.3$ million in 2002 and £31.5 million in 2003, representing a cost on profit for the financial year of -27.9% in 2001, -67.1% in 2002 and 14.4% in 2003.

The examples above demonstrate how non-core global financial risks affect different companies, the problems they face and how they try to solve them, and how they report the way in which they manage their global financial risks to their stockholders. It is fascinating to look at those manufacturing companies which purchase US dollars to purchase a hard commodity for use in making their products, but sell their end-product overseas, with the attendant currency translation risks. If both the US dollar and the hard commodity's price move adversely, by 10% each, say, the profit margin of the manufacturer takes a 20% hit – this is all before the manufacturing process has begun and they have not sold a single product, which will in turn also be affected by currency risks.

I was invited to speak at a university in the United States, a world-renowned engineering school, which asked me to talk to the students and faculty about managing global financial risks

---

[13] 'Corporate disclosures', *Risk*, April 2002; 'Q1 scapegoats: Energy and weather', *Risk*, July 2002; and 'Real problems' *Risk*, January 2003.
[14] Ibid.

Table 2.1 Examples of published corporate risk disclosures

Risk type	Name of company	Date of disclosure	Disclosure statement
Single currency devaluation			
	Repsol	28 March 2002	Scrapped its second-half dividend for 2002 after write-offs from Argentina's currency devaluation caused profits to plummet 58% last year. (Argentina accounts for 42% of Repsol's operating profit since it bought oil driller YPF in 1999 for $15 billion.)
		13 November 2002	The Spanish oil and gas group said weaker refining margins and the continuing economic crisis in Argentina had eaten into net income for the third quarter.
	Coca-Cola	16 April 2002	For first quarter 2002 recorded a negative currency effect of $0.03 per share (after tax). Recorded a non-cash first-quarter charge of $157 million before taxes related to investments in Latin America caused by currency devaluation.
Home (source) currency			
	Toyota	13 May 2002	The weakness of the yen boosted its profits last year.
	Nestlé	11 April 2002	The Swiss food group said all major currencies, with the exception of the Mexican peso and US dollar, depreciated against the Swiss franc, resulting in an adverse foreign exchange effect of 2.8% on consolidated sales.
General currency movements			
	Crown, Cork and Seal	14 February 2002	Reported that fourth quarter results were affected by negative currency translation effects of $147 million.
		18 April 2002	Net sales in the first quarter were $1567 million, 5.5% below the prior period, reflecting the effects of currency translation ($43 million).
	Chiquita	11 February 2002	Said increases in sales over the year were offset by the effect of weak European currencies.
		8 May 2002	European currency weakness had a $9 million negative effect on quarterly earnings for first quarter 2002.

(continued)

Table 2.1   (*Continued*)

Risk type	Name of company	Date of disclosure	Disclosure statement
Currency risks affecting balance sheet			
	Nintendo	21 October 2002	The Japanese video game maker said the yen's rise against the dollar in the six months to September reduced group sales by ¥4.5 billion and resulted in an appraisal of ¥29 billion on foreign-currency denominated assets.
	Toyota and Nissan	19 November 2001	Both companies blamed the strength of sterling for mounting losses in the UK – the hub of their European manufacturing operations.
Positive currency translation			
	Porsche	19 November 2001	Forecast a positive earnings outlook for the year despite expectations of falling unit sales, and told investors it expected to profit from hedging against the dollar.
Accounting rules change			
	Hydro Quebec	10 May 2002	A new accounting rule meant that Hydro shaved about C$202 million from its 2001 first-quarter results for a forex loss caused by the weakness of the Canadian dollar versus the US dollar.
	Coca-Cola	16 April 2002	Implemented FAS 133, the cumulative effect of which was a one-time, non-cash charge of $10 million and decreased earnings by $16 million.
Commodity price volatility			
	Royal Dutch/Shell	7 October 2002	Royal Dutch/Shell, the world's third-largest oil company by market value, said margins from refining oil into fuel in the third quarter remained at an historic low, and blamed a 43% jump in crude oil prices, which increase raw materials costs.
Hedge deviation			
	Enterprise Products Partners	2 April 2002	Reported the effectiveness of its hedging strategy for natural gas deteriorated in first-quarter 2002, creating a $17 million cash loss from hedging. Announced that it would quit its remaining hedged positions.
		30 April 2002	First-quarter results included a $16.4 million cash loss from settlements of natural gas financial instruments used to hedge Enterprise's equity NGL production.

Table 2.1   (*Continued*)

Risk type	Name of company	Date of disclosure	Disclosure statement
	Carbon Energy Group	3 April 2002	2001 results recorded a charge of $1.4 million against net income to account for FAS 133. Fourth-quarter results were affected by charges related to Enron hedges totalling $328 000.
	Chaparral Resources	19 November 2001	Suffered losses of $607 000 due to the decline in the fair value of its hedge contracts during the first nine months of 2001.
		20 May 2002	Recognized a loss of $698 000 for first-quarter 2002 to record its crude oil derivatives' fair value.

because the engineering students focus on everything related to engineering a supply chain, except for the global financial risks, which may affect the supply chain they are engineering.

The fact of the matter is that many companies which opened operations and manufacturing facilities in Asia before the 1997 currency crisis would have seen their entire supply chain model thrown completely out of the window in the aftermath of the Asian crisis. They would have been impacted by many non-core global financial risks and events as a result of the crisis. The first is the actual currency devaluations which affected their transaction, as well as translation, risks; clearly their balance sheet risks were decimated by the currency devaluation throughout the Asian continent. Additionally, interest rates in each domestic market affected by currency devaluations were rising to protect the value of the Asian currencies. The currency or liquidity crisis turned into a major debt crisis as banking institutions throughout Asia were in default, bankrupt and were liquidated as institutions, recapitalized or merged with other financial institutions. There was social unrest throughout Asia which also affected any company trying to do any kind of business on the Asian continent. Lastly, as economic growth in Asia collapsed, debts were written off, commodity prices fell, and domestic and overseas demand for goods produced in Asia fell away. This entire episode was caused by currency devaluations; regardless of how it was caused or why, the financial impact was devastating for each company caught up in the hurricane. The point is that non-core financial risks have an enormous impact on corporate earnings and shareholder equity and the way we do business throughout the world.

Now that we have had a look at some examples of the global financial risks that companies face, it is time to look at a specific company in greater detail. We will look at *Ford Motor*, examining several years' reports and accounts to gain an insight into the problems it faces.

CASE STUDY: FORD MOTOR

As the line manager responsible for the running of a major product line, the Senior Vice President running Ford Truck, Gurminder Bedi, was constantly frustrated with the way his non-core global financial risks, such as currency and hard commodity, were impacting his bottom-line profitability. Much of his frustration with the non-core global financial risks affecting Ford's core business lay in the inability to forecast, manage and mitigate the impact of the unforeseen price volatility impacting the company's profitability.

I examined three years of financial accounts from 2001 to 2003 to explore the trials and tribulations that Ford particularly had to entertain, as well as the aftermath of 11 September 2001, Enron, WorldCom, the economic slump, falling stock market and a new set of rules and regulations that followed the Enron debacle.

On the day my colleague Keith Krenz and I arrived in Dearborn, Michigan, Ford announced a $1 billion write-off from hedging price risks on palladium, a hard commodity metal mined in Russia and used in the manufacturing of catalytic converters in automobiles. As I have just mentioned, Ford has two major non-core global financial risks impacting its car sales every day: currency and hard commodity price volatility. I will start with the currency risks and then move on to the commodity risks over the three-year period from 2001 to 2003.

An important aspect of the way Ford manages its global financial risks is its policy on quantitative and qualitative disclosures about market risk: 'We are exposed to a variety of market and other risks, including the effects of changes in foreign currency exchange rates, commodity prices, interest rates, as well as the availability of funding sources, hazard events, and specific asset risks. These risks affect our Automobile and Financial Services sectors differently. . . . Our risk management program recognizes the unpredictability of markets and seeks to reduce profit volatility.'[15] Clearly, profit translation affected by currency translation is an issue for Ford, along with any diminishing effect of either currency or commodities used in the manufacture of automobiles or trucks. It is an issue in which Ford would like to hedge, or at least diminish, the marginal return on sales arising from unforeseen price volatility coming from both hard commodities and currency translation risks.

We now know what is of concern to Ford management regarding their market risks management programme: starting with currency risks, the definition that Ford uses is also found on the same page as the market risk disclosures.

Foreign currency risk is the possibility that our financial results could be better or worse than planned because of changes in exchange rates. We use derivative instruments to hedge assets, liabilities, and firm commitments denominated in foreign currencies. Our hedging policy is designed to reduce income volatility and is based on clearly defined guidelines. Speculative actions are not permitted. In our hedging actions, we use primarily instruments commonly used by corporations to reduce foreign exchange, interest rates and other price risks.[16]

The Ford report continues with its definition and policy on managing foreign exchange risks: 'We use a value-at-risk ("VaR") analysis to evaluate our exposure to changes in foreign currency exchange rates.' Ford uses the RiskMetrics system for its VaR analysis. VaR provides an estimate of potential currency price volatility based upon historic price movements. Ford Motor managers who are executing the various global financial risk management strategies are salaried employees of Ford Motor and not professional capital market traders at an investment bank in New York or the City of London; there are no financial incentives for getting their hedging strategy right or wrong, nor is managing global financial risks their core professional competency.

Ford Motor is in business to build and sell automobiles and its executives are focused on the process of financially supporting the activity of building and selling automobiles and are a part of that entire supply chain. Whereas professional capital market traders, as

---

[15] Ford Motor, Inc., 2001 Annual Accounts, p. 42.
[16] Ford Motor, Inc., 2001 Annual Accounts, p. 42.

discussed in Chapter 1, are empowered in every conceivable way to make as much money as they possibly can by trading, for example, currency and commodities markets and all of their derivatives instruments. Therefore, a company such as Ford is well served by using a market standard capital markets price volatility model such as VaR, which allows it to develop a base in which to hedge potential unforeseen price volatility.

As we will discuss in a later chapter, there are new ways in which to manage global financial risks. At the moment, Ford is doing all the right things from a policy point of view. Ford is exposed to many currencies, such as Swedish krone, British pounds sterling, Japanese yen, Mexican pesos, and Brazilian reals.

Ford reported its VaR analysis and subsequent hedging results as follows;

Hedging actions substantially reduce our risk to changes in currency rates. Based on our overall currency exposure (including derivatives positions) during 2001, the risk during 2001 to our pre-tax cash flow from currency movements was on average $300 million, with a high of $350 million and a low of $275 million. At December 31, 2001, currency movements are projected to affect our pre-tax cash flow over the next 18 months by less than $275 million, with 99% confidence, primarily because of decreased currency rate volatility.

However, when we look at the actual effect of exchange rate changes on cash, the fluctuations and sums of money involved from year to year are enormous:

2000	2001	2002	2003
−$914 million	−$252 million	$373 million	$1370 million

The fundamental amount of money and effect these numbers have on a company such as Ford can be seen through the percentage of these amounts on the total consolidated income/(loss) before tax (the amount of money by which currency risks are impacting the net bottom-line profit):

2000	2001	2002	2003
$8234 million	−$7419 million	$951 million	$1370 million

The effect of exchange rate changes on cash impacted net income (or the percentage impact of foreign exchange losses on net income) before income taxes by 11.1% in 2000, a 3.32% contribution to Ford's losses in 2002, a 39.2% contribution to 2002 and a 59.2% contribution to pre-tax profits in 2003. This is a significant impact in three of the four years we studied.

One of the frustrations with dealing with foreign exchange risks is the way they are accounted in a backward-looking manner. For example, the Ford Annual Report 2002 defines foreign currency translation as follows:

Results of operations and cash flows are, in most cases, translated at average-period exchange rates and assets and liabilities are translated at end-of-period exchange rates.

So the effect of the foreign exchange risks will not be known until the end of the period of measurement. The huge swings in valuations and the effect on cash flow from year to year because of currency price volatility are an extremely frustrating experience.

In its 2003 Annual Accounts, Ford began to use a new risk model, derived from value-at-risk, and called *earnings-at-risk* (EaR). The value-at-risk approach quantifies the risks derived from a portfolio of assets, such as equities, bonds, currencies and hard commodities. Another approach within the VaR family is cash flow-at-risk, which answers the question of how large a deviation there is between actual cash flow and the planned cash flow used in the budgeting process. The deviation will arise from a number of underlying risk factors but the probability for deviation works in the same way as VaR, with 95% confidence based on historic volatility of the underlying risk factors. EaR is similar to cash flow-at-risk but based on book depreciation, with the focus not on financial accounting in-flows and out-flows, but instead on profits and losses. Therefore, the user of EaR will calculate how large the deviation between the probable profit and a planned yearly profit is with a probability of 95%.

Ford reports in its 2003 account that

At December 31, 2003, the EaR from foreign currency exchange movements over the next twelve months is projected at less than $350 million, within 95% confidence level for the unhedged exposure. When calculated at the end of each quarter throughout the year, the high was $550 million, the low was $350 million and the average was $460 million; the risks impacting financial instruments are offset with underlying exposure being hedged. The 2003 year-end projection is approximately $40 million lower than the EaR projection for 2003 calculated as at December 31, 2002. The decreased exposure results primarily from more diversification benefit due to lower correlation among major currency pairings. The effect of currency movements on business units will vary based on the currency profile of the business unit (including any hedging actions taken). It can also be affected by competitive responses to currency changes.

There are a number of discussion points in this statement. First, the use of a risk management model is useful and helpful, but I come back to the percentage effect that we looked at earlier in this case study. The fact of the matter is that currency price volatility is having an enormous and significant impact on profit/(loss) before tax. Second, a $350 million probable impact on currency price volatility cannot be ignored and must be mitigated in some way; I will talk about the way in which it can be mitigated in a later chapter, particularly using new ways for managing global financial risks. For the time being, Ford must live with this risk.

One of the issues that Ford brought to our attention, which I will discuss in greater detail in the next chapter, is the way it determines how and what global financial risks are hedged. Ford determines at the outset of its budget cycle how much money it can afford, within its treasury budget, to hedge currency and hard commodity price risks. The budget amount that Ford has available only allows it to hedge 25–30% of its foreign exchange risks. This is a problem that must be solved and a frustration that must grate on every senior executive throughout the world who is in the same position as Ford executives.

In the US, the Financial Accounting Standard Board (FASB) has enacted new accounting requirements, which I will touch on in the next chapter, known as FAS 133, affecting the way in which companies in the US report their derivative instruments usage and positions in their report and accounts. In Ford's case, it reports its use of derivative instruments in notes attached to the general financial reports. I will extract the main points from the derivatives statement. The first hedging activity is the *cash flow hedges*.

We use cash flow hedges to minimize financial exposures to foreign currency exchange, interest rate, and commodity price risks resulting in the normal course of business. Derivatives used to minimize financial exposures for foreign exchange and commodity risks generally mature within three years or less, with a maximum maturity of seven years. The impact to earnings associated with discontinuance of cash flow hedges ineffectiveness was a gain of $6 million in 2002 and charge to earnings of $32 million in 2001.

The last sentence in this statement tells us that they did not hedge themselves properly, and that in 2002 they made $6 million and in 2001 lost $32 million on hedging ineffectiveness – one of the main problems with using derivative instruments to be discussed later, but not getting the planned result from hedging activity it is a significant problem with the present solutions to risk mitigation. The value of a derivative instrument changes for a number of different reasons (to be discussed in the next chapter) and therefore the value of a derivative instrument may not move in exact proportion with the underlying cash market risks which cause hedge deviation or ineffectiveness. Hedge ineffectiveness is part of the process which you will read about in all accounts of fair value reporting; reporting the value of the underlying cash risks' value and comparing it to the value of the derivative instrument used to hedge the cash risks.

The next area that Ford discusses as a hedging activity is called *net investment hedges*.

We use designated foreign currency forward exchange contracts to hedge the net assets of certain foreign entities to offset the translation and economic exposures related to our investment in these entities. The change in value of these derivatives is recorded in 'OCI' [accumulated other comprehensive income], as a foreign currency translation adjustment. The ineffectiveness related to net investment hedges is recorded in Cost of sales. Gains of $95 million were recorded in 2003 and 2002, respectively.

The last area in which Ford uses derivatives to hedge its global financial risks on behalf of its automobile operations is defined under *other derivative instruments*.

In accordance with corporate risk management policies, we use derivatives, such as forward contracts and options that economically hedge certain exposures. As previously stated, in certain instances we elect not to apply hedge accounting, which results in recording in income on a quarterly basis, the change in fair value of the derivative. Both the unrealized and realized gains and losses on derivatives that economically hedge commodity and foreign exchange exposures are reported in Cost of sales. The impact to earnings associated with non-designated hedges was a gain of $106 million in 2003 and a loss of $541 million in 2002.

Note that Ford has a financial arm, Ford Credit, which also has many non-core global financial risks and uses derivative instruments to hedge the impact on its operations.

At the end of the day, all companies want to make as much profit as possible, but the way in which they manage their non-core global financial risks is often a huge impediment to achieving their financial goals. As an insurance client once warned me about non-core global financial risks, 'the last thing I want or need is to report to my shareholders that we had a great year in the insurance business but we lost it all in our investment portfolio.' On 16 October 2002, Ford Motor announced that 'operations in South America reported a loss of $138 million in the third quarter compared to a loss of $56 million a year ago.' It said that unfavourable exchange rates were to blame.[17]

Let us move on to another non-core global financial risk that Ford faces, one which has caused them enormous harm – hard commodities price volatility. According to Ford's 2003

---

[17] 'Real Problem', *Risk*, January 2003.

Annual Accounts,

Commodity price risk is the possibility of higher or lower costs due to changes in the prices of commodities, such as non-ferrous metals (e.g. aluminum) and precious metals (e.g. palladium, platinum, and rhodium), ferrous alloys (e.g. steel), energy (e.g. natural gas and electricity), and plastics/resins (e.g. polypropylene), which we use in the production of motor vehicles.

Ford uses derivative instruments to manage the price volatility of its hard commodities and it uses EaR as well for commodities risks. Once again, the policy is all very well, but when it comes to actual practice, the negative financial consequences for Ford, as for many other companies, are extreme and unforgiving. In January 2002, the company announced a write-down of a precious metal loss of $1billion. The story, as reported by *Turtle Trader*, makes interesting reading.

January 28, 2002
Ford Motor Blows $1 Billion on Palladium Trading
By Doron Levin

Southfield, Michigan, Jan. 28 (Bloomberg) – Ford Motor Co.'s $1 billion write-off in the fourth-quarter for trading losses in precious metals should worry investors, though not as much as the company's sly accounting of it.

A couple of years ago, Ford decided to load up on palladium, a metal mined mostly in Russia. Along with rhodium and platinum, it's used by automakers for catalytic converters to remove pollutants from engine exhaust. Ford feared Russia might cut off the supply.

Ford bought large amounts of palladium in 2000, helping drive the price from about $500 an ounce to a high of $1125. Then, in early 2001, palladium prices began to collapse, falling to a low just above $300 an ounce.

Ford's purchase in the face of a limited supply was a principal reason for palladium's rise, says Ross Norman, a former metals trader in London for Credit Suisse First Boston. At least one Ford manager, not realizing his company was creating the bubble, bragged to financial analysts of a billion dollar paper profit in palladium.

Then, after amassing enough palladium to last several years, Ford stopped buying, which likely played a role in the price collapse. Meantime, a technical breakthrough in catalyst design by Ford engineers meant that less palladium would be needed than in the past.

Financial Engineering

Suddenly a big windfall in palladium had turned into a big liability. Not to worry: Ford's financial engineers would pick up where the catalyst engineers left off.

Instead of accounting for the actual cost of palladium Ford had purchased as an expense – in the manner the company accounts for steel, glass and other materials – the automaker decided to write off the entire billion-dollar loss in one fell swoop.

Ford's fourth-quarter financial statement was slated to be a disaster in any case, due to multibillion-dollar charges to cover the firing of 35 000 workers and closure of five plants. Who would notice an extra billion for palladium in the $5.07 billion net loss for the period?

Financial analysts weren't caught napping. Robert Brizzolara, who follows transportation companies for Harris Bank & Trust (whose mutual funds owned about 200 000 Ford shares, according to the latest filing with the Securities & Exchange Commission), at an analyst meeting asked Martin Inglis, Ford's chief financial officer, the extent to which the palladium write-off will improve Ford's profit in 2002. Inglis's answer: by $300 million to $400 million.

Number Polishing

Brizzolara and other analysts understand, unlike many investors, that each Ford vehicle in 2002 will be equipped with a catalyst containing palladium at its written-down and not true cost. Lower cost, as every schoolboy knows, means greater profit.

No one disputes the legality or propriety of Ford's accounting; whether it's a good idea is another matter. The automaker's crisis stems from quality problems and a sinking share of the market, a result of stiffer competition. Polishing the numbers to look better than they are doesn't change that.

Ford says it can break even on a pretax operating basis in 2002. Restoring investor confidence depends not only on making the numbers it forecasts, but in making investors believe these numbers are solid and represent a true turnaround.

For now, Ford's prospects as a company are solid enough so that investors flocked to buy $4.5 billion of convertible trust-preferred securities at 6.5 percent last week, less than the 7.5 percent initially proposed. The yield approximates that of junk-rated companies.

Promises and Results

When General Motors Corp. stumbled into financial crisis in the early 1990s, it resorted to a series of accounting adjustments – all perfectly legal – designed to make net income look better than it was. Wall Street wasn't fooled.

Ford Motor executives in those days shook their heads, proclaiming that their company would never tolerate such shenanigans. The companies seem to have reversed roles, with straight-arrow John Devine, a former Ford official, now vice chairman and chief financial officer at General Motors.

Inglis, in an interview with Bloomberg last week, insisted that 'Ford does not speculate' in precious metals. While Ford may not have bought large amounts of palladium with the aim of making a profit, the company was proud of itself when that happened.

Nevertheless, the automaker demonstrated remarkable clumsiness in procuring the material – something it doesn't tolerate at its own suppliers, who are lectured on controlling costs when they do any work on the automaker's behalf.

As 2002 unfolds, portfolio managers will recall the automaker's promises and gauge the magnitude of the results. Few, if any, will be misled by the substance – or lack of same – behind the numbers.[18]

Risk magazine duly reported in April 2002 that on January 29, 2002 'A shareholder lawsuit was brought against the company due to accusations of artificial inflation of a stock price

---

[18] http://www.turtletrader.com/ford_palladium.html

in 2000 and 2001 by failure to disclose that Ford had made, and failed to hedge, large commitments to purchase the precious metal palladium at "very high prices." A $1 billion write-down for precious metal costs ensued.'

The financial relationships discussed above, currency and commodity price risks, are not core to Ford's business. They are a part of doing business, but the business of Ford Motor is to build and sell motor vehicles. They must use currencies as a means to an end. For example, they want to sell cars and trucks in Europe; these have to be sold in euros. If they build production facilities in Europe to enable them to sell cars and trucks in Europe, the manufacturing plant and its profit and loss are denominated in euros. Likewise with commodity price risks. In the case of palladium, Ford was concerned with a supply shock from Russia; but when they had a $1 billion profit, why didn't they hedge their price risks? The story is also shocking because the company's forecast for future palladium consumption also changed, which is to suggest that they do not actually know how much and for how long they may require palladium supplies. Their hedging strategies should be in line with their underlying cash policy.

This event at Ford came hot on the heels of the Enron bankruptcy and a $1 billion loss on something outside the auto business was the last thing Ford needed – they were having enough problems with the global economy in a post nine-eleven environment.

As we wind down on the Ford story over the past three years, there were a number of notable changes in the 2002 Annual Report after the palladium debacle. One of these was the inclusion of who is actually responsible for the global financial risk management operations, 'the fall guy':

> Direct responsibility for the execution of our market risk management strategies resides with our Treasurer's Office and is governed by written policies and procedures. Separation of duties is maintained between the development and authorization of derivative trades, the transaction of derivatives, and the settlement of cash flows. Regular audits are conducted to ensure that appropriate controls are in place and that they remain effective. In addition, our market risk exposures and our use of derivatives to manage these exposures are reviewed by the GRMC and the audit committee of our Board of Directors.

The Ford case represents the problems that so many endure and fail to manage as well. The problem is not with the way companies manage their global financial risks, but stems from the old pipeline system along with the type of risk mitigation products that are available. Managing non-core global financial risk requires professional acumen but also the right instrument to perform along the lines that the underlying hedger requires. Ford executives complained that derivative instruments used to hedge their financial risks were expensive and the hedge ineffective. This situation is creating an uncertain environment for any treasurer who wants to mitigate a risk but is afraid of the outcome if they do hedge it. They're damned if they do and damned if they don't.

The Ford accounts contain some fine words indicating that Ford knows what it is doing with hedging its non-core global financial risks such as currency and commodity risks, but its actions speak volumes. This problem is not confined to Ford Motor but applies to every corporate throughout the world, as we saw from the *Risk* magazine list of risk disclosures in Table 2.1. I will discuss the ways in which corporates manage their global financial risks in the next chapter.

THE INSURANCE COMPANY PROBLEM

According to *The Times*, the top 175 life insurers in the United States suffered unprecedented losses on their bond and preference share investments between 2001 and 2003.[19] These losses came about during a bond market bull market.

There are significant regulatory changes on the way for insurance companies in Europe, the US and the UK. The way in which they will be required to manage the price volatility arising from their equity and bond investments held in reserve is changing dramatically. In the UK, under two new Financial Services Authority (FSA) consultative papers published in summer 2003 – *Enhanced Capital Requirements and Individual Capital Assessments for Non-Life Insurers* (CP190) and *Enhanced Capital Requirements and Individual Capital Assessments for Life Insurers* (CP195) – insurance companies will have to mark-to-market insurance company reserve portfolios, and this process will have an enormous impact on the way they manage their regulatory capital. In Europe, the new solvency requirements under the new insurance company directive will have the same impact on the management of insurance industry reserves in Europe as in the United Kingdom. One insurer told me that they were doing the best they could with managing equity and bond portfolio price volatility, particularly as it affects their regulatory capital requirements.

The insurance industry was struck by lightning on 11 September 2001 and into 2003 as equity market prices collapsed dramatically, causing an enormous financial disaster for many life and non-life insurance companies throughout the world. Nine-eleven changed everything! Insurance groups had to pay out historic amounts in claims arising from the bevy of insurance risks from nine-eleven, such as property and casualty, airline, environmental, life, and business interruption. But these same insurance companies had to face the onslaught of dramatically falling global capital equity market values in their reserve (investment) portfolios. The combination of these two global man-made events has had an enormous impact, creating what to many insurance executives must have looked like a financial black hole for their industry.

The non-core global financial risks that insurance companies face are the way they manage their assets or their investment portfolio in relation to their insurance liabilities. Insurance companies sell insurance products and are not necessarily investment or money management professionals.

However, the way in which each country's insurance industry manages its assets or investment portfolio is a function of the historic structure of the national financial markets. Life and non-life insurance companies have very different investment profiles because they have very different liabilities. Life insurance companies have liabilities that are pegged to life expectancy, therefore they seek longer-term investment returns which achieve the necessary return-on-investment to meet life expectancy liabilities, which may or may not be linked to the rate of inflation or some other benchmark. Non-life insurance companies have to worry whether they must pay a customer claim if a building falls down, an aeroplane crashes, or an earthquake, hurricane, or any other unexpected property and casualty event occurs. Their investment profile is much shorter term in nature, to ensure that they get the best non-volatile return-on-investment available but with the ability to liquidate the investment to pay a claim.

With that in mind, the problem with the insurance industry's investments involves looking at the historic creation of their investment activities and how they matched their liabilities.

---

[19] 'US insurers lose $24 billion on bond investment,' *The Times*, 21 October 2003.

Table 2.2   Size of global financial markets (US$ billions; amounts outstanding), 2002[20]

	United States	United Kingdom	Euro area	Japan
Equity	11 871	2859	3279	2027
Bonds Of which:	14 831	2059	7977	7484
Government	9135	441	4122	6028
Financial corporate debt	2985	130	3293	298
Non-financial corporate debt	2711	370	562	1159
Bank loans to non-financial corporations	1066	692	3117	8824
GDP	10 446	1567	6670	3986

Different investment styles have evolved over the years: where US and Japanese insurers traditionally use credit instruments, UK insurers invest in equities and continental Europeans favour a mix of government bonds and equities. Table 2.2 shows the size of the global financial markets in 2002; the investment appetite of the national insurance groups has played a huge role in their development.

'Differences in national financial systems and capital markets are due to a variety of factors, including stages of development, levels of financial intermediation and regulations. In a bank-based system, where banks provide the bulk of financing to corporates, capital markets for credit remain less developed. Insurance companies (and other large institutional investors) therefore have fewer opportunities to invest in credit instruments and consequently have found less reason to build up credit risk management skills. This is particularly true since, until recently, in many countries, insurance companies had been largely required to invest in domestic markets (or in instruments denominated in domestic currencies). As such, their asset portfolios tend to reflect the structure of their national or regional capital markets. By contrast, in a market-based system, corporate bond markets are better developed, and insurance companies have a longer tradition of investing in and managing credit risk.'[21]

Before we look at the problems life insurance companies have with their investment practices and the difficulties faced by their managements, it would be as well to give a clearer picture of historic investment practices. Table 2.3 gives the asset allocations of life insurance companies in 2002, at a time of volatility in global capital markets and falling values in equity markets. Note that Japan was in the midst of a 14-year deflationary spiral and perhaps has greater industry-wide investment problems than any other country.[22] The Japanese have generational asset – liability issues and problems for their insurance and pension fund industries, a horrible mess as the Japanese people age and the working population decreases.

Let us now turn to the asset–liability problem that insurance companies face. I said earlier that 11 September 2001 changed everything. Over the two years or so that followed, US, UK and European insurance companies felt the earth quake beneath them as asset values, their investment portfolios, declined substantially in value, while their liabilities steadily rose. Nine-eleven triggered what has been termed the *perfect storm*. Insurance

---

[20] 'Global Financial Stability Report, Market Developments and Issues,' IMF, April 2004, p. 77.

[21] 'Global Financial Stability Report, Market Developments and Issues,' IMF, April 2004, p. 79.

[22] Michael Hyman (2004) *The Power of Global Capital: New International Rules – New Global Risks*, Thomson publishing.

Table 2.3 Asset allocation for the life insurance industry (as a percentage of total assets), 2002[23]

Asset class	United States	United Kingdom	Euro area	Japan
Equity	4%	43%	26%	9%
Government bonds	3%	21%	22%	27%
Corporate bonds	61%	18%	17%	7%
Loans	—	—	20%	32%
Deposits	—	—	—	2%
Foreign securities	—	—	—	15%
Other	18%	18%	16%	8%
Agency securities	14%	—	—	—

companies were liable for payments for airline, property and casualty, business interruption, life insurance, environmental insurance and other non-correlated losses – this was the extreme event that every insurance group fears. Additionally, the Enron and WorldCom bankruptcies caused a default on billions of US dollars in credit default swaps issued by the banks and reinsured by the insurance industry. All of the events affecting the liability payments that had to be made came as equity markets fell dramatically. Interest rates and bond yields fell, along with financial deregulation in the 1990s, and this led many insurance groups to seek assets with higher returns for investment; those countries that did not have well-developed credit markets invested greater proportions of their assets in equity markets. They actually reallocated assets from fixed income assets into equities. The year 2000 brought the beginning of what turned out to be the largest drop in equity market values since the 1929 stock market crash and subsequent economic depression: the UK FTSE index fell by 50% between January 2000 and March 2003, and the German DAX by more than 70%. Insolvency margins fell sharply for those insurers that had invested in equities. 'The episode highlighted to market participants, regulators, and many insurers themselves the need to improve risk management capabilities and the need to rethink the desirability of equity holdings.'[24]

The regulatory world changed as a result, and we now have a new regulatory framework and accounting standards. New problems affecting the same old asset–liability relationship are posing new challenges for insurance companies.

Insurance industry 'Regulations set a framework for insurance companies' balance sheet structures and risk management. There are wide differences between regulatory regimes, with regard to both investment portfolios and insurance products.'[25] The solvency regimes in various countries are very different. 'Approaches in the major jurisdictions generally can be split into two styles. The US and Japanese regulatory systems apply a risk-based capital framework to assets, as well as a component related to insurance risks, as a part of the overall solvency requirement, while the UK and Germany (like other EU countries) have adopted EU directives for minimum solvency standards. Swiss regulations have evolved independently; however, they have been influenced by those of their EU neighbours. Currently, the EU directives base the solvency calculation primarily on premiums, claims and loss reserves, and set asset limits regarding large exposures, rather than applying a relative risk weighting or risk assessment to different asset classes. However, some European countries, such as Denmark, the Netherlands

---

[23] Ibid, p. 81.

[24] Michael Hyman (2004) *The Power of Global Capital: New International Rules – New Global Risks*, Thomson Publishing. p. 94.

[25] Ibid, p. 86.

and (under current proposals) the United Kingdom, go beyond EU directives, incorporating elements of a risk-based system.'[26] 'A risk-based capital regime attributes a range of capital charges to different investment risks.'[27]

Recall that the UK has the largest asset content of equity investments. The regulatory changes introduced by the FSA are causing new industry-wide problems and issues for life and non-life insurance companies. The new solvency regulations, a risk-based capital regime, were published by the FSA in CP190 and CP195. According to a *Risk* magazine special report,

> The new world is expected to result in a more harmonious environment for life insurers, in which business and regulation are aligned. It is also expected to make hedging a more efficient way of protecting against downside risk as well as opening the door to a range of ambitious risk management solutions.[28]

The report added that

> The new rules require life insurers to use two different valuation methods for their portfolios, alongside a revamped capital requirement – the individual capital assessment (ICA). Each measure will bite for different companies at different times.[29]

The UK story is an interesting one, because the regulations issued by the FSA are coming into force at the time of writing. Because UK insurance institutions were heavily invested (43%) in equities, they had to liquidate equity portfolios in an effort to meet the new solvency requirements. They must reduce the risk profile of their investment portfolio because of the impact of the risk-based capital weighting being implemented. An investment in bond portfolios, which are less sensitive to price volatility requires less reserve capital as part of their solvency requirement. Insurers saw the bottom fall out of the equity market from 2000 to 2003, and invested in bonds or other fixed interest investments at a time when interest rates were expecting to start their rise in July 2003, as US Treasury bonds started their bear market sell-off. Germany reacted differently in early 2002 to this problem of reducing their equities exposure by allowing German insurers to account and value their equity portfolios at an 'estimated ultimate realizable value' – basically the price of the equity for the valuation of the portfolio would be above the present market value. Japan did something like this with its banking system, investing regulatory capital in the Japanese equity market, and thereby, instead of being insolvent, doctored the books. The only thing achieved by mispricing one's investment position is the creation of less market transparency, less trust in the system, which will feed into more industry uncertainty, which has been the case for many major insurance companies. The UK authorities took a more pragmatic approach to UK life insurance companies as they started to make asset allocations from equity to fixed income, for example, by looking at each company and applying stress tests to ensure solvency. These companies continued to value their portfolios at market prices, which maintained transparency for the marketplace, the preferred route.

The headlines in the UK press have been telling a very different story as the insurance industry in the UK undergoes a generational change affecting life and non-life companies' risk management practices, investment management activities and risk–return profiles, causing many problems for the insurance industry.

I will look at Equitable Life because it represents a typical life insurance company in the UK which offered annuity products in the 1970s that have been affected by market and investment

---

[26] Michael Hyman (2004) *The Power of Global Capital: New International Rules – New Global Risks*, Thomson Publishing. p. 86.
[27] Ibid.
[28] 'Risk management for insurance companies, "A new regulatory world" ' *Risk*, August 2004.
[29] Ibid.

conditions in the 1990s. When the financial environment changed in the 1990s, Equitable did not have enough money to meet its life insurance liabilities from the returns-on-investment generated from its investment portfolio. Equitable Life was founded in 1762, the UK's first life insurer and the second largest life insurer and largest mutual insurance company in the UK until recently. It was named pension provider of the year in 1999 awarded by *Pensions Industry* magazine. So how did it all go wrong?

CASE STUDY: EQUITABLE LIFE

From the 1950s Equitable Life started to sell life insurance policies with a guaranteed annuity rate which allowed policyholders to opt for minimum pension payouts and a bonus when the policy matured. Typically, the policy would yield £12 000 a year based on £100 000 in pension savings. Equitable Life stopped selling guaranteed policies in 1988, but the asset–liability problem grew more difficult with time. Equitable was locked into liability payments when inflation and interest rates were high, deflation entered into the market in the 1990s, and interest rates fell dramatically, making Equitable's task of meeting policyholder liabilities impossible. Equitable reneged on guaranteed payouts affecting 90 000 policyholders, attempting to preserve a potential liability for Equitable totalling £1.5 billion.

The House of Lords ruled against Equitable Life in July 2001, and the company had to meet the promised liability to its policyholders. Lord Penrose was appointed in August 2001 to conduct an inquiry into the Equitable Life affair and reported its findings in March 2004. Lord Penrose 'identified . . . Equitable's policy of "over-bonusing" – promising more bonus payments to policyholders than was justified by their underlying share of the mutual assets.'[30] He concluded that 'Equitable Life's 1m-plus policyholders were failed by a combination of "manipulation and concealment" by its senior management and "complacent" government regulation.'[31] 'One independent report had previously estimated the cost of compensating policyholders for their Equitable losses at £3 billion.'[32]

In fact, many life insurance companies in the UK market experienced the same problems as Equitable Life – with-profits business accounts for about half the value of life insurance policies issued in the UK. 'With-profits funds aim to smooth investment returns by holding back profits from good years to pay out in lean times.'[33] However, contrary to its advertised selling points, 'Millions of people holding with-profits investments face a bleak and uncertain future as life companies fight a losing battle to keep the smoothed investment approach alive.'[34] And this is their problem, managing the non-core financial risk, the investment portfolio, in relation to their insurance liabilities. One could argue that the inability to assess and manage the asset–liability profile of an insurance company is core to their business and that is why they employ large numbers of actuaries. Calculating the necessary or required asset–liability return profile is one thing, but actually managing and delivering the required return-on-investment to meet insurance company product liabilities, the actual practice of managing that investment portfolio, may not be a core competency for many insurance groups. Insurance companies must take on certain global financial risks in order to sell their insurance products. Managing

---

[30] 'Inquiry inflames Equitable row,' *Financial Times*, 9 March 2004, pp 1.
[31] Ibid.
[32] Ibid.
[33] 'Investors Face Lean Times as Payouts Fall,' *Financial Times*, 23 February 2004, p. 4.
[34] Ibid.

the investment portfolio volatility is as difficult for an insurance company fund manager as it is for the best performing bank proprietary trader, hedge fund or independent money manager. The risk mitigation instruments are also used in an imperfect manner; perhaps the time is right for new global financial risk mitigation instruments for the insurance industry.

The FSA's new rules for life insurance companies, as set out in CP195, 'will force life assurers to issue financial statements that reveal more rigorously the amounts they will have to pay to the 22m policyholders of the funds, which have assets worth £315 billion'.[35] The new regulations will require the life companies to manage their investment portfolios much more professionally, using a variety of investment and risk management disciplines to ensure that they achieve the necessary returns-on-investment, while maintaining sufficient liquidity to meet their insurance product liability streams.

There have been a number of extraordinary stories in the London capital markets about dramatic shifts by life insurance companies in asset allocations, from equity investments into bond portfolios. These shifts are designed to meet the new financial regulatory requirements of the new rules which came into force at the end of 2004. Standard Life announced that it had sold £7.5 billion in a secret operation over a six-week period to meet the stringent new capital regulatory requirements. The *Financial Times* reported that

> Europe's largest mutual insurer said that after taking this corrective action its surplus capital under the City regulator's new 'realistic' solvency rules was in excess of £4b.[36]

According to the FSA, realistic reporting is a key part of reforming the way the FSA regulates insurance companies. The realistic approach provides a better way of helping ensure that firms have enough financial reserves to cover all of their liabilities in future.

Under the existing rules, firms have not had to back all of their promises with hard financial resources. In some cases, this has meant that their calculations have not identified the funds required to cover fully payment of the terminal or final bonuses which the firm has indicated it is likely to pay. The new rules will require firms to make a more accurate assessment of these promises and to hold sufficient finances to cover them.

Realistic reporting will result in some financial consequences for some companies that will require them to make changes in the way they deal with their finances. These companies have to make proposals for covering future liabilities. This will affect the amount of money available for policyholders (and shareholders in a limited company). The FSA will examine the proposals that firms make and will want to be satisfied that they are treating policyholders fairly.

The full implications are not yet clear to firms, the FSA and policyholders. Consumers concerned about the implications for them and unsure whether they should cancel existing policies or make new investments might consider taking financial advice.

So there is the problem for the insurance industry in a nutshell: their non-core financial risks have risen to the top of the pile because they cannot continue to conduct their insurance activities until their financial houses are put in order. And part of that process is the way they manage their assets and investment portfolios, and particularly the way they manage their equity and bond portfolio risks. The process of matching investment return and its price volatility with their specific product liabilities will require a talent and expertise that has not been a core competency with insurance companies.

---

[35] 'Life Assurers Face Tighter Rules on Fund Management,' *Financial Times*, 26 June 2004, p. M28.
[36] 'Standard Life Sells £7.5bn Shares,' *Financial Times*, 19 February 2004, p. 19.

THE PENSION FUND PROBLEM

The pension industry is in worse shape than the insurance industry, although its problems are theoretically similar. Pension funds must pay a cash liability stream to their pensioners in order to see them through their retirement years. The problem once again stems from the way pension funds manage their non-core financial risks in the shape of the investment portfolio that is used to generate sufficient returns-on-investment in order to meet their pension liabilities into the future. The disinflation and deflationary pressures of the 1990s, accompanied by immense negative financial and economic forces in the aftermath of 11 September 2001, have caused pension fund asset values to plummet and the divide between assets and liabilities to become a grand canyon. According to Standard and Poor's, at the end of 1999, US pension funds were running a *surplus* of $300 billion – that is, they had $300 billion more than they needed to fund their pension liabilities. By June 2003, they were running a *deficit* of about $300 billion, a swing of $600 billion in three years! If no one learns a lesson from this example, perhaps we are talking to a wall.

According to David Blake of the Pension Fund Institute at CASS Business School, London,

> Pension funds . . . assumed that inflation and interest rates would remain high, [and] they have been struggling to meet their commitments to deliver a stream of returns. An unanticipated deflation like the one we've had is great for investors who have secured those fixed nominal returns but bad news for anyone who has made those promises.[37]

In July 2003 the *Financial Times* carried a warning from the Confederation of Business Industry (CBI) that corporate earnings growth in the UK would stagnate for the next three years as companies made additional payments into their corporate schemes to balance their pension fund asset–liability deficit, which amounted to £160 billion for the UK corporate pension industry.[38] In November of the same year a *Times* headline declared 'Pensions crisis to cost £27 billion a year'.[39] More recently, the *Financial Times* reported that the UK's public sector pension schemes 'have unfunded liabilities of about $580 billion, more than 50 per cent higher than the most recent estimate published two years ago, according to actuarial consultants Watson Wyatt.'[40] And with the equity market price rally in late 2003, a *Financial Times* headline noted that 'Share rises fail to fill pensions black hole,'[41] although the article suggested that the actual black hole reported by the CBI to be £160 billion five months before was now £120 billion. The headlines paint a very clear and horrific picture for our future retirements.

Pension funds must be realistic in the approach they use in determining the correct sum of money needed to meet future pension fund liabilities and get on with funding the deficit and investing properly. For example, about one-third of the 'typical U.K. pension fund's liabilities represents claims by people contributing to the scheme who have yet to retire. Two-thirds reflect the claim of retirees, which should normally be matched by bonds. But bonds represent only 12.2 per cent of the average U.K. balance portfolio.'[42] And let us not forget the enormous macro problem that infects the pension fund industry, where it is predicted that by the year 2050, while the world's population is expected to grow by 50%, those of most western countries

---

[37] 'The Hunt for Yield Hots Up: Investors and Pension Funds Plunge Deeper into Illiquid and Riskier Assets', *Financial Times*, Comment & Analysis, 22 July 2003, p. 15.

[38] 'Pensions black hole is threat to profits', *Financial Times*, 28 July 2003, p. 1.

[39] 'Pensions crisis to cost £27 billion a year,' *The Times*, 11 November 2003, p. 1.

[40] 'Public sector pension deficit hits £580 bn,' *Financial Times*, 11 August 2004.

[41] 'Share rises fail to fill pensions black hole,' *Financial Times*, 17 January 2004, p. 1.

[42] Weekly Review of the Investment Industry, *Financial Times*, 26 January 2004, p. 1.

are expected to fall – Russia's by 19%, Germany's by 9%, and Japan's by 20%. Eventually, every working person may have to fund the pension of at least one other person.

With almost a decade and a half of deflation in Japan, their pension funding problems and macroeconomic problems are the most difficult and financially the largest to solve. Recall from the insurance company section that Japanese life insurance companies were the only ones to invest in foreign markets, with an asset allocation of 15%. The Japanese insurance company and pension fund institutions are desperate for return-on-investment in an effort to meet their life and pension liabilities, because bond yields were nearly 0% and equity markets in Japan were going down or sideways.

The global demographics are changing dramatically and will continue to do so in the coming years. According to a recent study by the IMF, in its World Economic Outlook, there are three forces driving global demographic changes:

1. Fertility rates – the number of children produced by each woman – are falling rapidly almost everywhere.
2. Life expectancy is also rising.
3. Developing countries are well behind the advanced countries.[43]

Martin Wolf says that,

> As a result of these changes, annual world population growth fell from 1.8 per cent in 1950 to 1.2 per cent in 2000 and is forecast by the United Nations to reach just 0.3 per cent by 2050. The proportion of the world's population under 15 fell from 34 per cent in 1950 to 30 per cent in 2000 but it is now forecast to reach 20 per cent by 2050. Average life expectancy jumped from 47 in 1950 to 65 in 2000 and it is forecasted to reach 74 by 2050. Consequently, the proportion of people over 65 rose from 5 per cent in 1950 to 7 per cent in 2000, and it is forecasted to reach 16 per cent by 2050. Finally, the countries we call "least developed" contained only 8 per cent of the global population in 1950, while the advanced countries contained 32 per cent. By 2000 these proportions had shifted to 11 and 20 per cent, respectively. By 2050, they are forecasted to reach 19 and 14 per cent.... Even in Africa life expectancy is forecast to reach 63 by 2050, up from just 48 in 2000 (itself a fall from 50 in 1990). In advanced countries, too, life expectancies are forecast to rise further, to 83 in 2050, from 77 in 2000.[44]

The percentage of workers' salaries contributed to pension funds will have to rise as well, a situation which most young people will reject. The problem must be solved today. According to *The Economist*,

> Europe is currently witnessing the slow-motion explosion of the most predictable economic and social time bomb in its history. As life expectancy began to increase quickly in the second half of the 20th century and fertility began to decline in the 1970s, the foundations of Europe's generous state-pension systems began slowly to crumble.[45]

In an article about the Lisbon Strategy under the chairmanship of Wim Kok, former prime minister of the Netherlands, Martin Wolf notes that

> the pure impact of ageing populations will be to reduce the potential [economic] growth rate of the EU from the present rate of 2–2.25 per cent to around 1.25 per cent by 2040... Already from 2015, potential economic growth will fall to around 1.5 per cent if the present use of the labour potential remains unchanged.[46]

---

[43] Martin Wolf, 'Through the demographic window of opportunity,' *Financial Times*, 29 September 2004, p. 17.
[44] Ibid.
[45] 'Work longer, have more babies: How to solve Europe's pension crisis', *The Economist*, 27 September 2003, p. 13.
[46] Martin Wolf, 'Europe must grow up if it wants to be taken seriously,' *Financial Times*, 10 November 2004, p. 17.

Part of the problem with the pension fund investment function has to do with the way in which traditional investment managers are mandated by the pension funds' trustees; portfolios are being measured or benchmarked against a performance index based on the assets of the portfolio itself. For example, a UK domestic equity portfolio's success or failure is based upon the portfolio manager's ability to outperform a FTSE-100-based benchmark index. A global bond investment manager may be measured against the JP Morgan World Government Bond Index. But the traditional performance measurement standards for pension fund investments are not being measured or indexed against the actual pensioner's liability required by the investment portfolio's return-on-investment.

At this point I should define the different types of pension fund out there and discuss the way in which investment risk is managed in relation to achieving a pension's expected liability cash flow stream. There are a variety of types of pension scheme available.[47] *Funded pensions* make pension payments from a fund that is an accumulation of financial assets built up over a period of years from the contributions of its members. These plans may be either private or government-run.

In contrast to funded pensions, *pay-as-you-go (PAYG)* systems pay pensions out of current contributions or taxes. They are usually run by governments from current tax revenues, and the amounts of the benefits are based on commitments, or promises, made by governments.

Defined contribution plans are funded accounts in the name of specific individuals. The contribution rate is fixed. The individual's pension is an annuity whose size – at a given life expectancy and rate of interest – is determined only by the size of his or her lifetime pension accumulation. Members of these schemes face the uncertainties associated with varying real rates of return to the pension's assets.

Often run at the level of firms or industries, *defined benefit plans* pay an annuity based on the employee's wage and length of service. In older schemes, the pension was often based on the employee's wage in his or her last year, or last few years, of service. The recent trend has been to base benefits on a person's real wages averaged over an extended period. Either way, a person's annuity is, in effect, wage-indexed until retirement.

In these schemes, the employer, not the employee, bears the primary risk of a fall in the return on plan assets, but also gets the benefit of any higher-than-required return. In reality, these risks (or gains) to the employer are shared more broadly, rippling through to current workers (whose wages may be more or less dependent on the cost of the scheme to the employer), to shareholders and taxpayers (through effects on profits), to customers (through effects on prices), and even to past or future workers, if the company uses surpluses from some periods to boost pensions in others.

Social insurance schemes are typically government-run PAYG plans. Risk is shared even more broadly than in private defined benefit plans. The costs of adverse outcomes can be borne by the retiree (through reduced benefits), by current workers (through higher contributions), by the taxpayer (through tax-funded subsidies), and by future taxpayers (through subsidies financed by government borrowings).

Let us now define which pension funds we are talking about in this book. First of all, when I talked about the insurance companies' problems with their life assurance products, these are defined contribution funds. Individuals invest a sum of money in a life insurance company fund, and at retirement the entire net value of the fund is converted into an annuity that is meant to last the duration of their retirement. However, insurance companies such as Equitable Life and

---

[47] *The Pension Puzzle*, IMF, March 2002.

Standard Life have invested badly, and the value of these funds has dropped significantly – and with inflation falling dramatically, the annual income stream from the sum saved with the life insurance company will not provide the same level of income in the 2% inflation environment of today as it would have in the 7% environment of ten years ago. Investors have seen their savings drop significantly and the annuity conversion value fall in line with inflation.

The pension funds that we will be discussing in the rest of this chapter are the corporate pension fund schemes known as funded or defined benefit plans, as defined above. The 'black hole' that is discussed in the press concerns the assets that the company and the employee are saving, invested to ensure that they meet the defined benefit, which could be a proportion of the employee's final salary. There are two problems with these pension schemes. The first are the historic promises that the employer makes to his employee on the benefits that the pension will pay at retirement, based on the final salary of the employee. The employee may receive, for example, two-thirds of their final salary as their annual pension payment. The second problem is the way the saved pool of employee and employer contributions is invested in the capital markets in an effort to generate the required return-on-investment to meet the final cash flow payments that the employee will receive as pension payments at retirement. This is where we step in – we have no control over the promises made by the employer to the employee, but we will look at the way those funds are invested.

The problem with the investment strategy stems from the high-inflationary period of the 1970s and 1980s, which focused the investment management policy of the defined benefits funds on investing in equities, particularly in the United Kingdom. The equity content of a typical defined benefit corporate pension scheme would be about 75% invested in equity markets, but the contradiction is that two-thirds of the typical UK pension scheme is to be paid to retirees today, whilst only the last third are actually working. Therefore, the typical UK pension scheme should be 75% invested in fixed income investments which are generating the necessary investment income to meet today's pension liabilities, rather than 75% invested in equities. Unfortunately, the harsh reality in 2005 is that most corporate defined benefit schemes do not have sufficient investment capital to make an asset allocation of 75% to fixed income. Equity investments historically generate a higher investment return and the corporate sponsor of these pension funds needs as much investment return as possible in an effort to make up the asset–liability deficit. The alternative is to make the fixed income investment allocation, but the corporate sponsor would be required to contribute significant sums of money to the pension scheme.

In the UK, for example, many corporate trustees feel that they do not have the expertise to make the correct investment decisions and they tend to outsource their funds to institutional investment managers who are known as balanced fund managers. Balanced fund managers manage a range of asset classes, such as equities, bonds and property, and they will determine the best asset allocation for the client's portfolio, diversify it amongst the various asset classes and get on with managing the pension fund scheme's money. The pension fund trustees have been taken completely out of the asset allocation decision-making process and to an extent responsibility for managing their portfolio's investments. According to the *Financial Times*,

> [Fund] managers are ignoring investment wisdom and are continuing to invest fortunes in equities. Traditional fund managers are defying the latest investment thinking by taking the biggest punt on the stock market since the early 1990s. These fund managers could be taking unreasonable risk with the retirement savings of thousands of people. There is also a concern that this gamble is motivated by the desire to produce the highest possible return and, in doing so, retain pension fund clients who have been turning to new-style specialist fund managers.[48]

---

[48] 'Funds gamble pensioners' money,' *Financial Times*, 26 January 2004, p. 1.

Starting with the past problem created by outsourcing the responsibility for managing their pension fund assets and allowing a huge investment in equities, by early 2003 defined benefit schemes found themselves with an enormous asset–liability deficit due to the fall in equity values. The impact of this colossal mistake left corporate defined benefit schemes unable to ensure that they can meet their pensioners' liabilities into the future. In April 2004, the *Financial Times* reported that 'Corporate contributions to schemes rose by 95% although the deficit was not lower than in 2002.' The article went on to say that 'The study by Watson Wyatt, the actuarial consultant that advises about half of the FTSE 100 companies, shows that corporate contributions to pension schemes rose on average by 95 per cent between 2002 and 2003. "Even if companies continue to contribute at the new increased levels it will take many years before the deficits are eliminated unless there is a dramatic improvement in the stock markets without the knock-on effect on corporate bond market or inflation expectations," said Robert Hails, partner at Watson Wyatt. Watson Wyatt also adds that the aggregate deficit of the FTSE 100 companies as at March 31, 2003 was £60 billion.'[49] Three months later, the *Financial Times* reported that 'FTSE 100 companies are doing far too little to plug [the] shortfall'.[50]

In the US, Bradley Pelt, executive director of the Pension Benefit Guarantee Corporation (PBGC), a US government-sponsored safety net, told a Senate Commerce Committee that 'while the agency could cover its current obligations, the longer-term solvency of the pension industry . . . is at risk.' The PBGC's single-employer insurance fund had a record deficit at the end of 2003 fiscal year of $11.2billion, and Mr Pelt said he expected to report a 'significantly increased deficit for the 2004 fiscal year.'[51] The PBGC estimates that overall underfunding of defined benefit plans among US companies has hit $278.6 billion, with the airlines accounting for more than 10%.[52]

A major US company that took necessary steps to start to fund its pension fund liabilities was General Motors (GM). According to a Reuters report of December 2003, GM expected to close a $19.3 billion gap in its pension plans, which was the largest deficit facing any single US company.[53] GM used a massive bond offering along with asset sales to plug its hole. It also announced that it thought the pension hole would cost shareholders $4 per share in 2003/2004 and $3.30 per share the following year. The financial pain may be too much for some, but it is better to take one's medicine today than to wait for the problem to compound and worsen over time.

The pension fund crisis reminds me of the Japanese debt and deflation crisis. When it first started to cause Japanese government officials sleepless nights in 1991, the Japanese hoped that the problem would take care of itself over time as they believed that the Japanese economy would improve in the near future. Fourteen years later, there may be signs that the debt and deflationary spiral is resolving itself. Note that the Japanese have the largest government deficit in the industrialized west; they continue to have billions of dollars of bank bad debts and their pension fund system is nearly bankrupt. Japanese insurance and pension funds are desperately seeking sufficient returns-on-investment to have a chance of meeting their pension liabilities. Many of these problems that the Japanese people have to live with could doubtless have been solved back in 1991. I hope the pension fund industry and corporate America, Britain and elsewhere will do the right thing – inject sufficient funds, realign their investment portfolios with their liabilities and put the problems behind them.

---

[49] 'Companies double their payments to pensions,' *Financial Times*, 11 April 2004, p. M1.
[50] 'Companies failing to plug pension shortfall,' *Financial Times*, 22 July 2004, p. 2.
[51] 'US Pensions Agency Issues Warning,' *Wall Street Journal*, 7 October 2004.
[52] 'Benefits or Bailout,' *Financial Times*, 3 September 2004, p. 15.
[53] 'GM Nearly Closes Pension Gap,' Reuters, 12 December 2003.

In the UK, many corporate schemes started to offload their equity portfolios for fixed income securities, as reported by the *Financial Times*: 'Pension funds could switch £150 billion out of equities into safer investments such as bonds over the next three years to help ensure pension payments are met'.[54] Unfortunately, the timing of these changes in asset allocations could not be worse, as inflation and interest rates are on the rise, and global economic growth is stabilizing after the past three years of economic and financial storm and chaos. Without making a cash infusion contribution into corporate defined benefit schemes, the chance of their asset base growing sufficiently quickly in order to meet their pension liabilities is at best slight.

'A return to a 1950s world of low interest rates and low nominal returns need not be cause for alarm', said the *Financial Times* in July 2004, although unfortunately the accompanying headline was 'The hunt for yield hots up: Investors and pension funds plunge deeper into illiquid and riskier assets'. [55] Pension fund trustees and executives are forgetting how quickly economic and financial events can move in our modern global society. What they do not seem to realize is that

> Today's 'high-yield bonds' generate about as much income as bank savings products did in the days when Michael Milken was pioneering the use of scorned non-investment-grade bonds in the 1980s. Some analysts suspect that the word 'junk' is in need of revival.[56]

Pension funds are investing more and more of their assets in much higher-risk junk bonds and other types of investment in an effort to improve return-on-investment in a low inflation, low nominal return era – isn't this what they used equity investments for when inflation was high?

> With the benefit of hindsight, many pension funds feel they were overly concerned with holding liquid investments during the stock market boom that ended in early 2000. Now they are so desperate for high yield that they are putting money into hedge funds, mezzanine funds and other alternative assets, knowing they may have to hold these investments for a considerable period of time.[57]

In the UK, the FSA

> worries that many investors are suffering from 'money illusion': the failure to understand that, because of falling inflation, a nominal return that seems low today could represent a better real return than a much higher nominal rate did a decade or two ago.[58]

The fact is that if inflation rises it will cause nominal yields to rise as well.

The problem with pension funds is that they have an enormous investment risk that they must solve in order to meet their investors' pension benefits. I suppose life would be a great deal easier if the corporate schemes merely injected sufficient funds to balance their asset–liability gap; however, since that is not likely, pension fund trustees must have a much better understanding of the global capital markets, the way to invest and how to hedge investment risk when needed.

Part of the problem with present pension funds stems from the way they value their assets and liabilities. According to *The Economist*,

> Perhaps the most egregious way in which companies smooth profits is by valuing pension assets using expected rather than actual returns. They are allowed to do this because the assets are invested to meet pension promises in the distant future, so they can dismiss short-term swings.... What

---

[54] 'Funds may move £150 bn from equities,' *Financial Times*, 27 May 2004, p. 3.
[55] 'The Hunt for Yield Hots Up: Investors and Pension Funds Plunge Deeper into Illiquid and Riskier Assets', *Financial Times*, 22 July 2004, p. 15.
[56] Ibid.
[57] Ibid.
[58] Ibid.

worries the SEC and many other investors is that using assumed returns, particularly high ones, is at best incredibly misleading and at worst gives the firms the flexibility to manipulate earnings.... Another assumption that has caught the SEC's eye is the discount rates used by companies to value pension liabilities. The higher the rate, the lower the present value of the pension obligations and the lower the pension expense.[59]

Elsewhere in the same issue, *The Economist* says that

> literally billions of dollars have been conjured on to firms' balance sheets and profit and loss accounts in recent years, flattering reported earnings.... The defined-benefit retirement funds of many big companies have huge deficits. But at the stroke of an actuary's pen a company can make heroic assumptions about the returns its pension assets will earn and so the rate at which its liabilities will grow in future, allowing it to claim that the pension-deficit problem is manageable.[60]

The solution to the problem is simple: proper capitalization of the pension fund, with matched liabilities, bearing in mind that a retirement liability is a certain prediction, unlike most insurance liabilities. Therefore, the investment profile for a properly capitalized pension scheme should match the liability stream. I suspect (and we are seeing it already) that many individuals will move toward a defined contribution scheme, although I would prefer a professional money manager to manage my money rather than a life insurance company annuity scheme. I dislike the annuity scheme – you are a hostage to the rate of inflation when your lump sum is converted into an annuity. If inflation is low when your fund is converted, and if inflation then rises, the value of your annuity will fall. I would prefer to take from my lump sum as I choose, thereby allowing me to live on the interest income from a pension fund bond portfolio, giving me greater flexibility with the future economic and financial environment.

To return to the US corporate funds with which we began this section, how could they allow a $300 billion surplus to dissolve and turn into a $300 billion deficit? Clearly this had better not happen again – when there is a pension fund surplus, reduce the investment risk, line up the assets with the liabilities and finish! What were people thinking? Like many government officials who were spending the fiscal surplus in Washington, which turned into the largest fiscal deficit the United States has ever seen, corporate executives facing a $300 billion pension fund surplus were probably thinking dividend.

CONCLUSION

In this chapter I have sought to explain the problems that exist within the corporate, insurance and pension fund world relating to non-core global financial risks. A pension fund scheme, for example, is a savings pool for an employee's retirement, a benefit offered by the company to its employees; the investment vehicle and consequences are a result of setting up the savings pool. If the savings pool were invested in money market instruments, none of the problems discussed above would happen.

The fact remains that the executives who make decisions in each of these categories must have a much better understanding of non-core global financial risks. The way in which different asset classes behave in the marketplace can be quite shocking when one looks at perceptions versus reality.

---

[59] 'Time to end a scandal,' *The Economist*, 30 October 2004, pp. 14–15.
[60] Ibid.

Many of the problems discussed in this chapter are also a result of the problems with the old pipeline system discussed in Chapter 1: more investment banks becoming proprietary traders, large money management firms forming part of a large banking or insurance institution, the type of risk management instruments available, how they are used and sold to the clients.

In Chapter 3 we will look at the many ways in which corporates, insurance companies and pension funds try to solve their problems using derivative instruments and also at the new regulations, corporate governance issues and laws that are changing corporate behaviour.

3

The Status Quo

Status Quo, you know, that is Latin for the mess we're in.

President Ronald Reagan March 16, 1981

Everyone chooses one of two roads in life – the old and the young, the rich and the poor, men and women alike. One is the broad, well-travelled road to mediocrity, the other road to greatness and meaning.

Stephen Covey, *The 8th Habit From Effectiveness to Greatness*,
Simon & Schuster, 2004, page 27

In this chapter, I will describe the ways in which corporates, insurance companies and pension funds presently manage the non-core global financial risks described in the previous chapter. Some corporates are doing better or getting luckier than others, while the insurance and pension fund industries tend to move in herds – slow moving and gigantic in size and in the scale of their problems.

> All business is risky. Logically, then, success or failure depends on a company's risk management savvy. While some may approach the management of risk with a flyswatter, the majority observe a more sophisticated approach wherein some risks are *avoided,* others *accepted,* some *transferred,* and others *mitigated*. These are the four classic risk treatments, and art and science inevitably come together in determining when and how to apply them.[1]

This chapter is divided into several sections. The first will look at derivative instruments and discuss their deficiencies when corporates, insurance companies and pension funds use them to manage their global financial risks. The second section will discuss how management behaviour is changing (corporate governance) and the way in which global financial risks are handled in the future. The third section will discuss the accounting implications for managing global financial risks and the new accounting regulations being introduced for hedging global financial risks. The fourth section takes a brief look at the Basel II capital accord, a new reserve capital regulation for global banking institutions which will come into force by 2007, and will have an impact on the way in which global banks do business with their institutional clients. The fifth section will look at specific examples of how corporates hedge their global financial risks today. The sixth section will look at the insurance industry and specifically at the new insurance regulations being brought into force around the world and how they will affect the way insurance groups manage their global financial risks as they impact their reserve capital requirements. The seventh section will briefly discuss the way in which pension funds are managing their non-core global financial risks: the way in which they outsource their investment management function to external investment managers and determine or outsource the asset allocation of their investments as well. Although I have touched on this subject in the previous chapter, I will provide a summary of the issues that they face today. The final section will provide a conclusion for this chapter and prepare the reader for the next.

---

[1] Mary Pat McCarthy and Timothy Flynn (2004) *Risk from the CEO and Board Perspective*. McGraw-Hill, p. 85.

DERIVATIVE INSTRUMENTS

Derivative instruments have been around for centuries. There is nothing new about derivatives. Aristotle, in his book *Politics*, written 2500 years ago, mentions an option on the use of olive-oil presses. In the 1700s, the Japanese traded futures-like contracts on rice or warehouse receipts. And the Chicago Board of Trade has been the scene of forward and futures contracts since 1849. Derivatives get their name because their prices are 'derived' from the price of some underlying security or commodity, or an index, interest rate or exchange rate. The term 'derivative' includes forwards, futures, options, swaps, combinations of such, plus traditional securities and loans. The Chairman of the Federal Reserve, Alan Greenspan, remarked in October 2004:

> No discussion of better risk management would be complete without mentioning derivatives and the technologies that spawned them and so many other changes in banking and finance. Derivatives have permitted financial risks to be unbundled in ways that have facilitated both their measurement and their management. Because risks can be unbundled, individual financial instruments can now be analyzed in terms of their common underlying risk factors, and risks can be managed on a portfolio basis. Concentrations of risk are more readily identified, and when such concentrations exceed the risk appetites of intermediaries, derivatives and other credit and interest rate risk instruments can be employed to transfer the underlying risks to other entities. As a result, not only have individual financial institutions become less vulnerable to shocks from underlying risk factors, but also the financial system as a whole has become more resilient.
>
> Derivatives have been used effectively by many banks to shift interest rate risks. In addition, while credit risks are transferred among financial intermediaries based on their ability and willingness to absorb such risk, increasingly credit risk has been transferred from highly leveraged financial institutions to those with much larger equity coverage. For example, not only has a significant part of the credit risks of an admittedly few large U.S. banks been shifted to other U.S. and foreign banks and to insurance and reinsurance firms here and abroad, but such risks also have been shifted to pension funds, to hedge funds, and to other organizations with diffuse long-term liabilities or no liabilities at all. Most of the credit-risk transfers were made early in the credit-granting process; but in the late 1990s and early in this decade, significant exposures to telecommunication firms were laid off through credit default swaps, collateralized debt obligations, and other financial instruments. Other risk transfers reflected later sales at discount prices as specific credits became riskier and banks rebalanced their portfolios. Some of these sales were at substantial concessions to entice buyers to accept substantial risk. Whether done as part of the original credit decision or in response to changing conditions, these transactions represent a new paradigm of active credit management and are a major part of the explanation of the banking system's strength during the most recent period of stress. Even the largest corporate defaults in history (WorldCom and Enron) and the largest sovereign default in history (Argentina) have not significantly impaired the capital of any major U.S. financial intermediary.[2]

Let us briefly outline the main derivative instruments. *Forward* contracts, the original and most basic derivative form, are agreements to buy or sell a certain quantity of an asset or commodity in the future, at a specified price, time and place.

Futures are standardized agreements to buy or sell a certain quantity of an asset or commodity in the future at a specified price, time and place. They differ from forward contracts in that they are standardized as to quantity, the underlying assets or commodities, and the time. Only the price and number of contracts are negotiated in the trading process. A daily margining system limits the risk of default.

Options give the buyer the right, but not the obligation, to buy or sell an asset or commodity at a specified *strike* price on or before a certain date. *Call* options are options to buy; *put*

---

[2] Alan Greenspan, American Bankers Association Annual Convention, 5 October 2004.

options are options to sell. Options sellers have the obligation to pay when buyers exercise their rights. An American option allows the buyer to exercise his right whenever he wants to – which in essence means whenever the price of the option is in-the-money. A European option only permits the buyer to exercise his right at the final expiry date, which means he will do so if the option is in-the-money at the expiry date.

Swaps are agreements to swap the net value of two series of payments where one is usually based on a fixed interest rate and the other is linked to a variable interest rate, another currency's interest rate, the total rate of return of a security or index, or a commodity.

The notional values of derivatives – the amounts used to calculate the payoff – can be staggering, but the actual liabilities involved are much lower. For example, the Bank of International Settlements found

> in 1995 that the notional values of all derivatives (excluding those traded in organized exchanges) were $41 trillion; however, if every obligated party had reneged, creditor loss would have been only $1.7 trillion, or 4.3% of the notional value.[3]

In addition to the derivative instruments defined above, the growing use of *credit derivatives* has revolutionized the way credit is managed and transferred from one counterparty to another. According to the IMF's Global Financial Stability report, insurers were the second largest group of credit protection sellers, after banking institutions. Life insurance companies use collateralized debt obligations to diversify or expand their existing credit exposures, while non-life companies acquire credit risk because it is seen to be uncorrelated with their traditional property and casualty business.[4]

> A credit derivative transaction involves one party shedding credit risk (in other words, buying credit protection) and another taking on this risk (i.e., selling credit protection). Credit risk can be transferred in part or in its entirety either by buying credit risk protection to reduce credit exposure or by directly selling the credit-risk bearing instrument. Sellers of credit protection take on credit risk in a manner similar to purchases of corporate bonds, loans, or other credit instruments.
>
> Credit instruments can be classified into two broad categories: those that transfer the credit risk relating to an individual borrower (single-name products) and those relating to a number of borrowers (portfolio products). Examples of these two categories are single-name credit default swaps (CDSs) and collateralized debt obligations (CDOs), respectively. In a CDS transaction, the protection seller agrees to pay the protection buyer if a reference entity (a company or sovereign) experiences a predefined 'credit event', such as a default on a debt obligation. The protection seller receives a premium (typically paid quarterly) from the protection buyer over the lifetime of the transaction.
>
> Typical 'cash' CDOs are debt securities issued by a special purpose vehicle (SPV), collateralized by a portfolio of loans and bonds. 'Synthetic' CDOs are created using portfolios of CDOs combined with highly rated debt securities (e.g., government bonds) to synthetically replicate credit securities. Investors who purchase CDOs from the SPV are selling credit protection, while the entities packaging the loans or bonds within (or entering into CDSs with) the SPV are protection buyers.[5]

When using derivative instruments to hedge any financial risk, understanding the technicalities, nuances and differences between the various instruments takes time and plenty of practice. There is an enormous amount of underlying financial activity going on between an underlying cash asset and the hedging instrument being used. Where forward and futures markets transfer risk (price volatility) from one party to another, an options contract mitigates the price volatility

[3] Ibid., pp. 97–98.
[4] 'Global Financial Stability Report, Market Developments and Issues,' IMF, April 2004, p. 90.
[5] Ibid.

risk of the underlying cash asset. Many people think (mistakenly) that an option is similar to an insurance policy, because one pays a premium to an options underwriter. Options differ from insurance in that options do not require one party to suffer an actual loss for payment to occur. In addition, the owner of an option need not have an insurable interest – such as ownership in the underlying asset – in the option.

Derivative instruments have their own unique behavioural patterns in relation to the underlying cash asset or risk. A futures contract behaves differently from an options contract. These behavioural characteristics, if not understood and, most importantly, not professionally managed, can cause untold financial harm. I am assuming that the reader has a basic working knowledge of the use of derivative instruments. We are not concerned with how to use derivative instruments but with the many things that can go wrong with them.

For example, there are a number of ways in which option instruments can go wrong. When purchasing an options contract, one has certain expectations about its behaviour in relation to the price of the underlying cash instrument. One would naturally expect the options price to move in close concert with the underlying instrument, in other words, the options contract correlates perfectly with the underlying cash risks – this is what goes wrong in so many ways.

The valuation of options contracts was dramatically improved in the 1960s when Fischer Black, Myron Scholes and Robert Merton created a model for this purpose which included several ingredients such as time, price spread (the ratio between the actual underlying cash instrument and the designated strike price of the option), interest rates and volatility. This widely used tool is now known as the Black–Scholes formula.

The Black–Scholes model makes six significant assumptions which, if not understood, can cause option prices to behave in a manner that is inconsistent with one's expectations:

1. The stock pays no dividend during the option's life. Most companies pay dividends to shareholders, so this is a serious drawback to the model, because if the company pays a dividend, the higher the dividend yield the lower the option premium.
2. European exercise terms are used. When using an American option and one exercises the option before the expiry date, the remaining time value of the option (see below) will be collected by the option buyer when selling the option before the expiry date.
3. Markets are efficient. This assumption means that investors cannot consistently predict the direction of the market or an individual stock. Furthermore, it means that prices move in a simple continuous fashion. This flies in the face of reality: price jumps often occur between one day's close and the next day's opening.
4. No commissions are charged. This is completely unrealistic, since everybody has to pay commissions.
5. Interest rates remain constant and known. The Black–Scholes model uses the risk-free interest rate usually associated with a 30-day US Treasury bill. There is no such thing as a risk-free interest rate and interest rates change daily, as indeed does the 30-day US Treasury bill yield.
6. The Black–Scholes model assumes that investment returns are log-normally distributed. This assumption means that the returns of the underlying cash stock prices move are normally distributed. There is no such thing as a normal distribution in the global capital markets – extreme events occur far more often than normal theory would have it.

The Black–Scholes model, while imperfect, allows investors to compare like with like. It offers a way to standardize the valuation of derivative assets or of risks and compare one investment with another. The important thing is to keep its limitations in mind.

There are a number of other little and independent things that can go wrong with options contracts. The things that can go wrong can be discovered as we explore the various options, *Greeks*, which relate to the various option price sensitivities that occur within the options' price versus, and in relation to, the underlying cash asset price action:

- *Delta risk*. This measures, for a certain underlying price, the impact on the option's price of a change in the underlying future price. Delta is defined as the change in the option price divided by the absolute value of the change in the asset price. This risk indicator gives you an idea of the speed of reaction of the option. A deep in-the-money option will usually have a delta close to ±1; a far out-of-the-money option will have a delta close to 0.
- *Gamma risk*. Since delta is not a constant and changes with the price of the underlying asset, the impact of the delta risk for a given change in the underlying asset is called gamma risk. Gamma can be positive or negative. It takes its highest value close to the strike price. A gamma of 0.05 means that the delta will increase by $0.05 for each dollar change in the underlying price.
- *Lambda risk*. This is very close to the gamma risk; lambda is defined as the percentage change in the option price for a 1% change in the underlying price. Lambda is always greater than (or close to) 1.
- *Theta risk*. Theta measures the impact on the option's price of a one-day change in the time remaining to expiration.
- *Kappa/vega risk*. The option's price is affected by changes in the market's valuation of implied volatility. This very important risk is referred to as kappa or vega risk. Vega is defined as the dollar change in option price for one positive point of implied volatility change.
- *Rho risk*. The last variable in the Black–Scholes model is the risk-free interest rate, discussed earlier. The impact on the option's price of a change in the risk-free interest rate is referred to as rho risk.[6]

Using options to play with risk is one thing; the attempt to hedge an underlying financial risk is quite another. There are so many moving parts in an options contract. As it tends to its expiry date, the time value decay will increase quite sharply, particularly if the option's strike price is out-of-the-money. A change in interest rates will change the value of an options contract. Investor anxieties and expectations will also change day by day and this is measured by implied volatility (the standard deviation that sets the model price equal to the market price). And lastly, the hedge ratio, or delta risk introduced above, can cause so many headaches as an investor attempts to control his/her delta, meaning having to ensure that there is nominal-for-nominal options contract exposure to the underlying cash asset risk. If an options value moves from out-of-the-money to in-the-money, the delta could move from 0.33 changes in the options value versus the underlying cash asset to 0.75 movements to the underlying cash asset. If this were to occur, and if the investor had used, let's say, three options contracts to hedge the underlying cash asset to ensure that they capture as close to a one-for-one hedge ratio with the underlying cash asset, and the delta moves to 0.75, the investor is now holding roughly twice as many options contracts than necessary to hedge a one-for-one relationship with the underlying cash asset.

Managing the delta ratio and implied volatility are full-time jobs for any market professional and can be a very cumbersome, difficult, and extremely frustrating exercise for any portfolio

---

[6] Analysis of Asset Allocation, 'Option: Greeks and Option's Risks.'

manager, let alone a corporate executive, pension fund manager or insurance company reserve manager. It is not their core competency and more importantly they do not have the time to stare at trading screens, keeping an eye on their options positions. No wonder there are so many hedge deviations in corporate accounts when they use options contracts as their hedging tool.

There is a place for the use of options, both for professional investment managers and those who are trying to mitigate price volatilities in the corporate sector. Those who use them successfully clearly understand the limitations of options as instruments and their pricing models that are used to value them.

A futures contract allows one to transfer the price volatility risk of the underlying cash asset to another counterparty. There are a few things that can go wrong with them.

A financial futures contract allows one to hedge interest rates, bonds and equity indices. The futures contract is standardized to represent a notional bond, or in the case of equities an entire index, such as the S&P 500 or FTSE 100. When an instrument is standardized its behaviour will reflect the underlying notional bond or index. For example, a US Treasury bond futures contract has a nominal value of $100 000 and usually a 30-year maturity. The actual underlying cash instrument deliverable by the futures contract is US Treasury bonds that, if callable, are not callable for at least 15 years from the first day of the delivery month or, if not callable, have a maturity of at least 15 years from the first day of the delivery month. The invoice price equals the contract's settlement price times a conversion factor plus accrued interest. The conversion factor is the price of the delivered bond ($1 par value) to yield 6%. The actual cash bond held with a client portfolio may not relate to the 30-year US Treasury bond futures contract because it is not exactly defined by the futures contract's established and generic characteristics. There may be several prospective cheapest deliverable bonds at the outset of the trading of the bond futures contract, but the individual cash bonds will change in price throughout this period of time and when the time comes to settle the cheapest-to-deliver bond with the bond futures contract, there will be only one cheapest-to-deliver cash bond and it may not be the cash bond originally thought to be deliverable when the bond futures contract was purchased. The futures contract will closely track the cheapest deliverable cash bond in terms of their respective price movements. However, if the user of the futures contract owns a portfolio of bonds that are not the cheapest to deliver to the bond futures contract, the actual cash bond portfolio will not correlate perfectly with the futures contract. This is a significant problem when using standardized futures contracts to hedge a portfolio of underlying cash assets – correlation deviation.

If one uses an equity index such as the S&P 500 futures contract, unless the investor owns the precise amounts of the underlying index in a cash portfolio, the index futures will correlate differently than the underlying futures contract. And that correlation deviation can come from many areas: the change in short-term interest rates, changes in the prices of the underlying futures index and adverse price movements relative to the portfolio against the futures index. When the exchanges change the make-up of an index, as happens from quarter to quarter, so too will the behaviour of the futures index.

Later in this chapter I will explore an interesting example of the use of hard commodity futures contracts by the airline Lufthansa, which hedged its jet fuel price volatility risk using crude oil and heating oil derivatives. It is an inexact science but unless one is watching the daily price changes and correlation deviations every day, there are too many factors that can go wrong and will go wrong, causing a potential for hedge deviation. Management, thinking they properly hedged their unforeseen price volatility on their non-core global financial risks soon recognize, when it is too late, that their hedging strategy has gone terribly wrong. They risk facing their shareholders reporting, perhaps, good earnings, but losses due to hedge deviations on their currency, bond, equity and hard commodity risks.

Derivative instruments are complicated. They require a good mathematics background and market understanding to use them and to understand the interrelationships between the derivative and the underlying cash asset. But also one must understand how derivatives behave between themselves – for example, options versus futures. Using derivatives is a full-time job and may not be the core competency of the treasurer or those who work in his office. Thus, their use leads to problems more often than not for those who are not professionally endowed to deal with them.

There are a number of other problems when using derivatives that I touched on in Chapter 1. I pointed out that seven banks in the US account for almost 96% of the total notional amount of derivatives in the commercial banking system (99% if one considers the top 25 banks). In addition, 'the top seven banks accounted for 79% of the trading revenue'[7] derived from derivative instruments – that only leaves 21% of the trading revenues for you and me. The capacity issue is a serious issue because when trying to buy and sell derivative instruments, the ultimate liquidity for the pricing, buying and selling is down to seven banking institutions (six if one takes into account the merger between JP Morgan Chase and Bank One).

Think of what might happen if one of these seven derivative market-makers suddenly withdrew from the market. Risk managers at JP Morgan Chase and Deutsche Bank are modelling their stress testing to anticipate this event – are you?

> When Citigroup's chairman Sandford Weil decided to pull Salomon Smith Barney out of the US fixed-income arbitrage business in mid-1998, the investment banking unit unveiled losses of $700 million related to withdrawal, along with Russian credit losses in the third quarter of that year. According to one school of thought, this exit was a significant contribution to the near-collapse of the LTCM hedge fund around the same time. Both Salomon and LTCM were taking similar views – for example, they were shorting dollar swap spreads – and Salomon's exit caused LTCM to mark down its positions. Other investment banks, also faced with mark-down problems, created a consortium to bail out LTCM to the tune of $3.6 billion to protect their own business.[8]

There are two points to be taken on board from this event. First, when a major bank pulls out of the derivatives business, the knock-on effect may be billions of dollars of losses as the market lacks sufficient liquidity to cushion the reversing of market positions. Second, when bank proprietary traders and investors are chasing the same investment and investment returns, the banks will win – they see the investment flows, they know who is winning and losing in the markets and in those specific positions, their market intelligence is therefore better than that of non-banking investors. They have the liquidity and capital to suffer those losses and recover; meanwhile LTCM, the hedge fund, went out of business.

> The disaster scenario is this: even a pre-planned withdrawal of one of the bulge-bracket derivatives dealers would cause a market disturbance that would make the near failure of LTCM look like a relatively minor blip on a dealing screen. LTCM had 'only' $1.25 trillion of derivative notional on its books in September 1998. JP Morgan Chase held $32.69 trillion at the end of the second quarter of this [2003] year. Furthermore, a large proportion of profits at leading dealers are generated by relatively illiquid long-dated instruments; including mortgaged-backed securities, collateralized debt obligation (CDOs), Bermudan swaptions and long-dated foreign exchange options. All these are credit-sensitive businesses. For complex derivatives, for which dealers act as warehouses of

---

[7] 'Seven US banks have lion's share of derivatives,' *Risk*, July 2003.
[8] 'The ultimate stress test: modelling the next liquidity crisis,' *Risk*, November 2003.

risk, the liquidity crisis would be especially acute. If a major counterparty pulled out of these businesses, hedging assumptions would become largely irrelevant. And fire-sale prices would mean huge mark-to-market losses.[9]

This is a very serious problem for market participants and it is a problem that has caught me out when I used over-the-counter options contracts. I was completely held hostage by the pricing of the option and the liquidity of that option strategy with my counterparty investment bank. When I wanted to sell my option strategy, I priced the options, I recognized that I would realize a loss on this position but when I sought a price for the options from my investment bank counterparty, they made a price that was substantially lower than the one I calculated – the investment banking market maker, making a price to me, couldn't care less about my options valuation, he offered me a price, 'take it or leave it'. I had to take it and realize a substantial loss on that options position – I have never used an over-the-counter product since that incident. The loss on those options nearly ruined me as I was trying to start up a money management business.

There are real differences of views developing on the value of using derivative instruments, particularly with regard to accounting issues in light of the Enron and WorldCom debacles. Warren Buffet, the renowned US billionaire investor, has been speaking loudly against their use. *Risk* magazine described Mr Buffet's remarks as

> a broadside [aimed] at the derivatives industry . . . by describing the instruments as 'time bombs' and 'financial weapons of mass destruction'. . . . Buffet's concerns . . . highlight general investor and analyst worries about how they should compare banks with large derivatives and risk management activities with those of more traditional lenders. Buffet's main areas of attack centred on the mark-to-modelling of some exotic derivatives positions, the leverage of total-return instruments and current incentives for bank executives to cheat in accounting for derivatives positions. He also expressed reservations about the relationship between corporate downgrades, collateral calls, and corporate meltdown, unpredicted correlations from seemingly diversified derivatives positions, the lack of central oversight, or monitoring of the industry, the concentration of credit risk in the hands of a few dealers, and the opaque nature of trying to analyse the financial condition of firms heavily involved in derivatives.[10]

Mr Buffet, on the whole, is correct. If he were not, there would be no need for this book or for a new generation of hedging instruments. As I hope I have made clear, derivative instruments are not easy to use, they have many complicated moving parts dependent upon various cash market changes that are occurring every second, and therefore many things that can go wrong within themselves and in relation to their underlying cash asset. Many over-the-counter products are difficult to value, because their valuation is produced by an econometric model of some sort. Hence Buffet's description of many derivatives as 'mark-to-model' and 'mark-to-myth'.

On the other hand, Alan Greenspan describes derivatives as powerful hedging tools that make the world's market safer. He, too, has a point: forward and futures markets allow risk to be transferred between counterparties, and options contracts allow the price volatility of a cash asset to be mitigated. The misuse, mispricing and mishandling of derivative instruments are due to management not really understanding them. Most managers do not want to have to deal with them at all, because they are not core to their business. They want an easy-to-use, simple-to-understand risk management solution and instrument.

---

[9] Ibid.
[10] 'Derivative disclosure calls mount,' *Risk*, April 2003.

WILL MANAGEMENT CHANGE THEIR BEHAVIOUR?

In this section I will look at the corporate governance issues driving necessary changes in managing one's unforeseen price volatility on non-core global financial risks. The question is: will management change? And, if they change, how will they change?

'If the corporation were a person, would that person be a psychopath?' asked *The Economist*. 'Like all psychopaths, the firm is singularly self-interested: its purpose is to create wealth for its shareholders. And, like all psychopaths, the firm is irresponsible, because it puts others at risk to satisfy its profit-maximising goal, harming employees and customers, and damaging the environment. The corporation manipulates everything. It is grandiose, always insisting that it is the best, or number one. It has no empathy, refuses to accept responsibility for its actions and feels no remorse. It relates to others only superficially, via make-believe versions of itself manufactured by public-relations consultants and marketing men. In short, if the metaphor of the firm as person is a valid one, then the corporation is clinically insane.'[11]

In the aftermath of corporate insanity, Enron and WorldCom, corporate governance is changing dramatically, causing corporate America and Europe to review the way in which they manage themselves. My focus is on the way in which these changes will shape the way in which non-core global financial risks are managed in the future.

A November 2002 Report of the National Association of Corporate Directors Blue Ribbon Commission on Risk Oversight stated that the 'Board's role, quite simply, is to provide risk oversight. This means making sure that management has instituted processes to identify, and bring to the board's attention, the major risk the enterprise faces. It also means the continual reevaluation of these monitoring processes and the risks with the help of the board and its committees.'[12]

Here is a great example of a corporate governance guideline in action:

> Our corporate governance guidelines [for board members] emphasize 'the qualities of strength of character, an inquiring and independent mind, practical wisdom and mature judgement.' It is no accident that we put 'strength of character' first. Like any successful company, we must have directors who start with what is right, who do not have hidden agendas, and who strive to make judgements about what is best for the company, and not about best for themselves or some constituency.

This is part of a speech that Kenneth Lay, CEO of Enron, made in April 1999 to the Center for Business Ethics on 'What a CEO Expects from a Board.'[13]

As the Association for Investment Management and Research (AIMR), now known as the CFA Institute, magazine, *CFA*, put it in spring 2004: 'The sorriest episode in recent corporate and financial market history is over. What will stop it from happening again?'[14] The 'perfect storm' years from mid-2000 until early 2003 opened up an immense can of worms living and feeding off the American, UK and European taxpayers and investors.

Here are some of the scandalous deeds perpetrated by companies:[15]

- *Off-balance-sheet entities.* US companies discovered that they could hide their less attractive parts in 'special-purpose entities' (SPEs), separate companies that did not appear on their creators' balance sheet. With enthusiastic help from banks and once-legitimate

---

[11] 'The lunatic you work for,' *The Economist*, 8 May 2004, p. 80.
[12] Mary Pat McCarthy and Timothy Flynn (2004), *Risk from the CEO and Board Perspective* McGraw-Hill, p. 154.
[13] 'Corporate [Mis]governance,' *CFA*, May/June 2004, front cover.
[14] Ibid.
[15] Ibid, pp. 31–36.

accounting firms such as Arthur Andersen, companies began dumping truckloads of toxic financial waste into SPEs. The Securities and Exchange Commission (SEC) defines off-balance-sheet arrangements as 'certain guarantee contracts, retained or contingent interests in assets transferred to an unconsolidated entity, derivative instruments that are classified as equity, or material variable interests in unconsolidated entities that conduct certain activities.'[16]

- *Earnings inflation.* CEOs who wanted their options to soar were forced to improvise. World-Com capitalized its operating expenses, inflating earnings by a total of $11 billion. Other telecoms firms cooked up 'bandwidth swaps' in which they exchanged similar stretches of fibre optic cable, booking the proceeds as profitable revenue. Other companies such as Coca-Cola resorted to channel stuffing, in which the company dumps excess inventory on its customers and books the shipments as sales.
- *Investment banker conflicts.* Investment bankers discovered that they could 'add value' by promising positive research coverage for client companies' stock. All stocks became buys and none were sells.
- *Auditors as advocates.* Accounting firms are, in theory, shareholder watchdogs; they discovered that designing sophisticated tax shelters paid much better than auditing.
- *Tax-rate arbitrage.* US accounting firms twisted the equipment lease into something called a SILO (sale-in, lease out). These complex deals allowed the avoidance of billions of dollars in taxes; such as buying a European city's sewer system and leasing it back to the city, creating no economic value, but generating a big taxable loss by depreciating the pipes of the sewer system. A Congressional Joint Committee on Taxation believes this scheme will cost the US taxpayer $33 billion over the next ten years. This strategy effectively reduced the corporate tax rate from 35% to 20%.
- *Regulatory arbitrage.* Derivatives make it possible to avoid some regulatory oversight; an insurance company that can legally speculate in the currency markets or junk bonds can create swaps or other derivatives without anyone really knowing. The result is that financial and quasi-financial institutions appear to be running free, with precious little oversight.
- *Clueless rating agencies.* Financial statements are so distorted and complex that they are beyond the understanding of the ratings agency analysts.
- *Insider dealing and flat-out theft.* There has been an amazing array of improprieties.
- *Mutual fund madness.* Mutual funds allowed their largest clients to move in and out of their mutual funds under favourable terms so that they could make an easy profit, costing shareholders about $5 billion a year.
- *Out-of-control executive pay.*
- *Captive boards.* At the epicentre of the corporate and financial earthquake was the board of directors, turning a blind eye to every excess.

With the ashes of the 1990s corporate and financial scandals still smouldering, new regulation and accounting rules are being implemented. The aim of the new rules is to force companies to account with greater financial transparency. As Warren Buffet says: 'If I cannot understand [a company's financial statement], management doesn't want me to understand.'[17]

In March 2002, John Morrissey, Deputy Chief Accountant of the SEC, offered the US House of Representatives Subcommittee on Oversight and Investigations the following definition of

---

[16] Ibid, page 48.
[17] 'Corporate [Mis]governance,' *CFA*, May/June 2004, p. 33.

financial transparency:

> A primary goal of the federal securities laws is to protect honest and efficient markets and informed
> investment decisions through full and fair disclosure. Transparency in financial reporting, that is,
> the extent to which financial information about a company is available and understandable to
> investors and other market participants, plays a fundamental role in making our markets the most
> efficient, liquid, and resilient in the world.[18]

In the aftermath of the 2001 and 2002 corporate scandals, and faced with the threat to confidence in the US securities market, the US Congress passed the Sarbanes–Oxley Act which is 'wide-ranging US corporate legislation, co-authored by the Democrat in charge of the Senate Banking Committee, Paul Sarbanes, and Republican congressman Michael Oxley. The Act, which became law in July 2002, lays down stringent procedures regarding the accuracy and reliability of corporate disclosures, places restrictions on auditors providing non-audit services and obliges top executives to verify their accounts personally.'[19] It requires new board oversight and internal controls, and promises to give investors better information.

But in the year following its passage, the number of firms that went dark and ceased to issue detailed financial reports tripled, meaning more investors were receiving no information at all. When a company goes dark it can no longer be listed on a big exchange like the NYSE but can continue to trade electronically, over-the-counter. Stocks that list here do not meet the minimum requirements or file with the SEC.[20]

The Sarbanes–Oxley Act requires at least one person on the audit committee of a US company to be a 'financial expert.' This carries the somewhat scary implication that board members sitting on an audit committee probably have no idea about the audit process. Section 407 stipulates that a financial expert must have all of the following five attributes:

1. Understand Generally Accepted Accounting Principles (GAAP) and financial statements.
2. Be able to assess the application of GAAP in connection with the accounting for estimates, accruals and reserves.
3. Have experience of preparing, auditing, analyzing, or evaluating financial statements with generally comparable breadth and complexity of accounting issues expected to be raised by issuers' financial statements, or have experience of actively supervising those engaged in such activities.
4. Understand internal control over financial reporting.
5. Understand audit committee functions.

The Sarbanes–Oxley Act is perhaps a knee jerk reaction to the corporate governance problem, but it is the beginning of a long process of reviewing and establishing consistent and standardized accounting procedures and practices. The way in which companies manage their non-core global financial risks will be simplified; the days of gaming with these risks are over.

In the division of responsibilities within the company, there are two fundamental ways in which to manage one's corporate risks: manage them in house or outsource them. A KPMG white paper refers to the former as centralized risk management and the latter as decentralized risk management.

---

[18] Mary Pat McCarthy and Timothy Flynn (2004), *Risk from the CEO and Board Perspective*. McGraw-Hill, pp. 130–131.
[19] 'Understanding Corporate Governance,' *Financial Times*, 5 September 2003, p. 11.
[20] 'Does Sarbanes–Oxley Hurt Shareholders and Hide Poor Management?' *Risk News*, 19 November 2004.

> Centralized risk management tends to focus on risks that affect the achievement of key corporate objectives and strategies and significantly affect most if not all functions and processes.... [A] decentralized risk management pushes the responsibility for risk management to those who live with it day to day.[21]

In my view, any risks that a company faces which are not core to its core business should be outsourced – let the risk professionals deal with them.

The effects of introducing the Sarbanes–Oxley Act have been substantial. On the negative side, the rise in the number of companies going dark is cause for concern. Whether the decision to deregister is due to the cost of maintaining corporate governance compliance, or to controlling insiders of the company wanting to evade the outside oversight of their company remains to be seen.

A survey by Korn/Ferry, an executive search firm, claimed in November 2004 that for the Fortune 1000 the total cost per firm of implementing Sarbanes–Oxley has reached $5.1 million, with a further cost of $3.7 million pending as a result of ongoing work.[22] The majority of German companies with US stock market listings would like to withdraw because of the cost and hassle of complying with the new corporate governance regulations.[23]

According to John Plender, 'When the bull roars and investors do well, there is a tendency not to look too closely at how money is made. Then, in the downturn, people forget that corporate accidents are part and parcel of creative destruction. They expect to enjoy the benefits of risk-free capitalism. It is, of course an illusion. Good corporate governance is a process, not an absolute destination. We forget that at our peril.'[24]

NEW ACCOUNTING RULES

In the United States the Financial Accounting Standards Board (FASB) is responsible for establishing best practice accounting and reporting, providing guidance on the implementation of transparent and accurate accounting procedures, and promoting the convergence of international accounting standards. The aim of the International Accounting Standards Board (IASB), based in the United Kingdom, is to develop a single set of accounting standards throughout the world. The introduction of new accounting rules in the United States under FAS 133, and in the European Union under IAS 39, will have an enormous impact on the way derivative instruments are accounted for and – perhaps most importantly – the way they will be used in the future.

> January 2005 will see the greatest revolution in financial reporting for a generation. A set of international financial reporting standards, promulgated by the International Accounting Standards Board, will come into force for listed companies in all member countries of the European Union and in many other countries around the world. Given the scale of the transition, it is hardly surprising that there have been arguments, nerves and the odd shouting match along the way. It was always going to be a difficult process.... The great controversy has been centred around IAS 32 and IAS 39, the two standards that deal with the disclosure of financial instruments, including the vexed question of derivatives and hedging. The IASB believes that derivatives should be stated at fair value on balance sheets, and that annual losses or gains on the instruments should be shown on profit and loss accounts. However, European banks have complained that this will introduce excessive volatility into balance sheets and income statements.[25]

---

[21] KPMG, 'Understanding Enterprise Risk Management: An Emerging Model for Building Shareholder Value', cited in Mary Pat McCarthy and Timothy Flynn (2004), *Risk from the CEO and Board Perspective*, McGraw-Hill, p. 260.

[22] 'Average US group Face $5m Compliance Bill,' *Financial Times*, 12 November 2004, p. 33.

[23] 'German Groups Rue US Listings,' *Financial Times*, 19 November 2004, p. 47.

[24] 'Understanding Corporate Governance,' *Financial Times*, 5 September 2003, p. 3.

[25] 'Understanding IFRS,' *Financial Times*, 29 September 2004, p. 2.

Ian Mackintosh, chairman of the UK's Accounting Standards Board (ASB), announced in mid-October 2004 that 'The position that the EU has reached on adoption of IAS 39 is unsatisfactory.'[26] UK companies were told to ignore it. 'the changes [IAS 39] followed intense lobbying by banks, especially those in France, which argued that the original IAS 39 proposal, based on US accounting rules, would disrupt their risk management practices.'[27] A few days later, a delay in implementation was announced: 'New corporate reporting requirements due to come into force January 1 are set to be delayed for at least three months after intense lobbying from business over the timing and substance of the changes.'[28] A *Financial Times* editorial outlined the problem:

> Just months before 7,000 EU companies adopt new accounting standards, the interpretation of IAS 39 remains embroiled in controversy. This is because EU ministers have agreed a carve-out allowing member countries to ignore parts of IAS 39, specifically some of the tough hedge-accounting and fair-value rules it contains. The carve-out involves striking nine paragraphs from the full standard and allowing companies to apply the rest of the rules without them. However, accounting standards are by their very nature interwoven and were designed to be adopted in full or not at all. No one seems to understand how the carve-out of IAS 39 will work.[29]

In this section I will briefly outline the new accountancy rules and look at the ways in which hedging global financial risks occurred under the old system and now under the new rules adopted in the US and proposed in Europe.

FAS 133 was issued by the FASB in June 1998: 'This Statement establishes accounting and reporting standards for derivative instruments, including certain derivative instruments embedded in other contracts (collectively referred to as derivatives), and for hedging activities. It requires that an entity recognize all derivatives as either assets or liabilities in the statement of [a] financial position and measure those instruments at fair value. If certain conditions are met, a derivative may be specifically designated as (a) a hedge of the exposure to changes in the fair value of a recognized asset or liability or an unrecognized firm commitment, (b) a hedge of the exposure to variable cash flows of a forecasted transaction, or (c) a hedge of the foreign currency exposure of a net investment in a foreign operation, an unrecognized firm commitment, an available-for-sale security, or a foreign-currency-denominated forecasted transaction.

The accounting for changes in the fair value of a derivative (that is, gains and losses) depends on the intended use of the derivative and the resulting designation.

- For a derivative designated as hedging the exposure to changes in the fair value of a recognized asset or liability or a firm commitment (referred to as a fair value hedge), the gain or loss is recognized in earnings in the period of change together with the offsetting loss or gain on the hedged item attributable to the risk being hedged. The effect of that accounting is to reflect in earnings the extent to which the hedge is not effective in achieving offsetting changes in fair value.
- For a derivative designated as hedging the exposure to variable cash flows of a forecasted transaction (referred to as a cash flow hedge), the effective portion of the derivative's gain or loss is initially reported as a component of other comprehensive income (outside earnings) and subsequently reclassified into earnings when the forecasted transaction affects earnings. The ineffective portion of the gain or loss is reported in earnings immediately.

---

[26] 'ASB Tells UK Companies to Ignore EU Ruling on Accounting Standards,' *Financial Times*, 12 October 2004, p. 1.
[27] Ibid.
[28] 'Corporate reporting shake-up faces delay,' *Financial Times*, 14 October 2004. p. 1.
[29] 'Thickening fog over accounting row,' Editorial, *Financial Times*, 14 October 2004, p. 18.

- For a derivative designated as hedging the foreign currency exposure of a net investment in a foreign operation, the gain or loss is reported in other comprehensive income (outside earnings) as part of the cumulative translation adjustment. The accounting for a fair value hedge described above applies to a derivative designated as a hedge of the foreign currency exposure of an unrecognized firm commitment or an available-for-sale security. Similarly, the accounting for a cash flow hedge described above applies to a derivative designated as a hedge of the foreign currency exposure of a foreign-currency-denominated forecasted transaction.
- For a derivative not designated as a hedging instrument, the gain or loss is recognized in earnings in the period of change.

Under this Statement, an entity that elects to apply hedge accounting is required to establish at the inception of the hedge the method it will use for assessing the effectiveness of the hedging derivative and the measurement approach for determining the ineffective aspect of the hedge. Those methods must be consistent with the entity's approach to managing risk.'[30]

In the EU, standards for financial instruments including derivatives are 'covered by IAS 32 and IAS 39. . . . IAS 32 sets out the requirements for the presentation of financial instruments and the disclosure of information about them. It is intended to enhance the market's understanding of the significance of these devices to a company's financial position, performance and cash flows. IAS 39 prescribes the principles for recognizing and measuring financial instruments. In particular, it sets strict conditions for the application of hedge accounting.'[31]

Under the old accounting standards, companies could treat the fair value of derivative instruments as an off-balance-sheet item, with the current period's net accrual being recognized in the income statement (i.e., accrual accounting model). The principle under which IAS 39 has been created requires all derivatives to be carried on the balance sheet at fair value, with changes in fair value being recognized in the income statement (i.e., fair value model). Hedge accounting treatment allows corporations to match changes in the fair value of the derivative with those associated with the underlying hedged item, and recognize these changes in the income statement in the same period.

Unless hedge accounting treatment is obtained, the changes in the fair value of the derivative will create additional volatility in the income statement. This volatility is caused by the change in fair value of the derivative being recognized in earnings without offsetting gains and losses in the underlying exposure. In order to qualify for hedge accounting, a derivative must be formally designated at inception as a hedging instrument in a specified hedge relationship. The hedge relationship must pass a numerical hedge effectiveness test both at inception and throughout its life.[32] The actual calculations to be used for hedge accounting effectiveness are technical and complicated, and therefore beyond the scope of this book.

Similarly to FAS 133, IAS 39 recognizes three types of hedge relationship:

- *Fair value hedge.* Hedges changes in the fair value of a recognized asset or liability that affects the reported net income; for example, a fixed-rate bond that is swapped, through an interest rate swap, to a floating-rate coupon.
- *Cash Flow Hedge.* Hedges the variability of cash flows of a particular asset or liability; for example, a fixed-rate loan swapped, using an interest rate swap, into a floating-rate loan, or

---

[30] 'Summary of Statement 133,' Financial Accounting Standards Board, June 1998.
[31] 'Understanding IFRS,' *Financial Times*, 29 September 2004, p. 9.
[32] 'Corporate Risk Management In An IAS 39 Framework,' Guy Coughlan, JP Morgan & Risk, pp. 5 and 6.

a highly probable forecasted transaction affecting reported net income such as the foreign currency cash flows hedged with a forward foreign exchange agreement.

- *Net investment hedge.* Hedges the changes in fair value coming from foreign exchange volatility of the value of an investment in foreign entity; for example, when balance sheet investments denominated in a foreign currency are hedged by using a currency swap.[33]

There are some fundamental problems with the hedge accounting definition and its ability to recognize hedge accounting and therefore to allow corporations to offset the hedging instrument with the underlying cash risk (if not, then it must go into the profit and loss statement). A company's earnings will fluctuate quite substantially, if not recognized as proper hedge accounting the derivative will be valued on its own, and the losses or gains could be extremely large. According to Guy Coughlan, Managing Director, Asset–Liability Management Advisory,

> The new accounting standard has forced corporations to document, monitor, evaluate and report hedging activities from a micro (i.e. exposure-by-exposure) perspective. Furthermore, the accounting effectiveness of hedge relationships must be evaluated in fair value terms only, and against arbitrary effectiveness thresholds.[34]

Coughlan's work also offered a number of examples which I will outline for you; these are transactions which, though economically sensible, would not qualify for hedge accounting and therefore lead to greater earnings volatility.

1. Foreign currency earnings translation:
   - A European multinational with a euro reporting currency has US dollar earnings through its US subsidiary, it uses forward foreign exchange agreements to hedge those US dollar revenues.
   - IAS 39 does not permit hedge accounting of foreign currency earnings translations.
2. Inter-company foreign currency exposure:
   - A UK parent company, with British pounds as its reporting currency has US dollar dividends paid by the US subsidiary to the UK parent company, a currency swap is used to hedge a proportion of the dividend flow for the next five years.
   - IAS 39 does not permit hedge accounting for hedging inter-company risk exposures, unless they are recognized assets or liabilities. The dividend must be declared before hedge accounting is permitted; in this case dividends are not known until they are announced.
3. Long-term foreign currency contracts:
   - A company wants to hedge the foreign currency payments of long-term projects, perhaps when they are completed.
   - IAS 39 does not allow it to be treated as hedge accounting because the timing of the payment is uncertain, this uncertainty rules out hedge accounting.
4. Options hedges:
   - A company wants to mitigate the unforeseen price volatility of a foreign currency payment to be made in one year's time, using an options contract.
   - In IAS 39, the full charge of the fair value of an option can be designated as part of a hedge relationship, but to be highly effective and received hedge accounting, only the intrinsic value of the option is designated, the time value of the option must be reflected in the company's earnings.

---

[33] 'Corporate Risk Management in An IAS 39 Framework,' Guy Coughlan, JP Morgan & Risk, pp. 5 and 6.
[34] Ibid.

5. Commodity hedges:
   — An airline wants to manage the price volatility of jet fuel, such as Lufthansa in Chapter 2, using a crude oil futures contracts hedge.
   — Commodity prices are a non-financial risk, IAS 39 does not allow hedge designation for just that portion of the price risk that corresponds to the exchange-traded futures contract.
6. Interest rate cap on interest payments that have been swapped to floating:
   — A company has net floating-rate interest rate payments due on a five-year fixed-rate bond issue that has been swapped to floating rates, hedging their exposure with a five-year interest-rate cap hedging against floating-rate interest rate payments above 5%.
   — IAS 39 does not permit a synthetic exposure to be an underlying hedged item on the basis that it would involve hedging a derivative with a derivative, which is not permitted.

In the light of these examples of effects that will hinder any treasurer or finance director from managing their non-core global financial risks, the uproar over the implementation of the new IAS rules is understandable.

An in-depth study published in November 2004 by Fitch Ratings of companies' derivatives usage and hedge accounting and reporting came up with a number of findings:

• The benefits of achieving lower income statement volatility are at the expense of distortions to balance sheet items.
• Changes in interest rates, exchange rates or commodity prices could exacerbate these effects, which is especially relevant considering Fitch's prediction that the federal funds rate will rise sharply and reach 4% by 2006.
• Disclosure is at best inconsistent and often inadequate, raising questions about derivatives usage and its impact on key credit metrics.
• Different applications of complex hedge accounting rules have the potential to result in a high level of restatement risk.

Roger Merritt, managing director of Fitch Ratings, summed up the problem:

Disclosure of derivatives must be improved substantially in order to achieve an acceptable level of transparency on which to base meaningful credit analysis. Without this, analysts and other market participants face a daunting task in understanding the risks associated with derivatives and their effects on financial statements.[35]

In the United States, FAS 133 has changed the way in which corporate treasurers are going about their business. In a Goldman Sachs survey publicly published through the Global Association of Risk Professionals (GARP) Newsletter (September 15, 2004), 'Treasurers in the United States are currently assessing the impact of the new rules and that there will likely be changes towards simpler hedging instruments.' Remember this quote when we get to the next chapter on the new instruments; many corporate executives are pleading for a new, innovative and easy-to-use instrument. The new accounting rules offer an opportunity to create the next generation of hedging instruments because management will have to change the way they behave.

---

[35] 'Hedge Accounting and Derivatives Study for Corporates,' Fitch Ratings, 23 November 2004.

BASEL II

Alongside the introduction of new corporate governance regulations and new accounting standards, new banking regulations are coming into force under Basel II. I touched on the impact of Basel II in Chapter 1, because of the way it will change the way banks deal with their institutional clients. I want to quickly address the way in which Basel II will affect the institutional clients, or perhaps explain why they must be more attentive to their risk management policies because banks will be pricing risk differently as a result of Basel II.

> Regulation aimed at curbing the excesses of the 1990's and promoting better corporate governance and accountability affects all industries, but few feel the pinch as much as the financial services sector.... The Basel II accord proposed by the Basel committee of banking regulators and due to be implemented at the end of 2006... aims to align regulatory capital more accurately with operational, credit and market risks that international banks face.... European banks will need to spend an average of €115 million to get their IT and risk management systems up to the required standard.... In the US Basel II will only be mandatory for the top 10 banks.[36]

The Basel Committee on Banking Supervision was set up in 1974 and is an international regulatory body for the world's financial institutions. In 1988, it introduced adequacy rules for banks in member countries, which required them to implement a financial risk measurement framework. The Committee is currently creating a new set of regulations to replace the original rules that would cover operational risk as well as financial risk. The new framework, usually called Basel II, is based around three *pillars*: the first determines minimum capital requirements; the second stipulates an effective supervisory review process; and the third sets out to strengthen market discipline by greater disclosure of banks' financial status.[37]

Those that do not implement the standards will be considered to be poor at risk management, and this will determine their credit ratings and access to capital markets. As a recent white paper from software company PeopleSoft put it, Basel II 'promises to dramatically change the landscape of the financial services industry, spurring continued industry consolidation as more efficient banks acquire less efficient ones to boost capital reserves and improve operational efficiencies.'[38]

The implications for corporate, insurance company and pension fund customers could be quite severe, as I mentioned in Chapter 1. The IMF pointed out four significant changes in a bank's business strategy that will affect their institutional customers.

1. Banks may scale back business lines that could attract higher capital charges. These include securitization, non-OECD lending, equity holdings (particularly large cross-shareholdings), and non-banking activities such as insurance and asset management.
2. Institutional clients may see their risk adjusted cost of doing business with their bank rise as more regulatory capital is required for less creditworthy companies.
3. Capital flows to developing and potentially lower-rated countries could be affected, as capital requirements for lending to such countries and domestic corporates may increase.
4. Premature implementation may weaken a banking system rather than strengthen [it].[39]

---

[36] 'Understanding Corporate Governance,' *Financial Times*, Part 3, 16 January 2004, p. 9.

[37] 'Corporate Governance,' Part 1, *Financial Times*, 5 September 2003, p. 11.

[38] 'Understanding Corporate Governance,' Part 3, *Financial Times*, 16 January 2004, p. 9.

[39] Global Financial Stability Report, 'The Revised Basel Capital Framework for Banks (Basel II),' IMF, September 2004, pp. 70 and 71.

CORPORATES

There are a variety of ways in which corporates tackle their non-core global financial risks. We have already looked in Chapter 2 at Ford's bungled attempts to hedge a key hard commodity, palladium, for the manufacture of their core product – the automobile. Management incompetence has led to shareholder lawsuits, their outcome unknown at the time of writing. In trying to avoid and/or mitigate the unforeseen price volatility on purchasing palladium, Ford created a price bubble as it built up its stockpile and then caused a price collapse when it stopped purchasing. And to add insult to the injury, Ford discovered a year later that its long-term need for palladium for catalytic converter production would be significantly less than originally forecast. This is one way to manage one's hard commodity price risks for which I suspect there will be few takers.

In studying the corporate accounts of Caterpillar Inc., I discovered a very interesting aspect of hedge deviation arising from the use of currency options.

CASE STUDY: CATERPILLAR INC.

A currency option allows one counterparty to exchange one currency for another at a predetermined exchange rate on or until the maturity date. In its General and Financial Information (Proxy Appendix) 2002, an appendix to its Annual Report and Accounts, Caterpillar defined its foreign exchange risks as follows:

> Foreign currency exchange rate movements create a degree of risk affecting the U.S. dollar value of sales made and costs incurred in foreign currencies. Movements in foreign currency rates also affect our competitive position as these changes may affect business practices and/or strategies of non-U.S. based competitors. Additionally, we have balance sheet positions denominated in foreign currency, thereby creating exposure to movements in exchange rates. Our machinery and engines operations purchase, manufacture and sell products in many locations around the world. As we have diversified revenue and cost base, we manage our future foreign currency cash flow exposure on a net enterprise basis. We use foreign currency forward and options contracts to manage unmatched foreign currency cash inflow and outflow. Our objective is to minimize the risk of exchange rate movements that would reduce the U.S. dollar value of our foreign currency cash flow. Our policy allows for managing anticipated foreign currency cash flow for up to four years.

One of the problems with the many derivative instruments available lies in the way they are used. The different types of instrument manage the risk very differently and therefore a very different risk outcome will occur, causing hedging mistakes and deviations. Certain instruments, such as options contracts, mitigate risk instead of transferring it to another counterparty. Options have a number of unique characteristics which pose problems when they are misunderstood; one of these is time value decay. Time value decay is the variation in option value due to the passage of time – in other words, options contracts lose value over time.[40]

Caterpillar announced the outcomes from its foreign exchange hedging activities as follows:

> We generally designate as cash flow hedges at inception of the contract any Australian dollar, Brazilian real, British pound, Canadian dollar, euro, Japanese yen, Mexican peso, or Singapore dollar forward or option contracts that exceed 90 days in duration. Designation is performed on a

---

[40] Philippe Jorion (2003), *Financial Risk Manager's Handbook*, 2nd edn, Chichester: John Wiley & Sons, Ltd, p. 339.

specific exposure basis to support hedge accounting. The remainder of machinery and equipment foreign currency contracts is undesignated. Losses of $.4 and $2 on the undesignated contracts were recorded in current earnings ('Other income (expense)') for 2001 and 2002, respectively. Gains/(losses) of $(.5) and $.3 due to changes in time value on options were excluded from effectiveness calculations and included in current earnings ('Other income (expense)') for 2001 and 2002, respectively.

The reason for quoting these accounting notes is also to point out that Caterpillar lost 50 cents per share in 2001 and gained 30 cents per share on the change in time value from the use of currency options. I am not in a position to say that they are misusing options and the volatility arising from the valuation in their option strategy is unforeseen, but the fact remains that a hedge deviation is occurring when Caterpillar used currency options to manage its various currency risks. It is worth noting as well that the company does not offer these notes in its published Annual Report and Accounts; one has to seek out an SEC-required financial appendix to discover this information.

CASE STUDY: LUFTHANSA

An example of a successful hedging programme for managing non-core global risks is that of the German airline Lufthansa. In 2004, the price of oil rose by more than 40% to over $50 per barrel. Many airlines were fighting for their lives in the aftermath of the World Trade Center attacks, the SARS epidemic in the Far East and the general lack of economic enthusiasm, many requiring central government financial help in order to survive. The US dollar was falling in value, as the euro strengthened by more than 20%, causing a great deal of additional financial stress on non-US airline companies. Airlines must purchase oil with US dollars, their US travellers purchase their tickets in US dollars and – perhaps more important – airlines purchase or lease their aircraft fleet in US dollars. Airlines operate on very thin profit margins, therefore any adverse movements in exchange rates, jet fuel and interest rates can have a catastrophic impact. Yet, while other airlines were adding a surcharge to their ticket prices because of rising jet fuel prices, Lufthansa did not, but was still able to hold on to its revenues and profit margins.

Lufthansa has clearly established a hedging programme for managing its non-core global financial risks – its jet fuel price and exchange rate risks. According to the Annual Report 2003, Lufthansa's major financial risk exposures 'are exchange rate fluctuations between the euro and other currencies, interest rate fluctuations on the international money and capital markets as well as price fluctuations on the crude oil and oil products markets.' Focusing on the oil risks first, in 2003, Lufthansa reported that 'the share of fuel expenses accounted for 7.6 per cent (prior year: 7.7 per cent) of the operating expenses of the Lufthansa Group.' They used 'Different hedging instruments with regard to the crude and heating oil market . . . to limit the fuel price risk. The Group's policy aims at hedging up to 90 per cent of the fuel consumption in the next 24 months on a revolving basis.' Of course, had oil prices fallen, needless to say many would argue that Lufthansa had mismanaged its oil price risks. I will argue, however, that this view is incorrect. Lufthansa is trying its best to budget for two years in advance, enabling it to price its airline tickets relative to its hedged costs such as jet fuel. Therefore, if the price of jet fuel falls, it is an opportunity loss, but not mismanaged. Lufthansa must protect itself, particularly with its slim profit margins, competing with many new no-frills budget airlines. It must manage the adverse movement of these non-core global financial risks to ensure that its budget projections are protected along with its profit margins. Also, Lufthansa is using a variety of hedging instruments in an attempt to hedge its jet fuel price risks, using oil and heating oil derivative instruments, it is trying to mitigate these risks which need to be managed, controlled and fine-tuned by experienced treasury staff at Lufthansa.

When it comes to foreign exchange risks, Lufthansa has over $2 billion of airline purchasing risks and €7.4 billion of operational exposure.[41] Lufthansa reports in its Annual Report 2003 that it is

in a net payer position with respect to the US dollar, in particular due to investments in aircraft. These investments in aircraft are hedged at 50 per cent against the exchange rate fluctuations as soon as they signed the contract. The hedging of the second part is effected subject to expected market developments. With all other currencies, there is generally a net surplus of deposits. The expected cash flows with individual currencies are hedged up to 75 per cent of the related currency exposures over a period of up to 36 months.

According to a *Risk* magazine article of August 2004, Lufthansa's financial risks are managed by a treasurer based in Cologne, while the commodity risks are managed in Hamburg. According to the treasurer Axel Tillmann, the company uses currency options to mitigate its currency fluctuations, it purchases out-of-the-money call options on the US dollar/euro and sells out-of-the-money put options to finance the purchase of its call options, attempting to achieve a zero cost for its hedging programme. This means that it sells the put option and uses the money to purchase the call option. There is a natural flow of US dollars coming back into euros, which allows it to sell a put option, not gambling or leveraging its existing position. When one sells or writes an option, whether it is a call or put option, one is underwriting that risk from the point of the strike price, plus the premium received by selling the option. If one does not have the underlying cash position risks, writing an option of this nature is known as uncovered, whereas in Lufthansa's case, it is writing a covered position because it has the underlying cash to cover an option becoming exercisable.

Many senior executives and treasurers claim that they do not hedge certain risks because their competitors do not hedge these risks. They say that they want the upside but not the downside or adverse movements in these risks. Others do not hedge because it is too expensive or the appropriate hedge strategy mitigates or transfers all of the upside potential. Other treasurers and CFOs believe that what goes around comes around, particularly for exchange rate movements (meaning a bad year this year may be a good year next year), therefore they do nothing. But of course the days of going around and coming around are long gone, and an adverse movement in a non-core global financial risk, as described in the Lufthansa case, is so severe that the upside potential or opportunity is not worth the risk. In other cases, senior management are so fed up with the adverse impact of non-core global financial risks that they want to ensure that they can protect their budget, and any opportunity lost does not form part of their core business anyway.

As a colleague of mine would say, the stock market does not pat any company on the back if they make money from non-core global financial risks, but woe betide them if they lose money on a non-core element of their business. In the case of Lufthansa, it seems to be standing alone in its ability to make appropriate risk management policy which in difficult times bears fruit

---

[41] 'Lufthansa Seeks a Clearer View,' *Risk*, 4 August 2004.

and in the good times will be lost in the background, whilst other airlines struggle to stay afloat in Europe, the United States, Asia and Africa. In the airline industry, effectively managing one's non-core global financial risks is the difference between success and failure.

CASE STUDY: REXAM

The can manufacturer Rexam offers a very good example of managing hard commodity price volatility risks through supply chain management rather than using hedging instruments such as derivatives. This example also highlights a preferred method for managing one's unforeseen price volatility arising from non-core global financial risks, although I have not found this strategy with many companies. Rexam enjoys a very privileged position with its customers along their supply chain.

> Rexam is one the world's top five consumer packaging groups and the world's leading beverage can maker. [Their] global operations span Europe, Asia, and the Americas and employ some 22,000 people in more than 20 countries. [They] provide packing solutions for many of the world's most famous brands. [They] supply billions of aluminium and steel cans for global soft drinks and beer brands. [They] produce glass and plastic bottles for global and regional beverage, food and pharmaceutical companies. [They] manufacture plastic containers for dairy and food products as well as plastic pharmaceutical packaging. [They] are a leading global supplier to the beauty packaging industry.[42]

Rexam uses 'long-term supply deals and client buyer power to ward off threat[s] from higher metal prices.'[43] The company is able to pass higher manufacturing prices on to its customers – if only we could all do this! Its metals hedging strategy used a 'combination of hedging, pushing through price increases and using the buying power of its largest customers.'[44] Rexam spends about £900 million a year on aluminium used to manufacture cans. The company was protected from the rising price of metals, including aluminium, by its largest customer Coca-Cola, which used its greater market purchasing clout to buy the aluminium. The price of aluminium has been protected for the next three years as a result, and all Rexam has to do is use the aluminium to manufacture the cans for Coca-Cola. Aluminium prices soared by 20 % in the first half of 2004, although the impact on Rexam's profit and loss account is zero. Rexam transferred the hedging of the aluminium price to Coca-Cola – not bad if you have the customer for it.

Additionally, Rexam's £100 million energy bill was offset by passing on to its customers average price increases of just under 1%.[45] Furthermore, Rexam reported that other raw materials costs such as resin for plastic packaging (about £70 million a year) and steel (about £75 million a year) are passed on to its customers.[46] Again, if only every company were able to do this. In spring 2004, Sarah Lee announced a drop in quarterly earnings because of higher manufacturing costs for their foods which they could not pass on to their consumer customers. There are very few companies in Rexam's position, but perhaps, as the global economy strengthens, the Rexam example may give readers food for thought.

---

[42] Rexam Annual Report & Accounts 2003, p. 3.
[43] 'Canny Hedging Gives Rexam 14% Profits Rise,' *Financial Times*, 26 August 2004, p. 19.
[44] Ibid.
[45] Ibid.
[46] Ibid.

Another good example of the way companies manage the unforeseen price volatility arising from non-core global financial risks is Nokia. It manufactures and distributes cell phones, and was one of the first companies to use value-at-risk methodology to measure its non-core global financial risks such as foreign exchange exposures, treasury investment and equity investment portfolios.

CASE STUDY: NOKIA

In its 2003 Annual Report, Nokia claims that its general risk management 'is based on visibility of the key risks preventing Nokia from reaching its business objectives.' Of its financial risks it says: 'The key financial targets for Nokia are growth, profitability, operational efficiency and a strong balance sheet. The objective for the Treasury function is twofold: to guarantee cost-efficient funding for the Group at all times, and to identify, evaluate and hedge financial risks in close cooperation with the business groups. There is a strong focus in Nokia on creating shareholder value. The Treasury function supports this aim by minimizing the adverse effects caused by fluctuations in the financial markets on the profitability of the underlying businesses and managing the balance sheet structure of the group.

Nokia has Treasury Centers in Geneva, Singapore/Beijing and Dallas/Sao Paolo, and a corporate treasury operation in Espoo in Finland. This international organization enables Nokia to provide the Group companies with financial services according to local needs and requirements.

The Treasury function is governed by policies approved by top management. Treasury policy provides principles for overall financial risk management and determines the allocation of responsibilities for financial risk management in Nokia. Operating policies cover specific areas such as foreign exchange risk, interest rate risk, use of derivative financial instruments, as well as liquidity and credit risk. Nokia is risk averse in its Treasury activities. Business Groups have detailed standard operating procedures supplementing the Treasury policy in financial risk management related issues.'

On foreign exchange risk it is stated that Nokia operates globally and is thus exposed to foreign exchange risk arising from various currency combinations. Foreign currency denominated assets and liabilities together with expected cash flows from highly probable purchases and sales give rise to foreign exchange exposures. These transaction exposures are managed against various local currencies because of Nokia's substantial production and sales outside the euro zone. Due to the changes in the business environment, currency combinations may also change within the financial year. The most significant non-euro sales currencies during the year were US dollar (USD), UK pound sterling (GBP) and Australian dollar (AUD). In general, depreciation of another currency relative to the euro has an adverse effect on Nokia's sales and operating profit, while appreciation of another currency has a positive effect, with the exception of Japanese yen, being the only significant foreign currency in which Nokia has more purchases than sales.

Nokia uses the Value-at-Risk (VaR) methodology to assess the foreign exchange risk related to the Treasury management of the Group exposures. The VaR figure represents the potential fair value losses for a portfolio resulting from adverse changes in market factors using specified time period and confidence level based on historical data. To correctly take into account the non-linear price function of certain derivative instruments, Nokia uses

Monte Carlo simulation. Volatilities and correlations are calculated from a one-year set of daily data. The VaR figures assume that the forecasted cash flows materialize as expected. The VaR figures for the Group transaction foreign exchange exposure, including hedging transactions and Treasury exposures for netting and risk management purposes, with a one-week horizon and 95% confidence level, are shown below.

Transaction foreign exchange position Value-at-Risk (EURm)

VaR	2003	2002
At December 31	16.7	5.9
Average for the year	9.3	14.3
Range for the year	5.8–16.7	4.9–27.6

Since Nokia has subsidiaries outside the euro zone, the euro-denominated value of share-holders' equity . . . is also exposed to fluctuations in exchange rates. Equity changes caused by movements in foreign exchange rates are shown as a translation difference in the Group consolidation. Nokia uses, from time to time, foreign exchange contracts and foreign currency denominated loans to hedge its equity exposure arising from foreign net investment.

Nokia has the following currency exposures: UK sterling 30%, Japanese yen 26%, US dollar 15%, Swedish krone 5%, Australian dollar 7%, and others 17%. Let us now explore the VaR analysis that Nokia uses as its risk management model methodology. To remind the reader, 'Value-at-Risk is the maximum loss over a target horizon such that there is low, prespecified probability that the actual loss will be larger.'[47] In other words, 'VaR is a statistical measure of downside risk that is simple to explain. VaR measures the total portfolio risk, taking into account portfolio diversification and leverage.'[48] Value-at-risk is providing a single sum of money answer to the question: with 95% confidence, over a 1 day, 1 week, 1 month, or 1 year period, based upon the historic volatility of the capital market investments that I have in my portfolio, how much money can I lose? VaR does not offer an answer for extreme events causing either a profit or loss on the portfolio using this methodology. The value-at-risk calculation is merely saying that over a specified period of time, the historic daily price movements of an investment such as currencies, equities and bonds will move in value in relation to the past historic price movements. It is also used for historic cash flow-at-risk and earnings-at-risk, as mentioned in connection with Ford Motor. There are many applications in which to use VaR. It is also a measure to compare like-with-like; meaning that as more companies, banks and insurance companies use, for example, the RiskMetrics Value-at-Risk system and formulae, investors will be able to easily compare one company's or bank's risk position with another's. It does not, however, tell me how much money I can lose under an extreme event – VaR assumes a normal distribution curve, but life does not follow a normal distribution curve.

I believe that the value-at-risk model is an extremely important and powerful tool; it enables corporate governance transparency as a risk management tool and reporting methodology for non-core global financial risks for corporates. It is also a way to compare banking institutions, particularly after the introduction of the new Basel II capital accord.

---

[47] Philippe Jorion (2003), *Financial Risk Manager's Handbook*, 2nd edn, Chichester: John Wiley & Sons, Ltd, p. 246.
[48] Ibid, p. 243.

Nokia's results quoted above suggest two things: either Nokia has a great deal more foreign exchange exposure in 2003 or the historic price volatility over the past year was significantly higher than in 2002. Interestingly, however, Nokia's average VaR in 2003 was €9.3 million and in 2002 €14.3 million, and the average weekly VaR ranged higher in 2002 than in 2003. The ranges are interesting as well: in 2003 the one-week VaR ranged from €5.8 million to €16.7 million and in 2002 from €4.9 million to €27.6 million, which in effect says that, based on historic price volatility, there was either an increase in foreign exchange exposure or price volatility, both of which could affect Nokia's profitability. The VaR ranged from as little as €4.9 million to as much as €27.6 million in 2002. Can you imagine a company's labour costs fluctuating this much over the year?

Remember these points when we get to the innovation section in Chapter 5. The volatility in the cost of doing business overseas must drive financial directors and managers nuts as they try to estimate profit margins at the beginning of each fiscal year. The best any treasurer can do when confronted with annual currency price volatilities, when they cannot net them off internally, is to mitigate them through the use of one kind of derivative instrument or another. We saw the outcome of Caterpillar's use of options contracts and Ford Motor's attempt to hedge palladium and currency risks. But we also saw the ability of Rexam to transfer its non-core global financial risks, specifically hard commodities, and also the way Lufthansa used options in a proactive way to mitigate the impact of foreign exchange fluctuations and jet fuel price rises. Both Rexam and Lufthansa view their non-core global financial risks, such as currencies and commodities, as a cost of doing business. Therefore, they want to assure themselves as best they can that they are protecting their forecasted or budgeted profit margins. They prefer budget assurance, profit margin predictability versus the unknown and potential upside gain from a positive currency or commodity price movement.

THE INSURANCE INDUSTRY

For insurance companies, solving non-core global financial risks entails addressing the way they manage their asset–liability relationships, ensuring that they have enough assets to meet their present and future insurance liabilities. I reviewed the problems that they face in Chapter 2, and I now want to turn to the way they are trying to solve their problems in light of the past few years' experience and the upcoming changes in insurance regulation.

Changes in regulations throughout the world are affecting the way the insurance industry must manage its asset–liability relationships. Common regulation throughout the European Union and the United States, along with the introduction of the Basel II capital accord, is forcing insurance companies to manage their assets in conjunction with their liabilities in a similar way to banking institutions. The long-term objective for regulation is the introduction of a risk-based capital regulatory structure for both banks and insurance companies. 'Regulators are bearing down on insurers as the market looks to establish better risk management practices. . . . Regulatory pressure is currently the major driver of risk management changes in the insurance industry.'[49]

In Europe the new regulations are referred to as the 'Solvency II' project which

> will further develop the capital adequacy framework for EU insurers. It aims to implement a three-pillar approach: standardized capital requirements, supervisory requirements, and risk-oriented

---

[49] 'Risk Management For Insurance Companies,' Special report, *Risk*, August 2004, p. 16.

public disclosure. It is thus a similar framework to the Basel II approach for banks. There is a great deal of agreement between member states over Pillars II and III of Solvency II, and work can now begin on drafting the framework directive. Adoption of the directive is expected by 2009. The detailed technical work will concentrate initially on Pillar I risk-based issues of setting appropriate levels for target capital and technical reserves. The Commission has stated its aim for a higher degree of harmonization which would reduce member states' need to set their own additional flexibility shown under the existing directives and continuing under Basel II.[50]

It is a little premature to talk about the solutions that will come from the adoption of the Solvency II proposal, because it is only a proposal at the time of writing and, from experience with the European Union, as it comes closer to implementation there are bound to be bitter arguments among EU members, particularly because of the cost of implementation for the EU member states.

The UK is working with the EU on Solvency II but has jumped the gun by implementing its own new regulations in 2004 in the form of Financial Services Authority (FSA) Consultative Papers (CP) 190 for non-life insurance companies and CP 195 for life insurance companies. The UK 'has proposed its own risk-oriented prudential approach, which anticipates or even goes beyond much of Solvency II's expected approach. The proposed U.K. system . . . will introduce closer links between investment risks and the requirements for capital and reserves, especially for "with-profits" business [defined in Chapter 2]. The required capital buffer will reflect market, credit, and persistency risks, while reserves will include an element to cover reinvestment rate risk. It includes stress tests designed to better reflect changing market conditions.'[51]

Since they are covered by different regulations, we should consider non-life and life companies separately. Several important points may be made about the FSA's intentions with the introduction of CP 190 for non-life insurance companies.

First, a main requirement of the Integrated Prudential Sourcebook is as follows:

A firm must at all times maintain overall financial resources, including capital and liquidity resources, both as to the amount and quality, to ensure that there is no significant risk that its liabilities cannot be met as they fall due.

The second point is the definition that the FSA uses for market risks:

the risk that arises from exposure to an adverse variation in costs or returns resulting from a change in market price or rate.

Remember this definition because the words 'adverse variation in costs or returns' had an impact on the development of the next generation instrument as well.

Thirdly, 'the more firms are able to demonstrate that their risk assessment processes capture and quantify all the issues in our guidance, then the lower we are likely to assess their ICG (Individual Capital Guidance) (and vice versa), thereby providing an incentive for good risk management.' In other words, the better an insurance company's management is with their risk management operations, procedures, transparency and ability to match their assets with their liabilities, the better their relationship with the FSA. Not a bad thing, and less oversight and interference will allow the insurance company to get on with its business.

The last aspect of the FSA's intentions relates to the way asset value risks are now one of the three components of the Enhanced Capital Requirement (ECR). The ECR is the name for the additional capital the UK authorities are requiring above and beyond the EU's Solvency II proposal. The ECR will be calculated by summing the asset-related values, the

---

[50] 'Global Financial Stability Report, Market Developments and Issues,' IMF, April 2004, p. 92.
[51] Ibid.

insurance-related values and the net written premiums and their respective asset, reserve and premium factor ratios. The risk ratios used for the asset values are: cash 0%, bonds 3.5% and equities 16.8%. The new ECR formula is:

$$ECR = \text{Asset-related Values} \times \text{Asset Factors} (\%)$$
$$+ \text{Insurance-related Values} \times \text{Reserve Factor} (\%)$$
$$+ \text{Net Written Premiums} \times \text{Reserve Factor} (\%)$$

Total ECR = X

The capital risk ratio means that every £1 held in equity investments instead of cash investments will require the insurance company to have an additional 16.8p more capital in its reserves.

Paul Clarke, a Partner with PricewaterhouseCoopers, offered a very good example of how the new risk factor ratio will impact the way in which non-life insurance companies will invest their assets:[52]

Impact on capital of change in asset mix

Asset strategy	Current allocation	New allocation
Cash and deposits	2%	3%
Equities, others	78%	26%
Debt/fixed interest	12%	63%
Reinsurance claims	8%	8%

Under the current allocation, this example non-life insurance company will require a further £3586, and under the new asset allocation £1936. With billions of pounds of assets to manage, the new risk asset value ratio is having a significant financial impact on non-life companies. They have to reposition their investments in order to ensure that they have sufficient capital to meet the new ECR of CP 190. If non-life companies move a majority of their investment portfolios into assets, which historically offer a smaller return-on-investment, they may have to raise capital to ensure that they have enough money to ensure that their assets can meet liabilities. Clearly this problem has been made more acute in the aftermath of the 'perfect storm' years beginning with the technology bubble crash in 2000.

Turning to life insurance companies, the FSA states in the Executive Summary to CP 195,

This CP develops the 'twin peaks' approach for with-profits business, to link provisioning and capital requirements more directly to how bonus payments are made to policyholders in practice. The twin peaks approach provides a useful benchmark for the assessment of financial resources required to support with-profits business and a degree of standardisation between firms. This CP also provides greater detail on how the individual capital adequacy framework (ICAS) will apply to life firms. The framework requires a firm to self-assess capital appropriate to its individual risk profile, as a complement to the minimum capital requirements for the with-profits business (in the twin peaks approach) and other life business.

As Iain Wright of the FSA argued,

The introduction of new rules to bring about risk-based regulation of the U.K. insurance industry was not a case of a busybody regulator imposing unnecessary market restrictions, but much-needed modernisation of rules that were well past their sell-by date.[53]

---

[52] Paul Clarke, paper presented to HSBC seminar on 'FSA compliance for insurers', *Insurance Regulations Change – The Integrated Prudential Sourcebook*, London, 27 January 2004.

[53] 'Risk Management for Insurance Companies,' Special report, *Risk*, August 2004, p. 23.

In the United States, life insurance companies are facing similar changes in regulation, which are affecting the way in which these companies manage their assets in relation to their liabilities. In the past, life companies in the US used reinsurance to transfer their risks, but regulation changes are altering that strategy. US life insurance companies are looking at securitization as a way to transfer their risks to the marketplace, leaving them with sufficient capital to continue to write life insurance policies. Securitization involves the economic or legal transfer of assets to a third party.

Securitization could be used to sell off a closed book of insurance business, enabling the life company to raise capital for new business products or opportunities or to be used as fresh regulatory capital, matching the asset–liability relationship for that company. They could also securitize future cash flows; premiums that are due to be received in the future can be discounted and securitized into a bond structure. This securitization allows the life insurance company to realize its future cash flows immediately, again helping to improve the balance sheet structures for the new capital regulations.

In the UK, life insurance companies are also using or considering securitization. The issue for life insurance company solutions is requiring life companies to look at their assets and liabilities in conjunction with each other rather than separately. 'The regulatory response has had two main thrusts. First, the insurance industry is being moved swiftly towards a fair-value model accounting (in the UK, the FSA calls it the "realistic peak" valuation). Insurers will be forced to recognise changes in the value of their liabilities as markets rise and fall, rather than being able to defer or disguise that recognition until the situation is too serious to ignore. Second, industry capital – which was often based on simple ratios – will now be based on risk, as laid out in the FSA's new rules. Other markets, such as the Netherlands, Denmark, and Switzerland, are taking a similar path.'[54]

CP 195 has not suggested a particular strategy that life insurance companies should follow; no doubt many new solutions will be created for life companies over the next few years, one of which we will discuss in later chapters.

Since the FSA is requiring the marking-to-market of assets and liabilities, under stress test scenarios, there is a sense that bankers are breaking out their options strategies in an effort to contain extreme movements in asset values. A product that has been offered by banks for many years but is being brought out of the closet is a technique known as constant proportion portfolio insurance (CPPI). 'CPPI works by tinkering with the allocation of assets, sometimes on a daily basis, so that an insurer always has enough assets to achieve the required minimum value of the portfolio – if stocks tumble, but the insurer can still sell out of equities and buy enough bonds to meet its guarantees, there's no problem. Banks offer to undertake portfolio rebalancing to ensure there are always enough assets to cover the insurer's liabilities over a specific time-horizon – and also construct a hedging programme to offer protection for market falls beyond the insurer's tolerance.'[55]

Other bankers are trying to create new products, 'in particular hybrid options that would enable insurers to manage the risk of a fall in the value of their assets and a simultaneous rise in the value of their liabilities.'[56]

In the United States, the US National Association of Insurance Commissioners issued a new regulation in January 2001 known as Triple-X, to prevent life insurance companies from allowing their capital reserves to run too low. According to market professionals, Triple-X

[54] 'Risk Management for Insurance Companies,' Special report, *Risk*, August 2004, p. 7.
[55] Ibid, p. 8.
[56] Ibid, p. 8.

requires life insurance companies to hold larger reserves than in the past; needless to say, holding these reserves will cost the insurer money. US insurance companies are using offshore reinsurance companies, which require less regulatory capital than US companies, to issue letters of credit which are used to cover the difference between the economic reserves and the needed additional regulatory capital.[57]

The key for any insurance company, however, is the actual amount of reserves and assets that it has to meet its liabilities at any time. The insurance problem is very similar to the pension fund problem, ensuring that sufficient capital is raised, invested in fixed interest instruments and investments, meeting their liabilities. However, the gap between assets and liabilities is enormous. Many are trying to raise funds to meet their regulatory obligations, such as Standard Life, mentioned in the previous chapter; unless sufficient funds are raised, all the risk management, sleight-of-hand transactions will not help insurers to access the sufficient regulatory capital to meet their liabilities:

> No financial institution needs capital quite like life insurers. Their capital levels dictate the kind of products they sell, their operational scale and any expansion plans – not to mention their solvency requirements. . . . Assets minus liabilities equals capital – that is the restrictive regulatory code that insurance companies operate under. In determining liabilities, they have to include all debt and all shares except ordinary shares and, within certain limits, perpetual and dated preferred shares or subordinated debt. In addition, changes to EU regulations are making things more difficult, and there is more in store. In 2009, the EU will introduce Solvency II, the industry equivalent of Basel II. And all of this follows a three-year bear market and difficult trading conditions in which a number of life companies need to increase their capital. No wonder life insurance groups are looking to find new ways of raising additional capital that could provide attractive alternatives to subordinated debt and equity issuance.[58]

The way insurance companies invest their funds has had an enormous negative impact over their asset base. With equity markets collapsing since the technology bubble burst in late 2000, the insurance industry suffered from being on the frontline of these perfect storm years. Japan has had 14 years of general economic and financial decline, and it is difficult to imagine what this meant for the size of the Japanese insurance industry's asset–liability gap.

As European, UK and US companies seek to restore their balance sheets in preparation for regulatory regime change, they must reconsider the way they manage their reserves and assets within an investment portfolio. Many market commentators say that insurance companies must raise sufficient capital, invest in fixed-income securities and be able to meet their liabilities with comfort. However, the insurance industry is unable, at least for the moment, to raise the necessary capital, either through equity rights issues or bond issues, therefore it must find alternatives. As discussed, rather than the buy-and-hold strategies of yesterday, alternative structures must be used today to raise, invest and actively manage additional capital. In other words, the insurance company that is raising fresh capital must manage these assets in investments to ensure that they meet the regulated capital requirements set by new regulatory standards. The investment portfolio should be predominantly invested in fixed-income, although many are seeking to use alternative investments to achieve additional returns-on-investment in an effort to create more capital through their investment portfolio.

US insurers are already investing 5–15% in alternative investments such as hedge funds (total return strategies), well ahead of UK and European insurers, and some commentators predict European insurers will invest up to 15% in alternative investment strategies at some time in

---

[57] Ibid, p. 14.
[58] 'A capital solution.' *Risk*, July 2004.

the future.[59] Hedge fund investment strategies may be reaching their zenith, in terms of their ability to generate the returns-on-investment that one would expect from past performance – too much money chasing too few investment opportunities. There are only so many types of investment available in which to invest, from the industrial to the developing and emerging markets, therefore, when one particular investment area or sector is offering good investment return expectations, there are too many investors chasing that same investment – too much investment leads to inflated or asset price bubbles. The perfect example was the technology (Internet) stock boom of the late 1990s.

PENSION FUNDS

The pension fund industry is going through a great deal of introspection at the moment. To an extent, pension fund trustees are like deer looking into the oncoming headlights of an eighteen-wheeler truck travelling at 75 miles per hour right for them. Pension fund trustees are afraid to jump one way or the other, although they recognize they have to jump and quickly. Pension trustees are responsible for the way in which pension schemes are managed, but not, according to Jon Exley of Mercer Consulting Group, one of the major pension fund consultants and actuaries, for any asset–liability deficit, which is the responsibility of the corporate sponsor. The pension fund trustee is responsible for ensuring that the funds available in the pension fund scheme meet the liabilities required today and as best they can for the future. The corporate sponsor, on the other hand, is responsible for the pension fund scheme's deficit.

As I mentioned in the previous chapter, part of the problem for the pension industry has been the way its institutional money managers are mandated to manage their investment portfolios. These investments are intended to ensure that the assets ultimately meet the pensioners' liabilities for as long as the company has members in its defined benefit schemes. Investment managers are benchmarked or measured against a relative index related to the assets that they are managing. The investment manager is therefore managing a portfolio in relation to that index, for better or worse, but not in relation to the actual liability profile of the pension scheme itself.

Many pension fund trustees actually outsource their asset allocation decisions to a balanced investment manager, as outlined in the previous chapter. In so doing, trustees are delegating the entire process to the institutional investment manager and, as I pointed out, the institutional investment manager is seeking to outperform a relative benchmark and not allocating the pension scheme's assets in accordance with the required liability return requirement. When this process goes well, meaning investment returns are strong, it is easy for the pension trustees to think that they have made the correct decision. However, when performance falls, as it has since 2000, the pension fund trustees don't look so good (they seem more like a herd of ostriches with their heads in the sand), and the corporate sponsor has a large pension fund deficit to fund as a result.

Presently, pension funds are doing very little to combat the problems that they face after four years of poor investment returns. They have not altered their asset allocations away from equity investments in favour of fixed income because they desperately need the high equity returns on investment that they have grown accustomed to over the past decades, and fixed income returns and yields are now at historically low levels. And they now need equity returns-on-investment to make up the pension fund deficit that has been exacerbated since 2000.

---

[59] 'A capital solution,' *Risk*, July 2004, p. 2.

As Jon Exley pointed out, the corporate sponsors do not have sufficient monies available for their pension fund scheme to enable them to invest their funds matched against their required pension liabilities. Unless the corporate sponsor starts to solve the investment deficit problem, the pension fund trustees will continue to do the best they can with the financial resources available to meet their pensioners' liabilities. However, as with any game of musical chairs, when the music stops and there are two people left standing with only one chair left, future pensioners may be left with the burden of fending for themselves during their retirement years – unless government bails the corporate sponsors out of their financial responsibilities.

CONCLUSION

There is no question that changing global rules and regulations are having an enormous impact on all companies around the globe. The time will soon come when the way managers and directors manage their non-core global financial risks will change for ever. Regulatory changes will force them to find 'keep it simple' strategies. But regulation should not and cannot stifle the entrepreneurial spirit which has been driving economic growth and expansion in all Anglo-Saxon economies. But according to the new Chairman of the Securities and Exchange Commission (SEC), William Donaldson, that is exactly what it is doing:

> Now, for the first time, Mr Donaldson is siding with those who argue that the crackdown is stifling entrepreneurialism, paralysing boardroom decision making. 'Sarbanes–Oxley unleashed batteries of lawyers across the country,' he says. The result is 'a huge preoccupation with the dangers and risk of making the slightest mistake, as opposed to a reasonable approach to legitimate business risk.'[60]

In the next two chapters I will introduce new and innovative methods, processes and solutions for managing the unforeseen price volatility arising from non-core global financial risks. These innovations are based on the discussions in these first three chapters. Chapter 4 will discuss the attributes and characteristics that market research is demanding of the next generation of risk management solutions, while Chapter 5 will introduce, define and discuss one such solution.

---

[60] 'After a year of US corporate clean-up, William Donaldson calls for a return to risk taking,' Interview in the *Financial Times*, 24 July 2003, p. 15.

Characteristics of the Next-Generation Financial Risk Management Solution

Don't worry about people stealing your ideas. If your ideas are any good, you'll have to ram them down people's throats.

Howard Aiken

Most people are more comfortable with old problems than with new solutions.

Anonymous

Discovery consists of looking at the same thing as everyone else does and thinking something different.

Albert Szent-Györgyi, 1937 Nobel Laureate in Physiology and Medicine

MANAGING THE UNEXPECTED

'On 4 August 1998 the Dow Jones index fell 3.5%, three weeks later, as news from Moscow worsened, stocks fell again 4.4%. And then again, on 31 August, it fell 6.8%'.[1] According to conventional stock market theory these events should have never happened; the probability of a sequence of events ending with the price fall on 31 August 1998 is one in 20 million, meaning if one were a trader this event would take more than 100 000 trading days[2] to occur. The probability of all three price declines in the same month is about one in 500 billion. In July 2002 the Dow index recorded three steep falls within a week, at a probability of one in 4 trillion. Financial theorists put at one in 100 000 000 000 000 000 000 000 000 000 000 000 000 000 000 000 000 the probability of the fall that occurred on the worst trading day in nearly 100 years, 19 October 1987. Looking at Dow movements from 1916 to 2003, according to financial theory there should be 58 days when the Dow moved more than 3.4%, but a study by Benoit Mandelbrot found that there were 1001 such days.[3] Theory suggests that there should be only six days of index swings beyond 4.5%, while there were in fact 366. Index swings greater than 7% should come once every 300 000 days, whereas in fact the twentieth century saw 48 days of such price swings.[4]

The point of these numbers and statistics is to demonstrate that so-called extreme events, no matter how they are calculated, occur too often! They are therefore not extreme events, expect the unexpected.

The financial theory referred to above is the efficient markets hypothesis introduced by Eugene Fama. I do not believe that markets are as efficient as this theory would have it – and Mandelbrot's study appears to back up my belief. The hypothesis states that in an ideal market, all relevant available information is accounted for in a security's price. Securities are also supposed to behave according to the postulates of random walk theory, introduced by the French mathematician Louis Bachelier in 1900, which says that prices will go up or down

---

[1] Benoit B. Mandelbrot (2004), *The (Mis)Behaviour of Markets*. Profile Books, p. 3.
[2] Ibid, p. 4.
[3] Ibid, p. 13.
[4] Ibid.

with equal probability, in the same way as a fair coin will land heads or tails. Random walk theory, however, also assumes that all price moves obey the normal distribution or bell curve. But it is evident that the normal distribution is not an adequate model for price changes, and that extreme events occur much more often than under the normal distribution – that is, the distribution of price moves has fatter tails than the normal.

Low-probability, extreme events (something of a misnomer!), as described in the first paragraph sometimes cause generational problems. They cause enormous financial distress and should be a concern for everyone.

Professor Mandelbrot uses movements in the price of the Japanese yen from 1986 to 2003 as an illustrative example. Nearly half of the decline in the US dollar versus the Japanese yen over this time period occurred on ten of the 4695 trading days. In other words, 46% of the price fall came on 0.21% of the days. Similar statistics apply to other markets. In the 1980s, 40% of the Standard & Poor's index positive returns came in only ten days.[5]

Another assumption made by theorists is that today's price movements occur independently of yesterday's. There is no doubt in my mind, as a professional trader, that this assumption is made purely for the sake of an easy life (theorists will call it a simplifying assumption, and it will be invoked to make the mathematics behave nicely) and that price movements are conditional on past price movements. You may have heard the saying 'the trend is my friend'. Professional market traders do have better knowledge of their markets than the man-on-the street, and they do not wake up in the morning completely oblivious of what happened yesterday.

Mandelbrot offers the argument that price changes in the financial markets can cluster into zones of high drama and slow evolution. He uses the analogy of the Noah effect, extreme life-changing events for the world, translating it into market speak – wild price swings with fat-tailed extreme events. An example of this is the stock market collapse of 19 October 1987 when the US stock market fell by 29.2%. The other type of event he uses is the predictability and forecasting of the Nile floods in Egypt – predicting the forthcoming floods which make or break crop production for all of Egypt. In market speak it is the interdependence of price changes and long memories of price movements that drive market prices.[6] The Nile floods represent stock market patterns when prices will move higher day after day and after days of rising prices the trend will change and prices will consistently fall day after day.

What all of this tells us is that markets are riskier than theory would have us believe. History is full of cases of extreme price movements that have caused untold financial harm for individuals, companies, pension funds and insurance companies. Look at the years 2000–2003: we now have a generational pension fund deficit because of extreme global financial market movements; the insurance industry nearly collapsed under the weight of its liabilities; and the United States has unprecedented fiscal and current deficits as a result of the slowdown in the global economy and the fallout from the events of 11 September 2001. In 1999, would anyone have predicted that the technology bubble would burst so spectacularly, or that the United States and then Europe would become embroiled in unparalleled corporate scandal?

According to Mandelbrot, we have little real clue as to the workings of financial markets:

> It is beyond belief that we know so little about how people get rich or poor, about how it is they dwell in comfort and health and die in penury and disease. Financial markets are the machines in which much of human welfare is decided; yet we know more about how our car engines work than about how our global financial system functions. We lurch from crisis to crisis. In a networked

---

[5] Benoit B. Mandelbrot (2004), *The (Mis)Behaviour of Markets*. Profile Books, p. 234.
[6] Ibid, p. 208.

world, mayhem in one market spreads instantaneously to all others – and we have only the vaguest notion how this happens, or how to regulate it.[7]

This chapter will outline the characteristics of the new instruments that are needed to help those who are faced with these non-core global financial risks, who are not market professionals and want an easy-to-use, simple-to-understand solution to deal with the uncertainty of managing non-core global financial risks. You can drive a car without having to understand how it works. Similarly, 'to invest in markets, you do not have to know why they behave the way they do'.[8] The new solution will allow you to hedge or lay off global financial risks without any knowledge of the way derivative instruments and global financial markets work.

From discussing global financial risk issues with many people in industry and financial services over a number of years, I have concluded that there are seven areas that they would like to see covered in the next generation of risk management solutions for financial risks. These are the subject of this chapter. They are driven by a single factor – the unprecedented regulatory environmental changes we are witnessing today.

Along with new corporate governance legislation in the United States, the Sarbanes–Oxley Act, there are significant accounting rules, FAS 133 in the United States and IAS 39 in Europe, causing havoc with the way the top public companies account for their financial risk management activities. And as if these are not enough to keep the accounting industry booking many hours of advisory work, the insurance and banking industries are being moved to a risk-based capital reserve structure which will affect every one of their customers in some way. Therefore, many of the characteristics that should go into the next generation of financial risk management solutions are being further driven by the need to comply with the new regulatory world.

The world of business is changing, greater globalization means more non-core global financial risks, and there is no question that an easy-to-use, easy-to-understand solution is needed more than ever. The seven characteristics of such a solution are as follows:

1. set and forget budget assurance;
2. cost efficiency;
3. hedge efficiency;
4. bundling non-core global financial risks into a single solution;
5. greater counterparty pricing – market pricing versus traditional proprietary bank pricing;
6. greater capacity for underwriting global financial risks;
7. simplicity.

In this chapter I will take each characteristic in turn. Bear in mind, however, there is one risk that cannot be eliminated – counterparty risk. In everything that we do in life, including the next-generation risk management instrument, counterparty risk will remain. The uncertainty over whether the counterparty – in our case the risk-taking underwriter – will honour their commitment to the contract is prevalent in every aspect of our business life.

SET AND FORGET BUDGET ASSURANCE

I first heard this term several years ago when a US senior executive was explaining his frustration with the way his treasury department was handling and managing his company's currency and interest rate risks. He was sick and tired of going to quarterly executive committee meetings

---

[7] Ibid, pp. 254–255.
[8] Ibid, p. 229.

and learning that the non-core global financial risk, which he thought was being managed and hedged, was in fact showing extreme hedge deviations from the previous meeting. The treasury department would demonstrate that they were using their European operations to internally hedge the natural currency translation risks in the United States and vice versa. But when it came to reading the management reports, he would see that the European operation was, for example, benefiting from currency translation whereas his operation was actually showing a loss because of the adverse currency movements affecting the company in the US. The company was not using natural internal hedging relationships as they had been explained to him, and the currency options contracts that they were using to hedge the balance of his unit's exposure were showing substantial hedge deviations. As a result, his unit was showing a pre-tax loss. This loss was completely outside his control, and he wondered why there was no solution or instrument available to him that behaved in a similar way to an insurance indemnification.

Set and forget budget assurance means that when executing a new instrument, companies can protect their budget assumptions for the coming fiscal year. The *forget* part means that they do not have to worry about it, they can put the instrument document away and only pull it out again when the time comes to settle the contract. They can forget about hedge deviation, time value decay, or any other issue that may cause the hedging instrument not to correlate with the underlying cash asset. Users of the new instrument would set it at the beginning of their fiscal cycle, fixing the cost to their entire budget of the impact of unforeseen price volatility on non-core global financial risks.

Managers do not have the time to think about and monitor the way their treasury departments manage their non-core global financial risks. They do not want any nasty surprises, particularly when these can cause so much damage to their profitability, and especially given that they tend not to learn about it until their next quarterly meeting. Set and forget budget assurance means that managers can lay off non-core global financial risks at the outset of the fiscal year.

Derivative instruments are difficult to understand and do not provide 'set and forget' budget assurance. The market for these products is extremely professional, with its own jargon, day-to-day fluctuations and movements, technical analysis, fundamental analysis, and inter-analysis between the underlying cash asset and the derivative instruments, as well as between the various derivative instruments themselves.

Using derivative instruments requires one to not only understand the strategies that they intend to employ, but also to understand the nuances of the markets themselves. Management must ask themselves what strategy to employ, which derivatives broker to use or whether to use their commercial banking relationship, and whose advice to take. Many corporate executives have an understanding of derivatives, whether they are futures or forward and options contracts, but, as I have repeatedly said, they are not part of their core competence. They don't know how to price a derivative, and how should they? If Nobel laureates are arguing over the right pricing model or strategy, what does this mean for the corporate executive and their treasury department?

Options and futures contracts behave very differently. As I mentioned in the previous chapter, futures are great for laying off a financial risk, while options are used to play with financial risks in many different ways or to mitigate financial risks using a variety of strategies. We saw Lufthansa doing it the right way and Caterpillar doing it the hard way. There are exchange-traded, as well as over-the-counter, derivatives which are aimed at very different types of underlying risks. Exchange-traded derivatives are standardized but have a liquid exchange which provides settlement, pricing efficiency, clearing and comfort when using them. But over-the-counter products are issued by the commercial or investment banks, who make the price and provide the liquidity for their product; this means that the user of such products is relying on the bank to provide the correct pricing and liquidity if the user wants to sell the instrument back. What happens when the bank and the client have an interest in the same risks? And what happens when both want to sell the same thing at the same time?

But what about those executives who do not want to think about the problem of using derivative instruments, who do not want to play craps on the outcome of a derivative solution? They do not understand the professional derivatives markets, they do not want to understand them, and they want to focus on their own company's products and services. They ask the question – why can't someone else sort this out for us?

The accounting for derivatives is complicated and with the introduction of new corporate governance regulations and accounting rules, companies would perhaps prefer to seek less derivatives usage rather than more. Companies now believe that the unforeseen price volatility on global financial risks may cost the company an enormous amount of money, but that derivatives are a worse evil. If they use derivatives incorrectly, executives will face embarrassment, shareholder disapproval, lawsuits and perhaps lose their jobs; in some cases they may even face legal prosecution.

Corporate executives do not want to have to worry about the probabilities and events as described in the opening paragraphs of this chapter. They have enough on their plates; they do not have the time to brood over financial theory about extreme events. They would prefer to use a solution or instrument which takes all of this pain out of their lives. They want a solution similar to an insurance indemnification which they set at the beginning of their fiscal year, protecting their budget from the impact arising from extreme events.

Non-core global financial risks should be seen as part of a company's enterprise-wide risk management scheme. Companies have many risks that are not core to their business model; these are the risks that fall into an enterprise-wide risk management policy.

An enterprise-wide risk management programme includes property and casualty insurance, business interruption, environmental, products and liability insurance, along with many more risks. When a company purchases insurance coverage, it has received an indemnification from its insurance underwriter that if an event occurs, which destroys a factory, for example, the company will receive from its insurance underwriter the funds needed to rebuild its factory and to cover the cost of the business interruption. The company does not have to worry about time decay for its insurance coverage; there is no insurance coverage deviation between the value of the property and the insurance cover. There may be disputes over the wording of the insurance coverage, but the performance attributes of an insurance indemnification are not the same as those of a capital market derivative instrument. An insurance indemnification provides perfect correlation with the underlying risk, such as the value of one's home, and in our case with a bundle of global financial risks. The company receives set and forget budget assurance against these insured risks.

Once the instrument is set and the risks are laid off into the market, companies do not want to worry about the risk, the instrument, the value of the instrument, the correlation between the instrument and their underlying cash asset. They want to be able to put the new instrument's document into a drawer, and take it out again when the fiscal quarter or year-end arrives and they either receive an indemnification payment from the underwriter or must make a payment to the underwriter. Companies do want to have to worry about pricing models, pricing discrepancies and accounting issues. They do not want any budget or profitability surprises.

Set and forget budget assurance is an experience for the risk-limiter customer – they receive, by way of a product, something that they can be assured is not going to go wrong, other than counterparty default, as I mentioned in the introduction to this chapter. The experience of the client when they take out set and forget budget assurance is 'peace of mind'. We are always going to have to rely upon someone's word or on a legal contract to make good on the promises made in that contract between the two or more counterparties. The experience economy[9] offers the customer goods and services that are unique and memorable experiences – hedging one's unforeseen price volatility on non-core global financial risks is an experience that many would certainly desire in this day and age.

COST EFFICIENCY

The next characteristic of the new solution and instrument is cost efficiency. The use of a derivative instrument incurs a physical cash cost. I am not referring now to hedge deviations or correlation deviations. When one uses a forward foreign exchange agreement to hedge a foreign exchange exposure, the cost of the instrument will be the interest rate differential between the two currencies. When one uses a futures contract to hedge a financial risk, the price of the contract will be the interest rate cost between the date of the transaction and the settlement date. When using options contracts, the cost is the premium that the options writer charges to the counterparty wanting to buy the option.

There are market standards and conventions governing the pricing of derivative instruments. These have been created for a reason, which is outside the scope of this book – suffice it to say that they have been created *by* market professionals *for* market professionals and may not make sense to non-professionals. Many companies are deterred by what they see as the excessive cost of using derivative instruments – they may reduce their usage or even refrain altogether. They may budget the cost of purchasing their derivatives, and once they spend their allotted funds on hedging their non-core global financial risks, they have to forgo the use of hedging strategies and instruments. Clearly, the cost of these instruments is an issue of concern to companies.

It is again worth making the point that derivative instruments lie outside the core competence of most company managers. There is a great deal of bitterness and frustration among managers in the corporate, insurance and pension fund world because they do not really understand the derivative instruments they are buying and clearly feel frustrated by the price they pay for them, particularly when they go wrong.

There is no escaping the need to consider hedging non-core global financial risks. Companies understand that the derivative instrument they select has underlying characteristics which may or may not provide the intended or expected result of hedging the unforeseen price volatility on these risks. They rely upon their bankers to select the right derivative instrument and price it correctly. Then they just hope for the best. If the hedging instrument or strategy goes wrong, the derivatives salesman blames it on the market, market standards and conventions; 'we did the best we could but it went wrong, it was out of our control. It is happening to everyone else, if it's any consolation.' Some companies will not hedge their foreign exchange exposures because their competitors are not hedging their foreign exchange exposures. They feel that following the herd is the safest strategy. This is madness, but understandable if one sees it as the result of an inability to understand what derivatives are all about and how to value them.

---

[9] B. Joseph Pine II and James H. Gilmore (1999) *The Experience Economy*. Boston: Harvard Business School Press.

Mandelbrot sums up the difficulty:

> Valuing options correctly is a high-roller game, but the rules are all messed up.... The most widely known formula was published in 1973 by Fischer Black and Myron Scholes, and it has been known for years that it is simply wrong. It makes unrealistic assumptions. It asserts that prices vary by a bell curve; volatility does not change through the life of the option; prices do not jump; taxes and commissions do not exist; and so on.... A fundamental problem is the Black–Scholes assumption of constant volatility – in essence, that the world does not change.[10]

Who is supposed to understand this harsh and uncertain reality? I am sure that few non-market professionals understand the pricing model and formula for valuing options contracts. Having said that, I also suspect that many market professionals are likewise unaware of the peculiarities of the Black–Scholes model; they just plug the numbers into their computers and up pops the answer, the value of the options contract, the price the options buyer should pay in premium, or the seller of the option should receive in premium, on their screens.

When a company must use a forward foreign exchange agreement to hedge its currency risks, it must arrange a credit line with its bankers. And sometimes, if it is not doing business with one of the top global banks, the company must organize credit lines for using forward foreign exchange agreements with more than one banking institution. This is a cumbersome and aggravating way to hedge one's unforeseen currency price volatility.

The pricing or valuing of derivatives instruments has also become commoditized; derivatives pricing has become undifferentiated between institutions, and there is very little price competition. One of the key characteristics that many non-professionals want is greater market and competitive pricing of hedge mitigation. They want the cost of a derivative instrument to be affordable – not the present pricing, but something new that cannot be commoditized by several large institutions. Recall from the first chapter that there are only six banking institutions presently underwriting 66% of all derivatives trades. With tens of trillions of dollars of derivatives transactions taking place, price discovery is limited to six banking institutions, therefore, when they make a price for a derivatives instrument of one kind or another, it's take it or leave it pricing.

We are back at square one: what is the right way to value a derivative instrument? Non-professionals do not want to get involved in figuring this out – it is not their business to understand the valuation process. But they would like to see greater price competition and would like to see a better valuing mechanism and an easier-to-understand way to budget and price derivative instruments.

In short, cost efficiency means the client wants to spend less money on a global financial risk management instrument or solution.

HEDGE EFFICIENCY

The third characteristic that risk-limiter corporates, insurance companies and pension funds want is hedge efficiency, which basically means that the product should do exactly what it says on the tin.

After suffering through the valuation process, whether doing it themselves or relying upon their bankers, the risk-limiter now has ownership of the derivative instrument, for example, an options contract. They have the right, but not the obligation, to buy or sell an asset at a

---

[10] Benoit B. Mandelbrot (2004) *The (Mis) Behaviour of Markets*. Profile Books, pp. 268–269.

specified price until the expiry date. Hedge inefficiency occurs when the derivative instrument, the options contract, behaves one way and the underlying asset behaves in another way. The cost implications of this can come as a nasty shock.

The major Fortune 50 company chairman we met earlier would shake his head in frustration with this problem. He would listen to the problem at every quarterly board meeting, aware that he was focusing his valuable time on a non-core business issue that could absorb more of his profitability than any labour negotiation. If the company's profitability falls into a loss, management can go back and renegotiate labour contracts, as is happening in the US airline industry at present, or cut costs – but how do you fix the unforeseen price volatility on non-core global financial risks? The company has paid a high premium for a derivative instrument, only to find it is costing even more in hedge deviation. If management do not hedge their global financial risks, they risk shareholder lawsuits. Some companies believe that what comes around will go around again, meaning that their currency price movements, for example, will move adversely this year but turn favourable the next year. Management may discover that this phenomenon in the global capital markets is long gone, and lose money. But at least if they try to do something they cannot lose their jobs or be judged as incompetent or negligent in their executive duties. However, now the corporate governance regulations and accounting rules for hedging non-core global financial risks are being changed, creating more uncertainty and anxiety for management.

The problem for the non-professional risk limiter is that they expect that their derivatives instrument and strategy will provide the required risk mitigation coverage – often mistakenly, as it turns out. Off-the-shelf futures contracts will not necessarily correlate with the underlying portfolio of bond or equity assets, for example. A futures contract tracks its underlying standardized index in the case of equities, or the cheapest-to-deliver bond in the case of bond futures contracts. Someone at either the company or their bankers must manage the correlation risks occurring each day. When using options contracts, the hedge deviations are more acute; recall the Greek relationships from the previous chapter, which will affect an option's value, minute by minute, day by day. As I discussed in Chapter 3, the delta of an option will affect the hedge ratio of the options value versus the underlying asset; the gamma of an option measures the change in the delta in relation to the underlying asset; the lambda risk measures the percentage change in the option price for a 1% change in the underlying assets price; the theta risk measures the impact on the option's price of a one-day change in the time remaining to expiration; vega risk measures the option's price and is affected by changes in the market's valuation of implied volatility; rho risk is the risk-free interest rate – there is no such thing as a risk-free interest rate, and interest rates, from official interest rates to money market interest rates, are changing every day, which is why the model is flawed in this way. There are too many moving parts that can and do go wrong all the time. I have always been amazed by the lack of understanding of options contracts; many think that they are insurance contracts and should behave similarly to an insurance indemnification contract – a perfectly correlated hedging instrument. Can you imagine if your automobile insurance would somehow change in value relative to your underlying asset, your car, over the time of the contract?

The other aspect of hedge inefficiency has to do with the strategies that many employ, whether a straight vanilla options strategy, buying a put or call option or using a forward, future and swap in a straightforward manner, or a combination of several derivatives in an attempt to mitigate the many hedge deviation risks. Of course many of the complicated and exotic options, futures, swap or forward transactions create or perhaps pile on hedge deviations rather than helping to mitigate them.

When I used to hedge currency risks for the portfolios that I used to manage, I always felt that currency risk was not my core competence but global bonds or fixed interest markets were my core acumen. Therefore, when I hedged currency risks, I would use forward foreign exchange contracts to lay those risks off; however, I would try to mitigate the cost of hedging those risks by taking a view on the interest rate differentials of the transaction. In effect, I would want to reduce the cost of hedging currency risks by playing with the rising or falling interest rate differentials between the currencies that I was hedging. The point of this story is that, as a market professional, I would watch and manage these two risks every minute of every day. Sometimes it would go wrong, I would misread the market, but I would take immediate action if it did go wrong. Non-professional market players don't necessarily understand their potential hedge deviation and no doubt their derivatives broker or bankers would suggest additional strategies to mitigate it. But the responsibility for the transaction rests with the risk-limiter client.

Senior management and executives understand their budgets and profit projections as they relate to their core business, but anything not core to their business they do not understand. They want to control those risks in relation to their budget assumptions and projections – the last thing they need or want is a negative hedge deviation negatively affecting their profits.

So the third characteristic that risk limiters want from a new and innovative financial risk instrument is perfect correlation, no hedge deviations, what you see is what you get – similar to insurance indemnification policies.

BUNDLING

The fourth desirable characteristic of our new instrument is concerned with bundling.

A typical corporate, insurance company or pension fund will have many assets and/or liabilities which affect their profit and loss statement or balance sheet. For example, some companies have a few foreign exchange translation or transaction price risks, while others have many; I know of one company that had 42 foreign exchange translation risks, representing 60% of its total revenues. Whether one has three or 33 currency translation and/or transaction risks, the traditional derivatives market allows companies to enter into forward foreign exchange contracts which represent a single and individual currency risk. A forward foreign exchange agreement requires the company to arrange credit lines with its bank to enable it to enter into a forward foreign exchange contract. In cases where forwards are not available, the risk-limiter must use over-the-counter options for those currencies which are generally available in developing and emerging market countries. Companies would like to bundle all of their currencies into one single instrument transaction – and then set and forget about it.

Unfortunately, the global capital markets are not set up in this way. A bank proprietary trading desk will price each individual risk and internally hedge that risk; there is no dynamic pricing or trading of client risk limiters' risks.

In other asset classes, an insurance company holding in reserve a wide array of bonds (with a wide spread of maturities, credits, currencies and coupon rates) may want to hedge the price volatility of its portfolio. Unfortunately, the only liquid instruments available are government bond futures and option contracts, or liquid interest rate swaps. But there is no way to hedge an entire bond portfolio or a large diversified equity portfolio with one instrument. Insurance companies and pension funds would like to bundle all of these risks into one single contract – once again, setting and forgetting about it.

Choices sometimes have to be made as to the type of instrument to use to hedge or mitigate non-core global financial risks. Today, companies have to rely on their derivatives brokers and bankers, but they recognize that they are being sold off-the-shelf traditional derivative instruments. They must talk to a vast multitude of salespeople representing different types of instrument. At the end of all this they may end up with a contract that doesn't quite match the risk that needs to be hedged, as in the case of Lufthansa, using crude oil futures contracts and heating oil as proxies to hedge jet fuel price volatility. With each potential transaction comes an overwhelming amount of paperwork, differing settlement dates, and differing conventions that have to be mastered. Dealing with all this is time-consuming and bewildering. Managers do not want to have to figure out which is the right instrument. So why can't there be one universal instrument that allows bundling of the risks into a simple indemnification contract?

MARKET PRICING

Market pricing refers to the way in which the derivative instrument is priced by the marketplace or bank counterparties. At present, the pricing of a derivative instrument is based upon traditional valuation formulae and models and has become commoditized, as I explained earlier. Therefore, the price quoted by one bank or broker will not be significantly different than that quoted by another. The key to successful derivatives broking is the ability to execute and fill the transaction order quickly, ensuring that the client receives the best price available in a trading pit on a derivatives exchange, particularly when prices are moving quickly and are volatile. In the case of over-the-counter products, bank counterparties may not offer sufficient liquidity to price, buy or sell one of their proprietary OTC derivatives because of their own risk trading positions. This can happen when the markets are at their most volatile.

Another key issue within this characteristic, which I explained in Chapter 1, and which constitutes a fundamental conflict of interest for banking institutions, is the proprietary pricing of derivative instruments for bank clients. As I mentioned in Chapter 1, banks use their capital to trade the global capital markets in an effort to generate capital gains revenues for themselves. These proprietary traders are competing for the same return-on-investment as many of their institutional clients, therefore creating a conflict of interest. The price that is offered to the client from a proprietary trading desk is based upon the view and/or valuation model of that banking institution. The price that the bank offers to its client will incorporate the conflict of interest: a high price is charged for risks that the bank does not want and a low price is shown to the client if the bank wants the client's risks. The client will not benefit from price discovery, but has to rely upon and accept what is offered by their relationship bank. The risk-limiting institution, the client, is held hostage by the price and counterparty liquidity offered by the bank.

Many managers accept that they are not getting the best price available for a derivative instrument, but also accept that their bank may not be making money on some of the services it is offering them. They accept that their bank must make up the difference or generate a profit on ancillary services such as derivatives trading. On the other hand, banks are becoming more competitive and are taking more and more proprietary trading positions in the global markets and are therefore becoming risk-averse, moving away from their fee revenue business model and creating a conflict of interest with their clients. The risk is that banks will look after their own proprietary position before that of their clients.

Market pricing is all about market discovery of the best available price for a given derivatives instrument – what the counterparty will seek in underwriting premiums for that client risk. Those futures exchanges that use open-outcry trading are the best at market price discovery. In open-outcry trading, a contract is made if one trader cries out that he wants to sell at a certain price and then another trader yells out that he will buy at that same price – in other words, for every buyer there must be a seller and vice versa. This is a great system for the exchange-traded standard derivatives, such as futures and options contracts, but what about the over-the-counter or more bespoke derivative instruments, such as forwards, swaps, swaptions and options contracts? The proprietary banking institution makes a two-way price for these – a bid price, which is the price the bank will pay for the derivative instrument, and an offer price, which is the price at which they will sell it.

The new derivative or hedge mitigation instrument will have to be priced differently than it is today. When seeking market pricing for the next-generation hedging instrument, we will seek out many competitive bidders from the banking industry, asset management groups and other global financial risk takers. There is value in a bundle of global financial risks, the portfolio effect will allow those financial institutions defined above to price the bundle of risks, and the value of the bundle is in the eye of the beholder. In other words, by placing value on a bundle of risks, some of those risks may be of greater value to one institution than another. The global financial risks of one client can be used to naturally hedge against another, or the bundle of risks may offer one an opportunity for capital gain. Therefore, a competitive bidding process such as a reverse auction will offer the client risk-limiter a market discovery process for the price of their risk mitigation solution. A reverse auction, also known as a Dutch auction, is the opposite of a traditional auction at Sotheby's or Christies auction houses. In a traditional auction process, the bidding process drives the price upward, whereas, in a reverse auction, the bidding process will drive the price, for the risk mitigation product premium, downward.

In order to create a more competitive marketplace for pricing global financial risks, the new instrument or solution will not have the traditional characteristics of derivatives. A new instrument will require a new pricing methodology.

UNDERWRITING CAPACITY – COUNTERPARTY DIVERSIFICATION

Many companies are stuck with their existing banking relationships as the only means of seeking ideas, products and pricing for derivative solutions. If they are using standardized exchange-traded products, needless to say, they receive the best executed price of the futures and/or options contract (the executed price is the price that the client receives when completing a derivatives transaction), but they assume all of the problems of correlation deviation etc., as described earlier. However, when it comes to bespoke financial engineering of a derivatives solution, the risk-limiter's banker will sell them what they have in their silo of product offerings, and the pricing of the solution will be based on proprietary trader pricing at the relationship bank. There is no price competition, and the client risk-limiter must take it or leave it.

The institutional risk-limiter wants to see greater price competition or have the ability to seek out the best price available at the time of executing a hedging strategy. But unfortunately, the global capital markets are not set up in that way for the client risk-limiter. They cannot seek out the best price from a range of counterparties. As I mentioned in Chapter 1, the capital available at banking institutions for underwriting global financial risk is shrinking rather than expanding. The number of bank counterparties underwriting the bulk of derivative instruments is shrinking as well. Therefore, client risk-limiters complain that they are held hostage by the credit line their relationship bank provides; and more importantly, it is their appetite for underwriting the entire package of global financial risks that causes problems.

I am probably not the only one who has been a victim of banking institutions who do not answer their direct telephone lines during times of extreme or high price volatility. When that happens you cannot do anything about your risk. If you have purchased an over-the-counter product from a specific bank, you must seek a price and the ability to sell via the same bank; you cannot go to anyone else.

John Nugee and Avinash Persaud point out that the new regulatory environment is causing the risk-taking institutions to pass on their global financial risks to pension funds and insurance companies, and the new accounting standards are causing pension funds, for example, to transfer or shift their risks to the pensioner. They argue that

> The logical outcome of this current approach is for regulation to increase and become more costly, driving risk from traditional risk-holders into ever more obscure areas that are unregulated. It would be unusually lucky coincidence if those areas turned out to be the best home for that risk.[11]

They suggest that

> We should start by asking where we would like risk to end up and focus regulation on moving it there. Risk will be held where we want it to be held, and regulation will be more focussed and less expensive. The best location for most risks would be in the hands of those who can afford to lose the shirt they are wearing because they have another in the closet – the wealthy and well-capitalized. Risks should be concentrated with long-term investors and experts who understand them and can diversify their holdings across time, asset-class and geography.[12]

I agree with these authors for the reasons outlined in Chapter 1. The global financial risks of the risk-limiter client are best held by the professional risk-taking individuals and institutions such as banking institutions and professional money managers. Bankers will price risk in a traditional manner, while the money management industry will dynamically price those bundles of global financial risks that risk-limiter clients want to outsource in a set and forget budget assurance manner.

Recall from Chapter 1 that in 1998 the assets under management by mature market institutional investors amounted to $30 trillion. As of summer 2004, the world's top 100 banks have approximately $1.5 trillion of capital to enable them to underwrite the world's global financial risks.[13] The institutional asset managers are very different from banking institutions; they are managing money in a dynamic way every day, and they are shifting their asset allocations from one part of the world to another or selling one stock in deference to another. Banking institutions, on the other hand, will price risk and underwrite it with any dynamic management; they will move the risk into their inventory or sell it on, but they are not in the business of dynamically managing portfolios in the same way as institutional money managers. Additionally, the institutional investor industry has greater capacity for underwriting global financial risk, with $30 trillion of assets under management, versus the banking industry's $1.5 trillion.

Therefore, the risk-limiter wants the ability to select risk underwriters from as many as possible, giving them the ability to diversify their risk among counterparties. Similar to the insurance industry business model, the client seeking to limit their risks would like to outsource the unforeseen day-to-day price volatility arising from their non-core global financial risks to an array of financial risk-taking institutions. And they want this type of policy through an instrument or solution at the outset of their financial year, similar to the way companies manage their enterprise-wide insurance policies.

---

[11] John Nugee and Avinash Persaud, 'The dangers of being risk-averse', *Financial Times*, 17 September 2004, p. 19.
[12] Ibid.
[13] Figures from *The Banker* website, summer 2004.

SIMPLICITY

Simplicity means that the client risk-limiter wants a new instrument that is easy-to-use, simple-to-understand, and easy to account and explain to auditors and shareholders. Mary Pat McCarthy and Timothy Flynn quote Richard Bressler, Chief Financial Officer of Viacom, as saying that

> Stakeholders and shareholders are rewarding people for simplicity in today's market. CFOs will stay away from elaborate types of financial instruments, . . . they may be doing a plain vanilla transaction when there's a better transaction out there, but they don't want to do it because of the accounting treatment, . . . people make bad economic decisions that may be good accounting answers.[14]

And needless to say, this is no way to run a business – making economic sacrifices for fear of the accounting treatment. But does simplicity have to be sacrificed for economic benefit from hedging the unforeseen price volatility on non-core global financial risks? In a word – no.

The experience of receiving a simple, easy-to-use instrument that bundles one's non-core global financial risks into a single instrument having set and forget budget assurance characteristics perfectly correlated is precisely what the client risk-limiters want – in a word, simplicity. They are willing to pay for this experience, according to Richard G. Barlow:

> What captivates us now is special stuff, stuff that only a few of us can get, stuff that stands for something or symbolizes something. And more compelling than stuff are experiences – events, trips, places, sights, sounds, tastes that are out of the ordinary, memorable in their own right, precious in their uniqueness and fulfilling in a way that seems to make us more than we were. . . . Some describe this phenomenon as the 'experience economy'.[15]

At the beginning of this chapter we talked about the chaos that flourishes in the global financial markets; they do not behave according to a standard bell curve, or normal distribution. There is no such thing as low-probability extreme volatility – extreme events happen all too frequently, with all the problems that ensue. A new and simple instrument is required to allow the necessary simplifications for managing extreme events – in other words, the client risk-limiter wants a perfectly correlated instrument to manage whatever can go wrong in one easy-to-use, simple-to-understand single instrument.

The client does not have the time to understand traditional derivative instruments and in fact, as the quote from Richard Bressler suggests, they do not intend to use complicated derivative strategies, even though there are economic consequences for not using them, but the risk of using them is much greater to the CFO or treasurer than not using them. Since the Enron and WorldCom debacles of 2001 and 2002 respectively, and the subsequent introduction of the Sarbanes–Oxley Act for corporate governance, chief financial officers are legally liable if their financial risk disclosures are not correct, and there is a growing trend for many CFOs to prefer not to use certain derivative instruments and not to hedge the specific global financial risk, in an effort to avoid falling foul of the legal authorities.

A final aspect of simplicity is the ability to manage unforeseen price volatility before the company's fiscal year begins, instead of in arrears or by rolling them over from quarter to quarter. At present, companies are marking-to-market their global financial risks at their fiscal quarterly reporting periods and at that time they learn of the effects of their risks on their profitability. It is not until the fiscal reporting periods that the derivative instrument and the

---

[14] Mary Pat McCarthy and Timothy Flynn (2004) *Risk from the CEO and Board Perspective*. McGraw-Hill.
[15] Richard G. Barlow, 'The Net upends tenets of loyalty marketing', *Advertising Age*, 17 April 2000.

underlying asset are valued and therefore the hedge deviation is accounted. The risk-limiter client wants to be able to set a hedging instrument at the beginning of the fiscal year which provides budget assurance, does not cause accounting discrepancies or hedge deviations. The client can simply set the instrument in place, knowing that the instrument provides perfect correlation throughout the life of the fiscal year or multiple years. Additionally, the client risk-limiter does not want too many moving parts to their hedging instrument; they want to be able to simplify the accounting process and procedures.

CONCLUSION

The characteristics that the institutional risk-limiters want from a risk management solution fly in the face of the traditional capital markets pipeline discussed in Chapter 1. Therefore, to create the next generation of risk management instruments will require a new capital market pipeline.

In order to create the new instrument, we need a new market pricing mechanism. And to create the new market pricing mechanism, we need a new instrument. The problems outlined in Chapter 2 illustrate the problems with the traditional capital market pipeline. And with the introduction of new corporate governance legislation, significant new accounting requirements and new regulations for the insurance and banking industry, the timing could be right for the introduction of new financial hedging instruments. Regulatory changes are driving many to think about adopting new thinking about managing non-core global financial risks, the next generation instrument and solutions for financial engineers.

Unless the traditional capital market pipeline is changed, the recent and forthcoming changes in corporate governance, accounting and insurance and banking regulations could result in a drop in hedging transaction volumes.

In the next chapter I will use the characteristics outlined in this chapter to explain the next-generation global financial hedging instrument.

5
The Next Generation – A New Method, Process and Solutions

Everything that can be invented has been invented.

Charles H. Duell
Commissioner of the US Patents Office, 1899

INTRODUCTION

The new method, process and solutions that will be introduced in this chapter can be thought of as a disruptive innovation. The disruptive innovation theory, introduced by Clayton Christensen,[1] points to situations in which new organizations can use relatively simple, convenient, low-cost innovations to create growth and triumph over powerful incumbents. The theory holds that existing companies have a high probability of beating entrant attackers when the contest is about sustaining innovations. But established companies almost always lose out to attackers armed with disruptive innovations. Disruptive innovations introduce a new value proposition. They either create new markets or reshape existing markets.

Let us remind ourselves of the basic hypothesis that has brought us to this stage. This consists of three salient points:

1. As globalization becomes a reality, businesses face growing numbers of non-core global financial risks.
2. Non-core global financial risks are being managed by salaried employees, *not* professional risk-takers.
3. Current risk management solutions do not provide truly effective protection.

The fact that corporate governance laws have been introduced, accounting rules are being redefined in generational proportions, and banking and insurance industry regulations have changed only adds to the necessity to introduce a new simple-to-use, easy-to-understand financial hedging instrument.

The importance of managing global financial risks is growing. The comments of Alan Greenspan, Chairman of the Federal Reserve Board, of 14 April 2000 are as important today as they were when he made them:

- New financial products that have been created in recent years contribute economic value by unbundling (therefore, bundling) risks in a highly calibrated manner . . . these new instruments and techniques enhance the process of wealth creation.
- Redistribution of risk induces more investment in real assets, presumably engendering a higher standard of living.

---

[1] Clayton Christensen (1997) *The Innovator's Dilemma*. Harvard Business School Press.

- Institutions need to balance emphasis on risk models that essentially have only dimly perceived sampling characteristics with emphasis on the skills, experience, and judgement of the people who have to apply those models.
- Were we to require bank risk management systems to provide capital to address all conceivable risks . . . rates of return on capital would fall, and the degree of financial intermediation and leverage, as a consequence, would inevitably decline.
- Any mechanism that shifts risk from those who choose to withdraw from it to those more willing to take it on increases investment without significantly raising the perceived degree of discomfort.

Before we go into details, let us also recall the seven key ingredients that go into the new proposed risk management solution, as discussed in the previous chapter: (i) it provides set and forget budget assurance; (ii) it is cost efficient; (iii) it provides perfect correlation or hedge efficiency; (iv) it can bundle many risks into one instrument; (v) it is market priced rather than traditionally priced by (vi) a wide array of potential and acceptable professional institutional risk-takers; (vii) it is simple to use and easy to understand.

A NEW METHOD

What is the first thing that comes to mind when you think of the words 'global financial risk'? In my case, it is 'chaos'. Managing global financial risks a year or more ahead is not easy – there are many instruments to choose from, and the entire process of setting up hedging strategies and their accounting creates as much uncertainty as the risks themselves.

However, I do not believe that global financial risks must be associated with chaos. On the contrary, there is now a way in which they can be treated without the confusion and mess that traditional risk management instruments engender. Global financial risks are a part of doing business; they will not go away, any more than one's labour force and labour costs. One could argue that if the world had a single currency, then currency risks and risk management would disappear. That may be true, but the global economy does not have a single currency, and I do not think we will see one in my lifetime. So we have to face the fact that companies doing business around the world have to deal with currency risks or hard commodity risks if they are manufacturing something. And financial institutions will continue to have their reserve assets, such as bond and equity portfolios, to manage.

Financial price volatility can be thought of as a cost of doing business. Currency risks, for example, can be thought of as a cost of doing business abroad. This is true for balance sheet as well as income statement risks. Think about these risks in terms of your company's budget; at the beginning of each fiscal year and perhaps at each fiscal quarter, management sits down and forecasts the year ahead. The budget and forecasting process includes all of one's costs, revenues, etc. But also think about the impact of the financial risks upon your budget.

The key question that you must answer is how much unforeseen price volatility you can absorb which will not upset or negatively impact your budget forecast for the year ahead. Think about these risks in terms of your profit margin for the goods and services you are selling abroad and ask how much unforeseen price volatility you can absorb within your profit margin or how you protect your profit margin from unforeseen price volatility arising from currency risks or any other non-global financial risks.

Figure 5.1 is the only graph that we will require to explain the new instrument – it is that easy! When we think about our business costs, such as labour or electricity, we forecast and

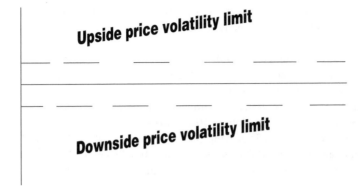

Figure 5.1 Graph depicting the range of upside and downside price volatility (the dashed lines) from an acceptable budget (the single straight line)

budget for that cost. The unforeseen price volatility on non-core global financial risks can be budgeted in the same way. Suppose a company has currency risks arising from the many countries in which it does business. During the budget process, determine the budget impact arising from potential currency price volatility. Ask yourself the question, at what point does currency price volatility impact your budget or profit margins or profitability projections? Suppose that you determine that an acceptable adverse price volatility is −1%, which was the case for one European company, meaning that beyond a negative 1% move in the foreign exchange value, the currency price volatility will be eating into profits. Think about laying off this negative price volatility as volatility deductible, as in insurance language. In Figure 5.1, think of the dashed lines as the volatility deductible (excess), the price or variation in a value of a portfolio of global financial risks that management finds acceptable for their fiscal budget or longer term business plan. The capital markets call this a *volatility collar*.

When we insure our homes, at the beginning of our policy we determine a deductible which we can live with in the event that something happens to our home. Beyond the deductible, we outsource an insured value of our home to an insurance underwriter. We do not worry about correlation deviation or any other problem once our home is insured. We know that we have a deductible for which we are responsible and beyond that we have insurance to cover an event of one kind or another. This is the way that I want you to think about global financial price volatility. What is the volatility deductible that my budget can afford? Beyond that volatility deductible, I want insurance to cover any event which may cause unforeseen price volatility.

When we construct the new instrument later in this chapter, one of the aspects of the new instrument is to determine and create a volatility deductible of upside and downside risks such as depicted in Figure 5.1. One of the research questions that I asked of all the risk-limiter clients was their willingness to give away all the upside potential of their non-core global financial risks in an effort to gain absolute protection from the downside or adverse price movements. This is a new method for managing global financial risk price volatility; we are creating new ways to think about managing our global financial risks.

The new method will allow the risk-limiter client to bundle their global financial risks into their analysis as part of the method. For example, if a company has many currency risks that impact its balance sheet or income statement risks (transactional and translational currency price risks), look at the total impact of those currencies and how they affect the budget or balance sheet. The way to analyze a currency bundle is through its weighted average index and the way its movements impact the budget and profit margin assumptions.

Another way to look at these currency risks is to look at each currency risk and how its price movements affect that country's overall return-on-investment. Once the individual country analysis is completed, create a weighted average currency impact, which in turn can be used to form the collar's up and down boundaries.

For example, a euro-denominated company may have balance sheet risks in many countries – say, 25% euro/US dollar, 10% euro/UK pound sterling, 5% euro/yen, 5% euro/yuan Remimbi, 5% euro/Thai baht, 5% euro/Taiwan dollar, 2% euro/Russian rouble, 3% euro/Hungarian forint, 5% Polish zloty, 5% euro/Brazilian real, 5% euro/Chilean peso, 5% euro/Argentine peso, 5% euro/Mexican peso, 5% euro/Canadian dollar and 10% euro/South African rand.

Once the weighted average basket is determined, using budget sensitivity analysis, determine the currency price volatility that can be afforded by the overall exposed budget – the weighted average price volatility sensitivity will allow management to determine a volatility deductible as depicted in Figure 5.1. The client risk-limiter can now determine what negative impact they can accept and if they seek some upside potential, thereafter draw the line on the upper bound of Figure 5.1, creating the upper and lower bands of acceptable currency price volatility.

For those companies which use value-at-risk methodology when determining the potential price volatility on a non-core global financial risk for the year ahead, such as Nokia, if the calculated VaR amount and range are budget-acceptable, then that amount acts as the volatility collar for the budget-acceptable amount of unforeseen price volatility for the financial year ahead. The upper and lower bounding of the basket of balance sheet currency risks acts as an extreme volatility budget assurance limit.

It may often be the case that one cannot accept any price volatility arising from one's foreign exchange price risks. Then, the price volatility deductible would look like Figure 5.2.

This analysis allows the client risk-limiter to determine in very precise terms the amount of price volatility they can accept as part of their budget analysis, working at the beginning of each fiscal year, rather than in arrears or haphazardly as the year progresses.

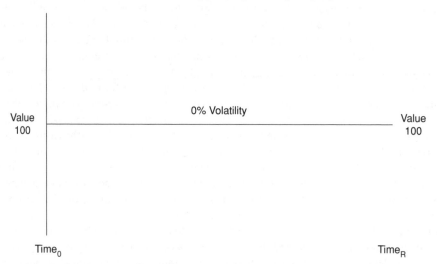

Figure 5.2 Graph depicting a picture of zero price volatility for a specific period of time

This process can be accomplished with bond or equity portfolios for those who hold these assets as reserves or as part of the relative volatility of an asset–liability relationship. I will present specific case studies in Chapter 6, but for now, think about global financial price volatility as a constant percentage change in price. Putting these risks together into one bundle is the same as, well, it all comes down to looking at their budgetary impact on the company.

In a later section of this chapter, I will explain the financial engineering difference, a very small one, that is needed to hedge the global financial risks for a balance sheet risk versus a profit and loss (income statement) risk, both of which will offer perfectly correlated set and forget budget assurance solutions.

There is no need for fancy risk models or valuation formulae; it is simply a matter of looking at the budget impact of the non-core global financial risks, much as one looks at labour costs or electricity costs. The new method is all about thinking about your non-core global financial risks as a cost of doing business. The method is simple to understand and simple to action.

Furthermore, the method provides an absolutely perfect correlation. At settlement date (for example, at the end of the fiscal year), the client risk-limiter receives a payment from the risk-taking underwriters if the basket's value is below the line, using the simplest scenario, zero volatility (see Figure 5.2 – the 0% volatility deductible), which is an adverse financial impact on the company. Alternatively, if the basket value is above the top line, the risk-limiter company will pay out to the risk-taking underwriters. The settlement date payment is made in the company's core currency – in the case of the euro-denominated (reporting) company the payment would be in euros. Therefore, the new instrument arising from the new methodology takes away all the aggravation of transacting individual hedging instruments such as forwards, options, swaps and/or futures contracts, which settle at different times and perhaps in a variety of currencies, absorbing and creating various credit line relationships. The analysis is all about the budget.

The new methodology and its new instrument will ultimately provide its user with budget assurance because the risk-limiter client now knows that they have an indemnification, an instrument that will compensate them against loss from unforeseen price volatility arising from their non-core global financial risks.

This method can be used for multiple-year analysis, as you will see from one case study. If a three- or five-year budget can be set for labour costs, it can be used for budgeting non-core global financial risk volatility for that number of years. The beauty of this methodology is that it is simple and provides an enjoyable experience.

Recall how Lufthansa would dynamically manage an options volatility collar strategy, using the sale of a call option to pay for a put option, which hedged the adverse movements in their many currency risks. The new instrument is much the same, except that it is much simpler to use and provides an absolutely perfect correlated set and forget budget assurance solution.

A NEW PROCESS

Having accomplished the methodology for creating the instrument, we need a new process for pricing it. We must succeed in creating a more competitive pricing mechanism to achieve market pricing, as opposed to traditional bank proprietary pricing. Greater underwriting capacity and greater numbers of counterparties seeking to take on the client risk-limiters' risks are also needed in a new process. The way the risk-limiter's risks are distributed will be improved dramatically, giving the client risk-limiter greater choice of counterparties and the ability to distribute their risks to those counterparties that they find acceptable, whether by credit rating, the price that they are willing to pay for the risk, and/or their ability to underwrite an amount of the client risks. Therefore, a new process will enable better pricing for the risk and its distribution to risk-taking counterparties.

The portfolio effect of bundling many global financial risks into one instrument will enable risk-takers to value the portfolio of global financial risks in their own unique way. In fact, to simplify it further, there is value in a bundle or portfolio of global financial risks and its value can be determined by the eye of the beholder. In other words, the value of a bundle or portfolio of currency, equity, bond and/or hard commodity risks will be determined by different types of counterparties who will value it in their own way. The portfolio effect presents opportunities for the risk-taker, as opposed to the valuation of a single cash asset, which in itself does not offer the opportunities found in a portfolio of many cash assets. I will talk about the valuation process and the investment discipline later in this chapter. The new method and process allow the client risk-limiter to outsource the entire valuation process to the professional risk-taking underwriting financial institutions.

This is a key ingredient to the new process because the client risk-limiter can focus on the appropriate analysis for managing their non-core global financial risks by seeking to manage them within their own budget constraints. The value of the hedging mechanism, the type of instrument that should be used to attain budget assurance for the client and the anxiety of pricing the individual risk management components are being outsourced to the professional risk-taker. The client risk-limiter wants a simplified and easy way to deal with their non-core global financial risk management, and obtains this by outsourcing the problem to the professional risk-taker.

The outsourcing model that I am introducing is no different than the typical insurance industry model that we all use individually and corporately. When I purchase insurance coverage for my home, for example, I go to my insurance broker; they in turn seek out bids for my personal home insurance needs. I receive a document which provides me with a set and forget insurance policy for my home. I do not have to figure out whether my home sits on top of a subway line, which may shake the house and cause damage, nor do I have to figure out whether my home sits on top of an earthquake fault line or any other detailed analysis which is part of pricing the insurance coverage that I seek for my home. This is the job of the insurance underwriter.

This is the type of outsourcing mechanism that I believe is required for the new method, process and solutions for managing global financial risks.

An article in the International Monetary Fund's semi-annual publication *International Capital Markets* (August 2001) had a profound effect upon my thinking about the new process. It said that

> Between 1990 and 1998, assets managed by mature market institutional investors more than doubled to over $30 trillion, about equal to world gross domestic product (GDP). Amid widespread capital account liberalization and increased reliance on securities markets, these investable funds became increasingly responsive to changing opportunities and risks in a widening set of regions and countries. Because global investment portfolios are large, proportionally small portfolio adjustments can be associated with large and volatile swings in capital flows. ... [Portfolio] adjustments sometimes had a significant impact on financial conditions in the recipient countries both when they flowed in and when they flowed out. This underscores the powerful impact that portfolio rebalancing by global investors can have on the volume, pricing, and direction of international capital flows and on conditions in both domestic and international markets.[2]

---

[2] 'International Capital Markets,' IMF, August 2001, p. 4.

As mentioned earlier, the top 100 banks in the world have $1.5 trillion of capital and the institutional investor has more than $30 trillion, representing nearly 100% of the world gross domestic product. The article makes the important point that the institutional asset manager companies now have a substantially greater ability to manage global financial risks than banking institutions. It also demonstrates the power of the professional risk-taker versus the non-professional risk-taker. How can a non-professional capital market risk-taker who is not watching the global capital markets on a minute-by-minute basis possibly know when professional managers make portfolio adjustments causing large and volatile swings in global capital markets?

So how do we turn a negative situation into a positive outcome for risk-limiters? As part of this outsourcing model, clearly the best outcome for the client risk-limiter is to outsource their global financial risks to the professional risk-taking institutions, in much the same way as the insurance industry works. There are professional risk specialists for professional indemnity, business interruption risks, insurance companies that specialize in underwriting home, car and life insurance. It is the same in the global capital markets, with specialists in currency, bond, equity and hard commodity risk-taking. These institutions may take the form of asset management companies, banking institutions that seek to add risk, regional banks or money managers. They are all seeking global financial risks of one kind or another; they will value those risks in their own unique dynamic way and manner. And perhaps more importantly, most risk-taking institutions are desperately seeking new ways to generate fee revenue and performance-related or trading revenues.

The client risk-limiter on the left-hand side of Figure 5.3 is receiving set and forget budget assurance for a bundle of non-core global financial risks, while the risk-taking institution on the right-hand side has underwritten the unforeseen price volatility arising from the client's

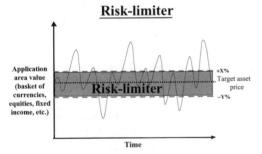
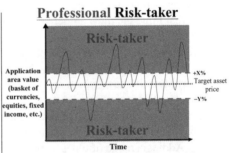

- Risk-limiter needs mechanism to assure budgeted performance of basket of key assets

- Not greatly interested in upside potential, rather needs to eliminate risk below a minimum level

- Willing to give away some or all upside potential so as to eliminate downside risk

- This mechanism must be affordable, totally effective, and timely

- Bundles downside risk with upside potential as a single financial instrument for *Professional* risk-takers (who can view the instrument as an 'investment-grade' opportunity)

- Professional risk-takers will understand the specific elements that comprise the basket of assets

- Professional risk-takers are free to unbundle and create their own hedge positions

- Classic principles of investment and underwriting

Figure 5.3   View of price volatilities from global financial risks taken by institutional risk-limiters and professional risk-taking financial institutions

non-core global financial risks. The risk-taking institution is now responsible for the client's price volatility above and below the volatility deductible. In other words, the unforeseen price volatility has been outsourced to the professional risk-taking institutions.

The risk-taking institutions have become commoditized in their product offering, pricing and underwriting capacity for global financial risks, as described in Chapter 1. They too need a new innovative global financial solution to enable them to perform better in a globally commoditized industry, and the new instrument provides these institutions with new revenue streams.

In summary thus far, the new process will allow client risk-limiters to bundle their non-core global financial risks into the new instrument and seek a price for their risks from a global counterparty pool which includes banks, asset management companies and other prospective risk-taking institutions. Let us now turn to the pricing or bidding process for allocating our clients' non-core global financial risks.

As I mentioned earlier, when seeking a price for a bundle or portfolio of global financial risks, there is value in that bundle and value is in the eye of the beholder – the beholder being the risk-taking institution. When seeking a price for the new instrument, as will be seen in the next section when I introduce the new instrument, a term sheet is created in collaboration with the client. Once this is accomplished, the term sheet is made available to as many acceptable institutional counterparties as possible – investment and commercial banks, asset managers, hedge fund managers, the investment department at some insurance companies and, in certain circumstances perhaps, development banks. The institutional risk-takers could be global or regional institutions. The key to an effective pricing or bidding process is the ability to have a diverse number of institutional risk-takers, all of whom have their own value and need for global financial risk-taking, or naturally hedging their own global financial risks.

The type of bidding process is important for an effective pricing mechanism. The bidding process that I find the most attractive is the reverse auction process developed by Freemarkets Online in Pittsburgh, Pennsylvania, during the boom period of the emerging Internet in order to drive downward the price of mechanical parts for manufacturing industry. The use of the Internet network to conduct a reverse auction process was a tectonic innovation. I am reminded of Robert Metcalf's law, which states that 'networks dramatically increase in value with each additional node or user.'

The reverse auction process introduces a market discovery pricing mechanism for the bundle of global financial risks, in contrast to the available price made by traditional proprietary bank pricing. Adding a range of types of risk-taking financial institutions, coupled with the various revenue generating opportunities, will lead to a highly competitive and dynamic market pricing system. The use of this process is demonstrated in the next chapter.

The reverse auction process also allows the client risk-limiter to lay off its risks, once the auction process is completed, to either a weighted average number of acceptable risk-taking bidders, or to layer price volatility allocations to different counterparties depending on the client's acceptance for the bidding counterparty.

In Figure 5.4(b), as the pie chart shows, the risk-limiter can allocate their risks to a variety of counterparties in a weighted average allocation. Figure 5.4(a) shows how the price volatility of the bundle of risks can be layered and laid off to a number of counterparties in this manner. Again, this risk distribution process is very similar to the one seen in the insurance industry. In fact, when we look at volatility layering, this is also an options strategy known as a barrier option, therefore the professional risk-takers have many tools available to them to properly

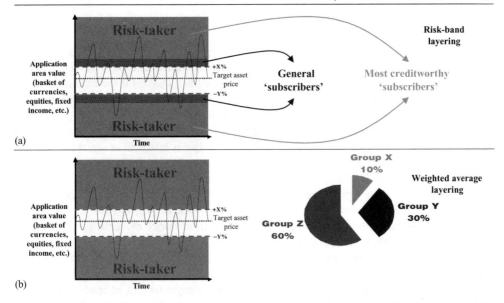

Figure 5.4   There are two ways in which client risk-limiters distribute their bundles of global financial risks to acceptable counterparty institutions. (a) How to layer price volatility, limiting an amount of financial exposure to specific counterparty underwriters; (b) distributing bundles of global financial risks in a weighted manner to different counterparties

value and price the way the risk-limiter wants to distribute those risks. Dynamic revenue opportunities will drive competitive pricing.

This risk distribution process also allows the risk-limiter to allocate to the best available price, but if they are anxious about the quality of their counterparty, they can layer the risks in such a way as to ensure the most creditworthy institutions underwrite the catastrophic price movements, while the less creditworthy can take perhaps lesser levels or more confined amounts of risk.

The competitive nature of a reverse auction process not only allows the client risk-limiter to realize the best available market price for their bundle of risks, but also provides absolute hedge efficiency, counterparty diversification unlike anything available in today's global capital markets, along with the capacity to underwrite their entire bundle of global financial risks in one simple single transaction and instrument. The simplicity of the process and its relationship to the well-known insurance model for outsourcing global financial risks helps the client risk-limiter greatly in their ability to quickly and easily outsource their global financial risks each year. And since these global financial risks are not core to the company's business, they can form part of that company's enterprise risk management scheme. Each year, during the fiscal review in preparation for the next fiscal year, non-core global financial risks can be treated in a manner similar to their property and casualty risks, etc., because the new instrument will provide set and forget budget assurance for the forthcoming financial year.

A NEW INSTRUMENT FOR MANAGING GLOBAL FINANCIAL RISKS

If there were a curtain, this would be the time to raise it! The new instrument is called a *volatility assurance transaction* (VAT). There is a whole family of VATs, all of which fall into two types:

the *absolute* VAT and the *relative* VAT, and these can cover currencies, bonds, equities and hard commodities.

An absolute VAT provides set and forget protection against the value of the [ ] basket falling from a certain initial base value. Under the transaction, (i) 'the client' pays the risk-taker an amount calculated by reference to the positive return of the [ ] basket if the final level of the [ ] basket is above ( ) % of its initial value; and (ii) 'the client' receives from the risk-taker an amount calculated by reference to the absolute value of the negative return of the [ ] basket if the final level of the [ ] basket is below ( ) % of its initial value. No payment is made by either party if the level of the [ ] basket on the final valuation date is less than or equal to ( ) % and greater than or equal to ( ) % of its initial value.

A relative VAT provides the same protection characteristics as an absolute VAT against the unforeseen price volatility of a bundle of global financial risks in relation to another index, such as interest rates, real interest rates, an equity index such as the S & P 500 or FTSE 100, a global bond index, commodities indices or relative currency price movements over a period time. I will discuss this subject in greater detail shortly.

As you can see from the definition, the VAT provides set and forget absolute volatility protection for a bundle of risks. The volatility deductible is set in accordance with the methodology described earlier and at the final settlement date, a payment will be made to the client if the settlement price of the basket is below the lower line and the client pays the risk-taking underwriter when the final settlement value is above the higher line of the volatility collar. If the settlement value settles within the volatility collar, as part of the deductible, there are no payments made, as the client has determined that they can absorb this amount of price volatility risk.

A typical absolute equity VAT constructed on behalf of a UK insurance company is shown in Box 5.1. I will review specific transactions in the next chapter; here I want to cover all the definitions and mechanics of the new instrument.

BOX 5.1   EQUITY VOLATILITY ASSURANCE TRANSACTION

INDICATIVE TERMS AND CONDITIONS

This term sheet sets out the indicative terms and conditions of the transaction described below. References in this term sheet to ISDA® shall be deemed to be made to the International Swaps and Derivatives Association, Inc. Certain capitalized terms used in this term sheet are based on the definitions and provisions contained in the 2002 ISDA Equity Derivatives Definitions and in the 2000 ISDA Definitions, as amended and supplemented (as published by ISDA®) (the 'Definitions'). In the event of any inconsistency between the Definitions and this term sheet, this term sheet will govern.

OVERVIEW:

1. This term sheet sets out the basic terms of an equity transaction on a share basket, intended to provide 'set-and-forget' protection against the value of the share basket falling from a certain initial base value. Under the transaction, (i) 'THE CLIENT' pays the Risk Taker an amount calculated by reference to the positive return of the Share Basket if the final level of the Share Basket is above 105% of its initial value; and

(ii) 'THE CLIENT' receives from the Risk Taker an amount calculated by reference to the absolute value of the negative return of the Share Basket if the final level of the Share Basket is below 95% of its initial value. No payment is made by either party if the level of the Share Basket on the Final Valuation Date is less than or equal to 105% and greater than or equal to 95% of its initial value.

2. The transaction (as is described in this term sheet) does not require the transfer of ownership of the Share Basket. Dividends are not required to be transferred to the Risk Taker. 'THE CLIENT' is not required to lend the components of the Share Basket.

Transaction:	[Share Basket Collar Transaction]
Trade Date:	
Premium:	
Premium Payment Date:	
Start Date:	30 April 2004
Initial Valuation Date:	The Start Date[a]
Final Valuation Date:	31 March 2005[b]
Expiration Date:	The Final Valuation Date
Exercise Date:	The Expiration Date
Automatic Exercise:	Applicable[c]
Settlement:	Cash Settlement applies[d]
Cash Settlement payment provisions:	On the Cash Settlement Payment Date, (i) the Risk Taker shall be entitled to receive from 'THE CLIENT' the Cash Settlement Amount where the Final Basket Price is greater than the Upper Basket Price; (ii) 'THE CLIENT' shall be entitled to receive from the Risk Taker the Cash Settlement Amount where the Final Basket Price is less than the Lower Basket Price; or (iii) if the Final Basket Price is greater than or equal to the Lower Basket Price and less than or equal to the Upper Basket Price, no payment shall be made by either party.
Cash Settlement Payment Date:	Three Business Days following the Final Valuation Date.[e]
Share Basket:	As described in the Schedule.
Cash Settlement Amount:	Means an amount in GBP calculated on the Final Valuation Date in accordance with the following: If the Final Basket Price is:

(i)   greater than the Upper Basket Price, an amount equal to the excess of the Final Basket Price over the Upper Basket Price; or

(ii)   less than the Lower Basket Price, an amount equal to the excess of the Lower Basket Price over the Final Basket Price; or

(iii)   less than or equal to the Upper Basket Price and greater than or equal to the Lower Basket Price, zero.

Upper Basket Price:	105% of Initial Basket Price.
Lower Basket Price:	95% of Initial Basket Price.
Initial Basket Price:	Means an amount in GBP calculated as the aggregate of the Initial Share Amounts.
Initial Share Amounts:	Means, in respect of each Share in the Share Basket, an amount in GBP determined as the product of (i) the Number of Shares, and (ii) its Initial Share Price.
Initial Share Price:	Means, in respect of each Share in the Share Basket, the price per Share on the Exchange determined by the Risk Taker in consultation with 'THE CLIENT' as at ( ) London time on the Initial Valuation Date.
Final Basket Price:	Means an amount in GBP calculated as the aggregate of the Final Share Amounts.
Final Share Amount:	Means, in respect of each Share in the Share Basket, an amount in GBP determined as the product of (i) the Number of Shares, and (ii) its Final Share Price.
Final Share Price:	Means, in respect of each Share in the Share Basket, the closing price per Share on the Exchange at the Valuation Time on the Final Valuation Date.
Number of Shares:	Means, in respect of each Share in the Share Basket, the number of shares set out in the table described in the Schedule.
Valuation Time	In respect of each Share in the Share Basket, the close of trading on the Exchange.
Exchange:	In respect of each Share in the Share Basket, as set out in the Schedule in relation to each Share.
Other terms:	
Risk Taker:	
Calculation Agent:	
Documentation:	ISDA
Arranger:	[Global Financial Risk Solutions/Regulated Entity]

DISCLAIMER

[This term sheet is indicative only and is subject to change without notice. We do not represent that it is complete or accurate. This term sheet does not constitute an offer or an agreement, or a solicitation of an offer or an agreement, to enter into any transaction. No assurance is given that any transaction on the terms indicated can or will be arranged or agreed. Before entering into any transaction, you should consider the suitability of the transaction to your particular circumstances and independently review (with your professional advisers as necessary) the specific financial risks, as well as the legal, regulatory, credit, tax and accounting consequences.]

SCHEDULE
The Share Basket

Share	ISIN	Exchange	Number of shares
United Utilities		The London Stock Exchange	
Lloyds TSB		The London Stock Exchange	
Bradford and Bingley		The London Stock Exchange	
Scottish Power		The London Stock Exchange	
Sainsbury's		The London Stock Exchange	
Scottish and Southern		The London Stock Exchange	
Friends Provident		The London Stock Exchange	
Alliance and Leicester		The London Stock Exchange	
Old Mutual		The London Stock Exchange	
Legal and General		The London Stock Exchange	
HSBC		The London Stock Exchange	
BAT		The London Stock Exchange	
Scottish and Newcastle		The London Stock Exchange	
Tomkins		The London Stock Exchange	

[a] Valuation Dates are subject to standard ISDA® postponement provisions in the event of non-Scheduled Trading Days or market disruption.

[b] It is being assumed that there is a single Final Valuation Date, following which, there will be a single payment to the party entitled to receive the Cash Settlement Amount.

[c] If Automatic Exercise applies, neither party needs to deliver notice of exercise and the party obliged to pay the Cash Settlement Amount on the Cash Settlement Payment Date shall do so without further request from the other party.

[d] If Cash Settlement applies, the transaction shall not entitle any party to deliver or take delivery of any security or underlying asset. It shall be settled with a cash payment calculated in accordance with the relevant formula.

[e] It is risky to set a fixed Cash Settlement Payment Date in relation to equity derivative transactions, given that Valuation Dates are subject to postponement in the event of market disruption. We recommend setting the Cash Settlement Payment Date as a date falling a certain number of Business Days after the Final Valuation Date.

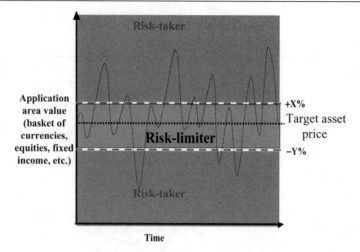

Figure 5.5 The institutional risk-limiter receives the protection desired during the life of the contract, whilst the institutional risk-taking underwriters are responsible for the all of the price volatility outside of the client volatility deductible. In effect, the risk-limiter has securitized the price volatility outside of their volatility deductible to the risk-taking institution – outsourcing all the nuances and vagaries of managing global financial risks

In the term sheet, the absolute equity VAT is settled as follows: The client determined a volatility deductible of ±5%, as depicted in Figure 5.5.

The client risk-limiter receives precisely what they require, a perfectly correlated set and forget budget assurance for a bundle (portfolio) of equity investments. The institutional risk-takers are responsible for all of the price volatility and market noise for that equity portfolio up to the settlement date. There is no time value decay, no hedge deviation and it is simple and easy to use.

When the final settlement date arrives, the portfolio or bundle is priced and valued as per the final official closing prices; the terms are defined in the ISDA term sheet. There are three prospective outcomes to the contract, as Figure 5.6 shows.

At the commencement of the equity VAT contract, the portfolio is valued. In our example ISDA term sheet, the total portfolio value is £100 million. During the life of the contract the value of the portfolio will rise and fall. As far as the client risk-limiter is concerned, all this volatility and market noise is immaterial because they have an indemnification for the unforeseen price volatility if the portfolio value rises by more than 5% or falls by 5%. The settlement payments are simple and very straightforward; if the bundle value finishes below the –5% line, shown in Figure 5.6(a), in other words if the portfolio falls in value below £95 million, the underwriter owes the UK insurance company client a difference cheque denominated in UK pounds sterling. If the portfolio value rises above the +5% line, or the value amount rises above £105 million, shown in Figure 5.6(b), the UK insurance company client owes the risk-taking underwriter institutions a sterling difference cheque. And if the final settlement value falls within the volatility deductible (collar), as shown in Figure 5.6(c), then no payments are made.

Another way in which to describe a volatility assurance transaction is to compare it to a typical derivative instrument. For example, the VAT contract specifies the exact timeframe but does not fix a forward price of the financial risks. A forward foreign exchange contract, futures and swap contracts fix the forward price of the financial risk, whereas the VAT protects the value of a portfolio of risks for the specified timeframe.

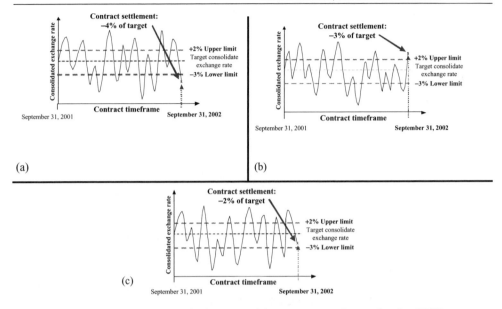

(a)   (b)

(c)

Figure 5.6   These three graphs show the three potential outcomes at settlement date for a VAT instrument. (a) The value of the bundle settled below the lower volatility line, therefore the underwriters owe the client a difference cheque; (b) the value of the bundle settled above the upper line of the volatility deductible and therefore the client owes the underwriting institutions a difference cheque; (c) the value of the bundle settled within the volatility deductible collar and therefore no payment is due from either party

The VAT contract draws an exact line of indemnification for a portfolio of global financial risks, whereas derivative contracts will not be able to draw an exact line of indemnification for a bundle of global financial risks, particularly when trying to use options contracts.

The VAT contract is not an options contract; it is an indemnification of the value of a portfolio of global financial risk against unforeseen price volatility. The differences between a VAT and traditional options (option price values can alter from the many characteristics described in Chapter 3), forward, futures and swaps can be seen in Figures 5.7–5.8.

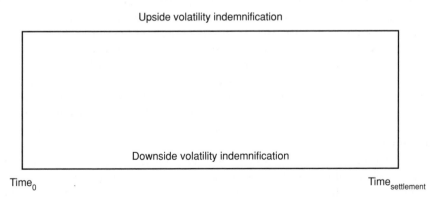

Figure 5.7   The volatility assurance transaction. The VAT creates a box, defining all four sides of the transaction, time and volatility

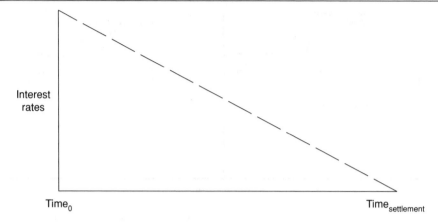

Time_0 ...... $\text{Time}_{\text{settlement}}$

Interest rates

Figure 5.8   Traditional forward, futures and swaps. The cost of fixing the forward price is a function of interest rate carrying costs

There are two ways, at least so far, in which a VAT can be applied; the first is to manage absolute volatility, and the second is for relative volatility.

Absolute Volatility

Absolute volatility, an example of which was described above, deals with the absolute movement of price volatility. This type of solution allows the client risk-limiter to create a set and forget budget assurance for the absolute price movement from one time period to another. The time period could be 1 year or many years, allowing the client to manage the absolute price volatility of their non-core global financial risks much as it treats the many other costs that it incurs in its day-to-day activities. In the example term sheet above, we dealt with the absolute price movements of an equity portfolio, setting the volatility deductible from the beginning of the fiscal year, and settling on the final day of the fiscal year.

There are two types of absolute volatility structure: one for the income statement and one for balance sheet risks. I will present two case studies in the next chapter on these two types of structure, but the difference requires additional financial engineering for a balance sheet risk.

Starting with the income or profit and loss statement, when creating an absolute VAT, the client risk-limiter has to make a payment if the final settlement value is above the top line of their volatility deductible. The client has the required funds to make a payment because the value of the bundle or portfolio has risen above that top deductible line. Therefore, the client can use the proceeds of the higher value to make a payment to the underwriter(s). And these processes protect the set and forget budget assurance characteristics of the transaction because the client has the necessary funds to make the payment to the risk-taking institutional underwriters arising from the unrealized value from the higher value of the portfolio. Therefore, the client company does not have to worry about where the money is coming from to pay their liability under the VAT contract.

However, if a client wants to use a VAT to hedge the absolute volatility arising from a balance sheet asset, such as currency risks from the many assets held abroad, we need to tweak the financial engineering. If a payment must be made from the client to the underwriter(s), the client does not have the necessary cash available to make the payment. A balance sheet asset

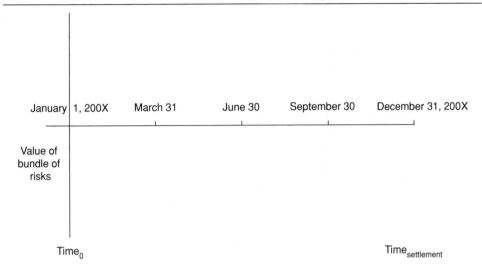

Figure 5.9   Accounting for the volatility assurance transaction. Using a typical fiscal calendar, the accounting treatment of the new VAT instrument is very straightforward. Since the new instrument provides perfect correlation in relation to the underlying cash assets, the accounting merely requires the provision or reserve above the line if the underlying cash assets' value is above the line – they must reserve for a payment for settlement date to the underwriter. If the value is below the line, the client can expect a payment from the underwriters. No money will actually be transferred until the defined settlement date

will have risen in value but it might be impossible to liquidate a portion of the asset to make a payment to the underwriter(s). And if the payment from the client to the underwriter(s) must come from the profit and loss account, unfortunately the payment to the underwriter(s) could be an enormous sum of money. The sum of money owed to the underwriter(s) could cause the company substantial profit uncertainty. Therefore, the solution to the balance sheet problem is to add a European exercise call option to the VAT contract, either embedded into the pricing of the VAT or priced separately. The client pays a premium for the call option and if the client is required to make a payment to the underwriter(s), the call option will fund that payment rather than having to rely upon the profit and loss account. By adding this call option to the VAT, we maintain the set and forget budget assurance characteristic, and the profit and loss account is protected from unforeseen payments that might be required.

On an accounting note, the simplicity of the VAT instrument allows for very easy accounting treatment (Figure 5.9).

Returning to Figure 5.1, the accounting of an indemnification, a perfectly correlated instrument, allows the client to mark-to-market each fiscal quarter, under FAS 133 and IAS 39, by valuing the underlying cash assets and either reserving above the line or below the line, as shown in Figure 5.7. But the line does not move as with traditional derivatives contracts. There is only one moving part, the underlying portfolio of global financial risks, and the VAT contract does not move in value because it is perfectly correlated with the risks. Additionally, this instrument provides much greater transparency in the hedging mechanism itself, the way it is used, the method and process that have created it. The entire method, process and instrument are simple to use, easy to understand, to account, value, settle and administer, all with greater transaction transparency.

For those who use value-at-risk models, as described earlier, the VAT is the ideal instrument for managing the extreme price volatility beyond the VaR output cash figure. The VaR model calculates a financial sum of money representing the amount of money that could be lost, based on historic price volatility, with 95% confidence. However, as we discussed in Chapter 4, the global financial markets do not obey the normal distribution or bell curve. Using the methodology or the technology of the VAT (method, process and solutions), given a VaR cash output over a one-year period, for example, with which a company is comfortable, construct the volatility deductible around that sum of money. In other words, if management is comfortable with the sums of money outputted by a value-at-risk model, their volatility deductible will be that sum of money, the VaR output.

Suppose, for example, on 31 December 2003, that a European company calculated for the coming fiscal year that its €2 billion foreign exchange VaR position was €16.7 million. If the company was satisfied that its budget along with profit margin assumptions could absorb the VaR position, it could seek to manage that risk using a currency VAT contract. The volatility deductible in this case would be ±€16.7 million on an insured sum of €2 billion.

Under the newly established corporate governance legislation, coupled with accounting changes, using a VAT in conjunction with VaR modelling offers all companies an attractive enterprise-wide risk management solution for their non-core global financial risks.

Relative Volatility

Relative price volatility occurs when the cash assets of a global financial risk portfolio are measured in comparison with something else, which is also dynamically moving, not in perfect correlation with the underlying cash assets being measured against, such as an equity index or a bond index. Relative price volatility also occurs when the underlying cash asset is dependent on, or interconnected with, something else, such as a liability index for life insurance companies and pension funds. I will discuss each in turn.

When an underlying cash asset such as an equity or bond portfolio is managed and bench-marked or measured against an index related to the underlying cash portfolio or bundle, both parts of the relationship are constantly and dynamically moving each day. Pension funds and insurance companies, for example, often either seek to index a portfolio versus a benchmark index or seek outside institutional asset managers to manage their portfolios on their behalf, using a benchmark index to measure the portfolio performance of the asset manager. The client risk-limiter, the insurance company and/or the pension fund, may want to manage the potential risk of a significant divergence of portfolio performance versus the benchmark index.

The use of a VAT can allow the client risk-limiter to hedge the portfolio's performance divergence from its benchmark index. We use the same methodology, process and solutions as for an absolute volatility problem, but in a relative volatility situation, instead of using the underlying cash asset prices as the measure for price volatility comparison, we use the benchmark index.

A client risk-limiter may want to manage the relative volatility of the two by measuring the budget sensitivity to the outcomes of the actual portfolio versus the benchmark index. For example, let us assume that a risk-limiter determines that their budget cannot underperform by a specific percentage amount in relation to a benchmark index. In this case, we create a VAT which is measured and marked-to-market on the settlement date; if the final valuation determines that the underlying cash portfolio has diverged from the benchmark index beyond the negative percentage, the risk-taking underwriters owe the client a difference cheque based

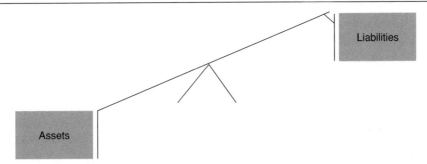

Figure 5.10 An asset–liability see-saw. The asset–liability relationship behaves similarly to a child's see-saw. Typically, as interest rates rise, the value of the assets falls, but the cost of the liability will decrease. As interest rates fall, the swing will move in the other direction, the value of the assets rise but so too does the cost of the liabilities

on the starting value of the portfolio, but if the valuation is a positive percentage, the client owes the risk-taking underwriters a difference cheque denominated in the client's source currency. It is that simple. This methodology is also a way to hedge active investment managers against passive investment managers. The application potential for this type of relative price volatility is enormous and yet it is very simple, easy to understand and to implement.

When the underlying cash assets are dependent on, or interconnected with, something else, such as a liability cost or assumption for a defined benefit pension fund or other annuity rate, the relative relationship is similar to a see-saw, as shown in Figure 5.10.

In the case of a pension fund, there is a relative risk between the value of its assets and expected value of its future liabilities. When price volatility occurs, the value of the pension scheme's assets will move in value relative to its liabilities. For example, as interest rates rise, the value of a bond portfolio will fall; however, the liability owed by the pension fund under a defined benefit scheme will reduce because the discount rate for those liabilities will rise as interest rates rise. A relative VAT solution could be used to lay off the relative price movement of the fixed income portfolio in relation to the value movement of the pension fund's liability real interest rate index used to calculate the scheme's cash liabilities to its pensioners. The pension fund could use a liability index of 20-year fixed income yield and index-linked bond yield as the composite index for composing and fixing the value of the liability index at the commencement of the contract. When interest rates fall, bond prices rise, the liability cost rises, and vice versa when interest rates rise; the payments are offset by the risk-taking underwriter. At settlement date, if the relative values of the portfolio versus the liability index diverge from the set relationship, coming in either lower or higher, a difference cheque is either received or paid by the client risk-limiter. The dynamic pricing for one of these solutions will be quite interesting.

Another approach is to use a relative VAT, but using extreme value theory to manage the asset price volatility in relation to the liability index volatility. In this case, the risk-limiter client may budget an asset–liability volatility relationship that meets the pension fund's actuarial assumptions. The pension fund may seek to protect itself from extreme adverse relative volatility events – wouldn't we all! The pension fund may want an indemnification solution in the event of an extreme or unforeseen occurrence, which causes an enormous breach of the accepted budget relative volatility asset–liability relationship (see Figure 5.11).

Note that I have added an acceptable band of price volatility for the assets and liabilities; the client has determined that budget assurance will allow a flex in the asset–liability relationship.

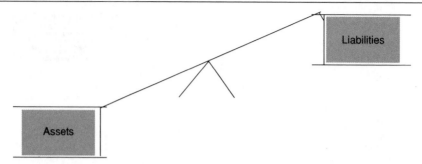

Figure 5.11   The client company can accept a specific amount of movement between its assets and liabilities, but it cannot accept an extreme movement in either the value of assets or the cost of liabilities widening, causing a greater asset–liability deficit

However, over the next one or more years, if that relative volatility or flex of acceptable volatility is breached at settlement date, payments will be received or made by the client to the risk-taking underwriters.

In both cases of relative price volatility, the client risk-limiter has created an easy-to-use, simple-to-understand set and forget budget assurance contract against unforeseen relative price volatility.

A NEW INVESTMENT DISCIPLINE

Let us now look at the opposite side of the VAT transaction, from the risk-limiter to the risk-taking institution. When a risk-taking underwriter looks at a VAT, they could traditionally price a volatility collar or they could dynamically price the risk. When an underwriter prices the VAT using a traditional method they are not seeking to extract any value from the portfolio of risks, merely to provide a price which takes into account the need for the underwriter to insure their risks. They will set a price based on laying off each risk contained in the portfolio, and may sell off each part using a derivative of one kind or another – their price will be based upon the cost of laying off the risk plus a profit margin.

However, a new investment discipline could be used to dynamically price the bundle or portfolio of global financial risks. When the risk-limiter enters into a VAT contract, they receive a payment from the underwriter if the settlement value is below the line and they make a payment to the underwriter if the settlement is above the line (Figure 5.12). This is a typical and traditional European exercise options contract – exercising the option will only take place at settlement date. Therefore, the underwriter is being given a covered call option; the client risk-limiter will pay to the underwriter a sum of money if the settlement value is above the line.

Dynamically pricing this portfolio of risks allows the underwriter to manage the risk within the bundle in their unique way throughout the life of the contract, which may include extracting value from the global financial risks. Another way to look at the situation is as follows: the underwriter must build a volatility-neutral or delta-neutral portfolio, assuming 0% volatility deductible. A strategy for the underwriter is to fund the derivatives positions required to build and manage a volatility-neutral portfolio, using margin monies to fund the derivatives to ensure that the hedge achieves as close to a volatility-neutral result as possible. During the life of the contract, the underwriter can use the covered call option to trade specific risks within the bundle

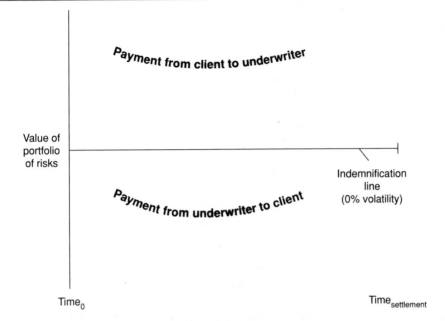

Figure 5.12   At settlement date, if the value of the portfolio or bundle of global financial risks settles above the line, the risk-limiting client will owe the risk-taking institutional underwriters a difference cheque and vice versa if the value of the bundle of risks falls below the line at settlement date

or portfolio. They can use options strategies to play with the underlying global financial risks, or they can seek out arbitrage or anomalies available in the marketplace arising from the underlying cash and derivatives relationships.

Remember that the client risk-limiter is outsourcing the entire risk management activity to the risk-taking underwriters; therefore, they are responsible for managing this entire activity. The underwriting financial institution can price the client risks either traditionally or dynamically.

By creating a diversified way to price a portfolio of global financial risks, the range of institutional underwriters is wide open, from traditional banks to asset management companies and other financial institutions. Asset management groups can create an entirely new investment operation, adding to their assets under management by bidding for and underwriting VAT global financial risks. They can charge a premium to underwrite the risks and extract, if they choose performance-related revenues by dynamically managing the client portfolio. The VAT instrument creates an entirely new investment discipline and revenue driver for asset management companies.

Using the example of Figure 5.5 above, if a client risk-limiter determines that they want a ±3% volatility deductible for a 12-month period on a portfolio of bonds, the underwriter has to create such a deductible using all available hedging instruments to achieve as close to a 100% correlation as possible. As we discussed, achieving a perfect hedge correlation is very difficult, although not impossible, depending upon the portfolio of risks.

However, the underwriter will charge a premium to the client. Putting my personal money management hat on, I would price the very first client that I was underwriting by determining how much margin money would be required to dynamically manage the ±3% volatility deductible. Once that was accomplished, I would look at the approximate cost for the correlation deviation that I would be exposed to for the next 12 months. The combination of these two factors would be part of the fee that I would charge. But now I would also look at the potential ways in which I could extract performance-related value, using an array of potential trading opportunities, from this portfolio of risks for the next 12 months. These two components would form the basis for the premium for underwriting the client risk-limiter's VAT terms.

Remember that the risk-taking underwriter would have to be an acceptable counterparty to the client risk-limiter. The dynamic bidding process shines through as a number of underwriting bidders seek to buy the client risk-limiter's risks in an effort to achieve a nice return-on-investment of their funds under management. Let us assume that due to the competitive bidding process during the reverse auction, a financial institution may charge a 1% underwriting fee and seek additional performance-related fees by dynamically managing the client's bundle or portfolio of global financial risks.

The performance fees are purely speculative, but I wanted to discuss the investment discipline, because the VAT pipeline generates an entirely new pipeline of revenues. This is particularly true for those assets or risks that have never been hedged, for example an insurance company in Europe has traditionally invested its reserve capital into bonds, portfolios that are bought and held to maturity, because it never had to mark-to-market the value. With the introduction of new insurance regulations requiring it to mark-to-market its insurance reserves, the insurance company bond portfolios must be actively managed and hedged, otherwise the insurance company may be required to add additional regulatory capital because of the new risk-based regulatory regime discussed earlier.

The insurance company does have the in-house expertise to manage its bond portfolio, therefore, what better way for it to manage its total bond portfolio price volatility for the coming financial year, but simply buy a bond VAT? When an underwriter takes the insurance company risks under management, using a volatility-neutral hedging strategy, they will be transacting and adding significant volumes of derivatives to the banking industry.

The client risk-limiter has outsourced the entire problem to the professional marketplace. The client risk-limiter gets exactly what they want, set and forget budget assurance in a simple-to-use, easy-to-understand instrument that provides greater transparency in terms of corporate governance and accounting requirements. The risk-taking underwriter gets exactly what they want, an entirely new pipeline of revenue streams as well as a boost in trading volumes for the traditional capital markets pipeline.

Financial engineering is creating a win–win situation for both sides of the transaction. With the introduction of the new VAT pipeline everyone wins – the client risk-limiter, the asset management and banking community as well as the traditional capital markets pipeline. The new VAT pipeline also fulfils the magic formula for disruptive innovation theory.

One final aspect of the VAT should be mentioned. Because of its perfect correlation with the underlying cash risks, with the instrument characteristics of an insurance indemnification, the VAT is issued as a capital markets instrument, in its ISDA form, as introduced earlier in this chapter. At present, developing an insurance indemnification document to enable insurance companies and brokers to issue a VAT to their customers is ongoing and one of the key ways to distribute the VAT to those client risk-limiters who seek to package their non-core global financial risks into an enterprise-wide risk management scheme. Typically, an enterprise-wide corporate risk management scheme forms the strategy and risks to be bundled and insured by insurance companies. The client risk-limiter's insurance broker is responsible for putting the enterprise-wide risk management package together. Although at present, the insurance executive within major corporations deals with the traditional insurance risks, while financial risks are being managed by the chief financial officer and their treasury department. But as more and more companies seek to bundle their non-core global financial risks into their enterprise-wide risk management policy, the communication process between insurance broker and client companies will hopefully improve, creating an additional distribution segment for VATs.

CONCLUSION

Before we move on to specific case studies, let us summarize all the points of innovation discussed in this chapter. The innovation of the next generation of hedging instrument for global financial risks is certainly far from over. Unlike others in my industry, I believe a great deal has yet to be discovered and invented for the global capital markets. But there will always be a difference between the professionals and non-professionals in the global capital markets and it is that segregation of professional discipline that must be considered in any future new innovative ideas. The act of managing a global company takes a great deal of time and energy today and I am a firm believer that one should focus on what one does best, outsourcing anything that does not form that core business or corporate competency.

In summary, the areas of innovation discussed in this chapter are as follows:

1. the instrument and its creation;
2. the pricing mechanism;
3. the risk distribution process;
4. document processing;
5. investment discipline (underwriting the instrument).

The Instrument and Its Creation

The method for creating a volatility assurance transaction focuses the client or buyer of the instrument on the cost of unforeseen price volatility arising from non-core global financial risks, such as currency translation and transaction exposures, bond and equity portfolios or hard commodities. Think of the unwanted price volatility as a predictable cost of doing business, as part of one's budget costs. The degree of financial protection needed will be a sum of money that management determines to be an acceptable amount of price volatility that can be absorbed within their annual budget forecast (think of that sum of money as volatility deductible as in insurance parlance).

The new method allows the client to take a portfolio of non-core global financial risks and combine them into one instrument. The client pays one premium, for an annual period or multi-year period (like house insurance). The instrument is perfectly correlated with the underlying cash assets or risks. The instruments provide the client with set and forget budget assurance from unforeseen price volatility arising from non-core global financial risks.

The objectives of the instrument are to provide the client with a more hedge-efficient, hedge cost-efficient, counterparty diversified, transparent solution to the problem of protecting against unforeseen price volatility arising from non-core global financial risks.

Turning to accounting objectives, the ability to account for the VAT ISDA instrument permits the client to simply reserve on either side of the volatility collar line rather than marking-to-market a range of derivative instruments which have correlation and hedge deviations. The VAT does not move in value, only the underlying cash assets or risks move in value from quarter to quarter, in contrast to traditional derivative instruments which move in value along with the underlying risks. When a client risk-limiter has many global financial risks to hedge, using many traditional derivative instruments to hedge them, the client's traditional derivative instruments have many moving parts which have to be marked-to-market and valued; this is complicated, inefficient and difficult, and creates unnecessary anxiety for corporate executives. The new VAT takes all of these issues off the table, providing a 'peace of mind' experience for the client.

The final objective is to improve client credit ratings, taking the uncertainty out of unforeseen price volatility arising from non-core global financial risks.

The Pricing Mechanism

The innovative process is needed to create the instrument, because the instrument could not exist without a new pricing mechanism – dynamic pricing through a reverse auction. This instrument enables and empowers the client to receive competitive bids from a wide range of client acceptable financial institutions to be the underwriters for the client's VAT risks. The collar has the attributes of providing a covered call option; pricing can begin with the cost of running a volatility-neutral portfolio; any price movement could be exploited for performance-related returns.

The instrument allows a client to bundle their non-core global financial risks into one instrument; there is value in the bundle and the value of the bundle is in the eye of the beholder.

A financial intermediary can act as the auctioneer, since the number of prospective bidders can number in the hundreds if the client chooses.

The Risk Distribution Process

Using an outsourcing model used by the insurance industry, the entire risk management process and value of the portfolio of global financial risks for the client are outsourced to the underwriting counterparties. The client determines the portfolio of risks, sets the timeframe and volatility deductible, and approves the counterparties for the bidding process.

The client can distribute the risk to the underwriters either by weighted average or layering price volatility. The instrument also allows layering for extreme event management.

Document Processing

The client's VAT can be documented as an ISDA contract. As mentioned earlier, an insurance indemnification contract is also being developed.

Investment Discipline (Underwriting the Instrument)

The business of underwriting the client risks through a VAT allows the underwriting institutions to generate a (premium) fixed fee from the client for taking on the client's risks, along with a performance-related fee or trading revenues from this business activity.

Dynamic pricing through a reverse auction allows underwriting institutions to dynamically price their premium and forecast performance-related revenue streams because the VAT collar attributes provide a covered call option. Pricing can begin by determining the cost of running a volatility-neutral portfolio. Any price movement could be exploited for performance-related returns. Additionally, natural internal hedging can be used because of the precise timing for the VAT pricing.

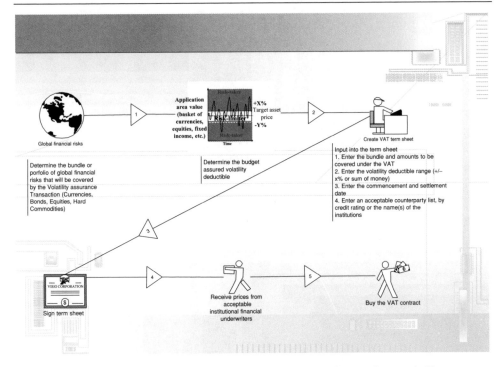

Figure 5.13 The volatility assurance transaction. The easy steps for creating a volatility assurance transaction. First, define the bundle of global financial risks to go into the contract. Second, determine the volatility deductible, the budget impact. Third, input into the VAT term sheet the bundle of risks and the amounts of risk, define the volatility deductible as plus or minus a percentage or as plus or minus a sum of money, and define the list of acceptable parties to underwrite the price volatility of the bundle of risks. Fourth, sign the term sheet. Fifth, conduct a reverse auction to price the VAT contract. Finally, sign the contract with your risk-taking institutional underwriter – and relax

The products created thus far for specific industry problems, using the VAT, are as follows:

- *Corporate.* Currency transaction and translation exposures, an absolute volatility budget assurance for profit and loss and balance sheet risks.
- *Insurance groups.* Equity and bond portfolio reserves, absolute and relative volatility budget assurance for regulatory capital requirements.
- *Pension funds.* Risk budgeting relative volatility budget assurance along with absolute and relative volatility budget assurance.

Additionally, the VAT products can be used by all three industry sectors for:

- *Extreme value theory (EVT).* For extreme events, absolute and relative volatility budget assurance.
- *Value-at-risk.* Bundles of global financial risks, absolute and relative volatility budget assurance.

The VAT provides a 'peace of mind' experience for the risk-limiter client and also provides the underwriter with a new pipeline to generate fees and trading revenues, a win–win proposition for all parties (Figure 5.13).

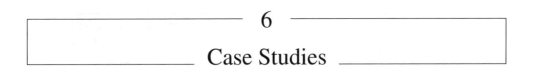

6

Case Studies

I hear and I forget. I see and I remember. I do and I understand.
Confucius

In this chapter I present half a dozen case studies from my early attempts to execute a few concept transactions with a number of clients who gave me the opportunity to gain insight into their global financial risk management, as well as to use the volatility assurance transaction to demonstrate its capabilities.

CASE STUDY ONE – EMERGING MARKET CURRENCIES

The first company in which we were able to generate an interest was a European development bank, based in London, whose report and accounts were denominated in UK pounds sterling. Its core business acumen was investment in growing companies located in developing and emerging market countries. This development bank took an equity position with these companies but had to suffer the trials and tribulations of the foreign exchange rate risks which accompanied its investment.

It had a relationship bank, which was supposed to offer solutions for managing its non-core global financial risks, which in this case were currency risks. The relationship bank did not, however, offer the underwriting capacity that this client required nor the forward foreign exchange and options pricing which would have constituted a sensible solution for the client. The client was losing 5–7% per annum on its foreign exchange exposures. These annual currency losses created a great deal of uncertainly for the treasurer. He never knew what to expect from year to year from foreign exchange risks and therefore could not effectively budget for them. The solutions being offered by the relationship bank, on average, would cost the client more than 10% per annum. The client preferred to accept the foreign exchange misfortunes rather than hedge because the cost of hedging the currency risks was substantially worse than the risk itself.

I met the treasurer of this firm in spring 2002 and found him very receptive to the new instrument, its method, process and solution. He immediately understood the new method for creating the volatility deductible. In fact, when I returned to his office for our second meeting to create a term sheet, we were able to finish the work within thirty minutes. He knew exactly what the volatility deductible would be, which he set at $+1^1/_2\%$ to -1%. He created a portfolio of ten emerging market currencies as follows:

For this portfolio, valued at a total of £214 756 000, he sought a five-year contract term. The reason for the five-year term was his desire to link the currency VAT with the average life of the company's investments in the developing and emerging market countries, which was five to seven years.

He agreed to allow me to seek bids for the term sheet from 15 counterparties; these included global banks, asset management companies, currency overlay investment managers and two hedge funds. When I placed the term sheet out for tender, I did not think that this bundle of

Currency	Amount (GBP equivalent)	Exchange rate vs GBP 31 September 2002
India rupee	64 456 000	70.18
Dominican Republic peso	33 923 000	23.71
South Africa rand	22 610 000	17.4
China yuan	18 550 000	12.04
Costa Rica colon	16 356 000	496.09
St Lucia Caribbean $	16 244 000	3.93
Guyana Guyana $	11 474 000	261.83
Swaziland lilengeni	10 449 000	17.4
Zimbabwe Zim $	10 351 000	80.66
Tanzania shilling	10 343 000	1332.41

emerging market currency risks would attract any bids. A few of the risks had value but some of the others are extremely difficult markets.

However, we asked the fifteen institutions to price and bid for the client risks outlined above – note the simplicity of the term sheet, the new methodology which creates the weighted average bundle of global financial risks, the volatility deductible (volatility collar), in other words, the acceptable budget price volatility arising from the unforeseen price volatility of developing and emerging market currencies. And the last item for the term sheet is the settlement date, in this case the contract will commence 1 October 2002 and settle 31 September 2007. It is this simple, with the actual term sheet looking like the one introduced in the previous chapter, and the details of the contract as shown in Figure 6.1.

The outcome of the bidding process was a surprise. We received bids ranging from 1.5% premiums to as high as 5.3% for the bundle of currency risks. The winning bidder was a major global bank. The complete outcome delivered to the development bank client was as follows:

Type of fee	Amount (%)
Underwriting fee	1.50
Financial engineering fee	1.50
Client deductible (adverse)	1.00
Total	4.00

Because the term of the VAT contract is five years, the worst-case annual cost (taking into account the client's adverse deductible price volatility) for the client development bank would

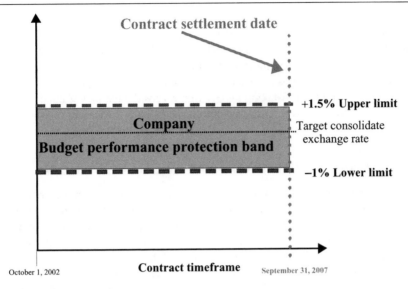

Figure 6.1 Emerging market currency example

be 0.80% per annum set and forget budget assurance. If the price volatility of the bundle of currencies were to settle at the top end of the volatility deductible, the annual set and forget budget assurance cost would be 0.30% per annum.

Instead of an uncertain 5–7% currency price volatility cost to the client development bank, it achieved a set and forget budget assurance VAT contract which enabled it to bundle ten emerging market currencies into one instrument for a five-year period. This enabled the client to budget for the cost of emerging market currency exposures for the next five years in much the same way as one budgets for labour costs.

After this initial concept transaction I was able to complete the following approach comparison between the traditional hedging instruments and the new approach using a volatility assurance transaction. The new VAT approach provided the client development bank with a much less expensive solution in terms of premiums paid. There is no hedge deviation, and the number of transactions was one instead of at least ten. The counterparty risks were reduced because the client was able to receive pricing from a wider array and number of counterparty bids instead of just their relationship bank, which could not deliver a solution anyway. Management time for putting this transaction in place was limited to hours of work at the outset of the fiscal year instead of an ongoing day-to-day ordeal for the next five years. The experience of using a VAT instrument was very pleasing for the client.

	Traditional	The VAT
Total cost	Expensive	Up to 50% reduction
Hedge deviation	Options – YES	NO
Counterparty risk	YES	Much reduced
Management time	Exhausting	Limited

In terms of the bidding process, we learned that the VAT instrument truly allows the risk underwriter to value the bundle of risks in terms of their own requirements. Remember that the

VAT is not a forward foreign exchange agreement, nor an options contract in the traditional sense, but allows one to value the bundle in terms of one's own internal requirements. In this case, the global bank used this particular VAT to fund local country reserves that it needed to hold in its emerging and developing market bank depots.

The client thus received exactly what they needed, a set and forget budget assurance for the next five years, and the risk taking underwriter received what they wanted, a way to fund local country reserves in a very cost-efficient manner. It was a win–win transaction for both parties.

CASE STUDY TWO – BALANCE SHEET RISKS

In Case Study One, the client development bank was hedging its currency risks against its balance sheet investments in developing and emerging markets. At this stage I did not recognize the difference between hedging a balance sheet and hedging an income or profit and loss statement. Because the client in Case Study One matched their hedging settlement date with their investment horizon, I was not able to distinguish between the two types of risk. It was not until I met our next company that I was able to make the distinction.

The client this time is a regional electricity company. It was investing in foreign electricity companies in Central and South America as well as in the United Kingdom. It invested over $1.2 billion, but had been making enormous foreign exchange losses for many years on its overseas investments. From information supplied, it was evident that these losses amounted to around 10% per annum on the investment, or about $100 million per year.

Both this case study and the previous one involved balance sheet management, because an equity investment in foreign countries comes from the balance sheet and not the income statement. The difference between them is that the electricity company did not have a timeline or expectation of when it would liquidate its investments overseas. The development bank of Case Study One estimated that its investment would be sold within five to seven years, therefore its currency VAT contract was lined up with its investment profile.

The electricity company used value-at-risk to analyze the future potential currency price volatility for one year, using the previous year's historical price volatility as the measure to calculate the future potential price volatility. Since the previous year's volatility was about 10%, the next year's volatility was 10%.

Since the investment portfolio was losing so much money from foreign exchange risks, the board of directors stopped making or adding to their overseas investment portfolio. They did not hedge their currency risks related to this investment portfolio because of the cost of the relevant options strategies, which did not necessarily hedge their currency price risks anyway. They asked us for help, and I duly prepared a term sheet for a six-currency portfolio with a volatility deductible of $\pm 10\%$ per annum.

While presenting the term sheet to the client, a problem arose. Where would the company find the money to pay to the risk-taking underwriters if it had to make a payment?

The company's balance sheet does not have the cash to make a payment, only the income or profit and loss statement has the cash available. The client company wanted a set and forget budget assurance instrument, but the balance sheet risks did not allow it to be created, at least at that time. If the client company had to make a payment to the risk-taking underwriters, since they were not realizing their overseas investments, there would be no natural cash available. Therefore, the payment to the underwriters had to come from the income statement. But the problem with relying upon the income statement for the cash payment from the client company to the underwriters is that the size of the potential payment is an unknown quantity. Therefore, the set and forget budget assurance characteristic is not met. The uncertainty of the payment and the amount of the payment prevented the transaction from happening.

The answer to this problem came to me later when I was working on another problem. When creating a VAT for balance sheet global financial risks, we merely have to add a currency basket (matching the currency basket of the client) call option. If a payment needs to be made from the client company to the underwriters, the call option will generate the necessary cash. When purchasing the call option, the client company achieves set and forget budget assurance, the premium paid is the only sum of money that the client has at risk, and therefore it is budgeted and forgotten.

CASE STUDY THREE – INSURANCE COMPANY RESERVES (A BOND PORTFOLIO)

One of the ways I have been introducing the new VAT, along with its method and process, is through banks. As I mentioned in Chapter 1, there are two types of commercial bank: those that focus on proprietary trading as their main source of revenue, and those that focus on fee-generating activities. The latter are bundling more and more products and services together in an effort to maintain their client relationship. It is these banks that I originally approached. They need more products and services and, as discussed in Chapter 1, many of them lack the ability to innovate, research and develop new products and services. The bank I was working with at this time was of this type.

One of its European insurance clients came to it with a problem in early summer 2003. The problem stemmed from the changes in insurance regulations that I discussed in Chapter 2. This insurance company had €14.5 billion of insurance reserves invested in European bonds. Their head of reinsurance was seeking protection against the bond price volatility which he was concerned would take the form of adverse price movements, because interest rates in the United States and elsewhere were soon to rise.

In the past, insurance companies in Europe were permitted to buy and hold bonds as part of their reserve accumulation. They did not have to mark-to-market the bond portfolio, but regulation is changing to a risk-based capital requirement for insurance companies throughout Europe. Additionally, after the 'perfect storm' years, many insurance groups sought to raise capital and repair their balance sheets. Many saw their credit ratings fall, which adversely affected their ability to underwrite preferable risks from creditworthy clients as these took their business to more creditworthy insurers. During this period, those insurers who saw their credit rating fall wanted to rebuild their balance sheets in an effort to restore their credit ratings as quickly as possible. Needless to say, a fall in insurance reserves weakens the ability to gain a higher credit rating.

Our case study insurer's credit rating fell in the aftermath of 11 September 2001. Its business plan for the next four years was to rebuild its reserves, and therefore regain its higher credit rating. The company came to the bank seeking to limit or manage its bond portfolio price volatility to ensure that its value would not fall dramatically as interest rates rose. They did not have the in-house expertise to figure out how to manage this for themselves, let alone to hedge it professionally, never having had to manage it in the past. The bank did not have an in-house solution to help its client, so it asked me.

The client's requirement to limit the price volatility of their bond portfolio would neatly fit into a bond VAT. Unfortunately, this transaction never took place, but the characteristics of the client, the problem that they faced, along with the products available to cope with the problem, are exactly why the VAT is needed. What is more unfortunate is that since summer

2003, the global bond markets have been selling off, and bond market values have been falling and will continue to fall as interest rates rise in the United States and Europe. The bond VAT would have saved this particular European insurance company perhaps as much as €1 billion of capital losses on its bond portfolio.

CASE STUDY FOUR – AN EQUITY VOLATILITY ASSURANCE TRANSACTION

I was approached by the finance director of a UK insurance company with a problem to which his several relationship banks could not offer a solution. UK tax rates on insurance company investments differ between fixed-income and equity dividends: fixed-income coupons or interest received are taxed at 30%, while UK equities are subject to a 10% withholding tax on dividends received. The client was seeking to maintain UK fixed-income price volatility while at the same time receiving equity dividends.

One would think of a transaction of this nature as seeking the Holy Grail, particularly since the insurance company must physically invest in the equities to receive the benefit of the equity dividend. The client could not create a synthetic equity investment nor use a derivative of an equity portfolio in an effort to take advantage of the income tax differentials.

We were able to create a solution for the client, the term sheet for which is illustrated in Box 6.1. The entire transaction was to be taken through a reverse, or Dutch, auction process, and all the constituent parts of the transaction – the sale of the UK fixed-income portfolio; the purchase of the UK equity portfolio using the proceeds from the sale of the UK fixed-income portfolio; the purchase of an equity VAT with a 0% volatility deductible; and the repurchase of the UK fixed-income portfolio one year forward – were to take place simultaneously. Then, at settlement date, one year on, the equity VAT contract would be settled and the UK equity portfolio sold, using the proceeds from the sale of the equity portfolio to repurchase the UK fixed-income portfolio at the price fixed at the transaction date (the year before).

BOX 6.1 UK FIXED-INCOME/UK EQUITY INCOME SWAP TRANSACTION

OVERVIEW:

1. The investment objective is to add investment income on behalf of [UK Insurance Company] arising from switching from a money market or UK Gilt-Edged Bond investment to equity dividends, with absolutely no equity price volatility.
2. At [ ] London Time [ ], the client [ ], will invest the proceeds arising from funds invested in fixed-time assets into a UK equity portfolio weighted and described in this term sheet in the schedule below.
3. Simultaneously, the client [ ] will purchase an Equity Volatility Assurance Transaction described in this term sheet below with a value date of [ ].
4. Simultaneously, at [ ] London Time [ ], the client, [ ] will repurchase the [UK fixed income portfolio] with a value date of [one year forward]; at which time, one year forward, the client, [ ], will sell the 10 equally weighted UK FTSE 100 stocks with a value date of [ ] and reinvest the equity proceeds into the fixed-income portfolio, settling the Equity Volatility Assurance Transaction.

EQUITY VOLATILITY ASSURANCE TRANSACTION

INDICATIVE TERMS AND CONDITIONS

This term sheet sets out the indicative terms and conditions of the transaction described below. References in this term sheet to ISDA® shall be deemed to be made to the International Transactions and Derivatives Association, Inc. Certain capitalized terms used in this term sheet are based on the definitions and provisions contained in the 2002 ISDA Equity Derivatives Definitions and in the 2000 ISDA Definitions, as amended and supplemented (as published by ISDA®) (the 'Definitions'). In the event of any inconsistency between the Definitions and this term sheet, this term sheet will govern.

OVERVIEW:

1. This term sheet sets out the basic terms of an equity transaction on a share basket, intended to provide 'set-and-forget' protection against the value of the share basket falling from its initial base value. Under the transaction: (i) the Equity Amount Payer [the client] pays the Risk Taker an amount calculated by reference to the positive return of the Share Basket if the final level of the Share Basket is above 100 (the base value of the Share Basket being equal to 100); (ii) the Equity Amount Payer receives from the Risk Taker an amount calculated by reference to the absolute value of the negative return of the Share Basket if the final level of the Share Basket is below 100. No payment is made by either party if the level of the Share Basket on the Final Valuation Date is exactly 100.
2. The transaction (as is described in this term sheet) does not require the transfer of ownership of the Share Basket. Dividends are not to be transferred to the Risk Taker. [The client] is not required to lend the components of the Share Basket.

Transaction:	[Share Basket Transaction]
Trade Date:	[ ] London Time [ ]
Premium:	•
Premium Payment Date:	•
Start Date:	[ ]
Initial Valuation Date:	The Start Date[a]
Final Valuation Date:	[ ][b]
Expiration Date:	The Final Valuation Date
Exercise Date:	The Expiration Date
Automatic Exercise:	Applicable[c]
Settlement:	Cash Settlement applies[d]
Cash Settlement payment provisions:	On the Cash Settlement Payment Date, (i) the Risk Taker shall be entitled to receive from [the client] the Cash Settlement Amount where the Final Basket Price is greater than 100; (ii) [The client] shall be entitled to receive from the Risk Taker the Cash Settlement Amount where the Final Basket Price is less than 100; or (iii) if the Final Basket Price is equal to 100, no payment shall be made by either party.

Cash Settlement Payment Date:	Three Business Days following the Final Valuation Date[e]
Share Basket:	As described in the Schedule.
Cash Settlement Amount:	Means an amount in GBP calculated on the Final Valuation Date in accordance with the following: If the Final Basket Price is:

(i)   greater than 100; or
(ii) less than 100 Lower Basket Price; or
(iii) Equal to 100 then no payment.

Initial Basket Price:	Means an amount in GBP calculated as the aggregate of the Initial Share Amounts.
Initial Share Amounts:	Means, in respect of each Share in the Share Basket, an amount in GBP determined as the product of (i) the Number of Shares, and (ii) its Initial Share Price.
Initial Share Price:	Means, in respect of each Share in the Share Basket, the price per Share at transaction determined by the Risk Taker in consultation with THE CLIENT as at [ ] London Time on the Initial Valuation Date.
Final Basket Price:	Means an amount in GBP calculated as the aggregate of the Final Share Amounts.
Final Share Amount:	Means, in respect of each Share in the Share Basket, an amount in GBP determined as the product of (i) the Number of Shares, and (ii) its Final Share Price.
Final Share Price:	Means, in respect of each Share in the Share Basket, the closing price per Share on the Exchange at the Valuation Time on the Final Valuation Date.
Number of Shares:	Means, in respect of each Share in the Share Basket, the number of shares set out in the table described in the Schedule.
Valuation Time	In respect of each Share in the Share Basket, the close of trading on the Exchange.
Exchange:	In respect of each Share in the Share Basket, as set out in the Schedule in relation to each Share.
Other terms:	●
Risk Taker:	●
Calculation Agent:	●
Documentation:	ISDA
Arranger:	Global Financial Risk Solutions Limited

Disclaimer

This term sheet is indicative only and is subject to change without notice. We do not represent that it is complete or accurate. This term sheet does not constitute an offer or an agreement, or a solicitation of an offer or an agreement, to enter into any transaction. No assurance is given that any transaction on the terms indicated can or will be arranged or agreed.

Before entering into any transaction, you should consider the suitability of the transaction to your particular circumstances and independently review (with your professional advisers as necessary) the specific financial risks as well as the legal, regulatory, credit, tax and accounting consequences.

Schedule

The Share Basket

Share	ISIN	Exchange	Percentage of portfolio
United Utilities	•	The London Stock Exchange	5%
Lloyds TSB	•	The London Stock Exchange	12%
Bradford and Bingley	•	The London Stock Exchange	5%
Scottish Power	•	The London Stock Exchange	10%
Sainsbury's	•	The London Stock Exchange	10%
Scottish and Southern	•	The London Stock Exchange	10%
Severn Trent	•	The London Stock Exchange	5%
Aviva	•	The London Stock Exchange	9%
Shell	•	The London Stock Exchange	8%
Dixons	•	The London Stock Exchange	4%
HSBC	•	The London Stock Exchange	8%
BAT	•	The London Stock Exchange	9%
Boots	•	The London Stock Exchange	5%

[a] Valuation Dates are subject to standard ISDA® postponement provisions in the event of non-Scheduled Trading Days or market disruption.

[b] It is being assumed that there is a single Final Valuation Date, following which, there will be a single payment to the party entitled to receive the Cash Settlement Amount.

[c] If Automatic Exercise applies, neither party needs to deliver notice of exercise and the party obliged to pay the Cash Settlement Amount on the Cash Settlement Payment Date shall do so without further request from the other party.

[d] If Cash Settlement applies, the transaction shall not entitle any party to deliver or take delivery of any security or underlying asset. It shall be settled with a cash payment calculated in accordance with the relevant formula.

[e] It is risky to set a fixed Cash Settlement Payment Date in relation to equity derivative transactions given that Valuation Dates are subject to postponement in the event of market disruption. We recommend setting the Cash Settlement Payment Date as a date falling a number of Business Days after the Final Valuation Date.

The client agreed to a list of counterparties with which to conduct the market pricing through the reverse auction process. As with the first case study transaction, the reverse auction that was conducted through an inter-dealer broker (inter-dealer brokers are securities brokers that trade between banking institutions who are either selling off or wanting to buy financial risks of one kind or another) was fascinating to watch, and the result surprised us all. The reverse auction was conducted on the basis of the entire transaction being priced and carried out by one winning bidder (the client-approved list of risk-taking banking institutions). The pricing was based on the cash flow pick-up between the UK fixed income and the equity dividend income. For example, if a bid came back offering the client £250 000, this meant that the benefit that the client received would be £250 000 of after-tax income over and above what they would have received by remaining invested in UK fixed income for the fiscal year ahead. We conducted two reverse auctions, the first to see what would happen, and the second was the actual competitive bidding from the approved counterparties.

During the first auction the best bid was £250 000, but after we introduced further competitive bidding, the actual benefit for the client rose to £1 million. The transaction size was £100 million, therefore the actual benefit to the client was a full 1% of additional cash flow revenues. It was a successful outcome for the client and an interesting way to use and implement an equity VAT.

The UK insurance company received exactly what it was seeking: protection against UK fixed-income price volatility while receiving UK equity dividend income for the fiscal year commencing 1 April 2004 and ending 31 March 2005.

CASE STUDY FIVE – A GLOBAL BANK USING A CURRENCY VOLATILITY ASSURANCE TRANSACTION

As I mentioned earlier, one of the ways in which I sought to introduce volatility assurance transactions was through existing client–bank relationships, particularly on behalf of those banks whose income derives from fee revenues. In this case study, the client was a global bank and it in turn would issue a mirror VAT contract document to its client.

This particular global bank was beginning to penetrate the Spanish corporate market, and many Spanish corporates have Latin American currency risks. The bank does not have a core competence in managing and pricing Latin American currency risks, therefore I helped it by creating a currency VAT which enabled it to offer its Spanish client a competitive product and pricing for their emerging market currency exposures in Latin America.

The term sheet for this transaction was as shown in Box 6.2.

**BOX 6.2   CURRENCY VOLATILITY ASSURANCE TRANSACTION
CURRENCY TRANSACTION EXPOSURES**

INDICATIVE TERMS AND CONDITIONS

This term sheet sets out the indicative terms and conditions of the transaction described below. References in this term sheet to ISDA® shall be deemed to be made to the International Swaps and Derivatives Association, Inc. Certain capitalized terms used in this term sheet are based on the definitions and provisions contained in the 2002 ISDA Equity Derivatives Definitions and in the 2000 ISDA Definitions, as amended and supplemented (as published by ISDA®) (the 'Definitions'). In the event of any inconsistency between the Definitions and this term sheet, this term sheet will govern.

OVERVIEW:

1. This term sheet sets out the basic terms of a currency transaction on a Currency Basket, intended to provide 'set-and-forget' protection against the value of the Currency Basket falling from a certain initial base value. Under the transaction: (i) The Global Bank Client pays the Risk Taker an amount calculated by reference to the positive return of the Currency Basket if the final level of the Currency Basket is above 105% of its initial value; and (ii) The Global Bank Client receives from the Risk Taker an amount

calculated by reference to the absolute value of the negative return of the Currency Basket if the final level of the Currency Basket is below 95% of its initial value. No payment is made by either party if the level of the Currency Basket on the Final Valuation Date is less than or equal to 105% and greater than or equal to 95% of its initial value.

2. The transaction (as is described in this term sheet) does not require the transfer of ownership of the Currency Basket.

Transaction:	[Currency Basket Collar Transaction]
Trade Date:	•
Premium:	•
Premium Payment Date:	•
Start Date:	1 January 2005
Initial Valuation Date:	The Start Date[a]
Final Valuation Date:	31 December 2005
Expiration Date:	The Final Valuation Date
Exercise Date:	The Expiration Date
Automatic Exercise:	Applicable[b]
Settlement:	Cash Settlement applies[c]
Cash Settlement payment provisions:	On the Cash Settlement Payment Date, (i) the Risk Taker shall be entitled to receive from The Global Bank Client the Cash Settlement Amount where the Final Basket Price is greater than the Upper Basket Price; (ii) The Global Bank Client shall be entitled to receive from the Risk Taker the Cash Settlement Amount where the Final Basket Price is less than the Lower Basket Price; or (iii) if the Final Basket Price is greater than or equal to the Lower Basket Price and less than or equal to the Upper Basket Price, no payment shall be made by either party.
Cash Settlement Payment Date:	Three Business Days following the Final Valuation Date.[d]
Currency Basket:	As described in the Schedule.
Cash Settlement Amount:	Means an amount in Euros calculated on the Final Valuation Date in accordance with the following: If the Final Basket Price is:

    (i)   greater than the Upper Basket Price, an amount equal to the excess of the Final Basket Price over the Upper Basket Price; or

    (ii) less than the Lower Basket Price, an amount equal to the excess of the Lower Basket Price over the Final Basket Price; or

    (iii) less than, or equal to, the Upper Basket Price and greater than, or equal to, the Lower Basket Price, zero.

Upper Basket Price:	105% of Initial Basket Price.

Lower Basket Price:	95% of Initial Basket Price.
Initial Basket Price:	Means an amount in Euros calculated as the aggregate of the Initial Currency Amounts.
Initial Currency Amounts:	Means, in respect of each Currency in the Currency Basket, an amount in Euros determined as the product of (i) the Number of Currencies, and (ii) its Initial Currency Price.
Initial Currency Price:	Means, in respect of each Currency in the Currency Basket, the price per Currency on the Exchange determined by the Risk Taker in consultation with The Global Bank Client as at [ ] London Time on the Initial Valuation Date.
Final Basket Price:	Means an amount in Euros calculated as the aggregate of the Final Currency Amounts.
Final Currency Amount:	Means, in respect of each Currency in the Currency Basket, an amount in Euros determined as the product of (i) the Number of Currencies, and (ii) its Final Currency Price.
Final Currency Price:	Means, in respect of each Currency in the Currency Basket, the closing price per Currency on the Exchange at the Valuation Time on the Final Valuation Date.
Number of Currencies:	Means, in respect of each Currency in the Currency Basket, the number of Currencies set out in the table described in the Schedule.
Valuation Time	In respect of each Currency in the Currency Basket, the close of trading on the Exchange.
Exchange:	In respect of each Currency in the Currency Basket, as set out in the Schedule in relation to each Currency.
Other terms:	•
Risk Taker:	•
Calculation Agent:	•
Documentation:	ISDA
Arranger:	[Global Financial Risk Solutions/Regulated Entity]

Disclaimer

This term sheet is indicative only and is subject to change without notice. We do not represent that it is complete or accurate. This term sheet does not constitute an offer or an agreement, or a solicitation of an offer or an agreement, to enter into any transaction. No assurance is given that any transaction on the terms indicated can or will be arranged or agreed. Before entering into any transaction, you should consider the suitability of the transaction to your particular circumstances and independently review (with your professional advisers as necessary) the specific financial risks as well as the legal, regulatory, credit, tax and accounting consequences.

Schedule
The Currency Basket

Currency	Euro Currency Amounts
Brazilian real (BRL)	€1 951 000 000
Chilean peso (CPL)	€551 000 000
Peru new sol (PNS)	€305 000 000
US dollar (USD)	€380 000 000

[a] Valuation Dates are subject to standard ISDA® postponement provisions in the event of non-Scheduled Trading Days or market disruption.

[b] If Automatic Exercise applies, neither party needs to deliver notice of exercise and the party obliged to pay the Cash Settlement Amount on the Cash Settlement Payment Date shall do so without further request from the other party.

[c] If Cash Settlement applies, the transaction shall not entitle any party to deliver or take delivery of any security or underlying asset. It shall be settled with a cash payment calculated in accordance with the relevant formula.

[d] It is risky to set a fixed Cash Settlement Payment Date in relation to equity derivative transactions given that Valuation Dates are subject to postponement in the event of market disruption. We recommend setting the Cash Settlement Payment Date as a date falling a number of Business Days after the Final Valuation Date.

To prepare the global bank to sell a VAT to its client, I spent time with the bank's sales personnel, teaching them the new method and process.

After consultation with their client, they asked me to create a term sheet for €3 187 000, made up of Brazilian real, Chilean peso, Peruvian new sol and US dollars. The client wanted ±5% volatility deductible for a one-year term. To price this bundle of euros I sought bids through a reverse auction. Once it was priced, the global bank would add a profit margin for itself and issue the currency VAT contract to the client. My client is the global bank and the counterparty risk is between the global bank and the ultimate risk-taking underwriter. This is a process that is very similar to the insurance and reinsurance market.

One risk-taking underwriter made a bid of 5.5%, meaning they would charge the client a 5.5% premium on the portfolio value of €3 187 000. This particular underwriter would only underwrite 25% of the total risk, €796 750 of the total portfolio. However, risk-taking underwriters are not permitted to cherry-pick the risks they want from the portfolio. If they only want 25% of the risk they can only underwrite a weighted average of the total portfolio.

However, another major global bank came in with a bid of zero; they were prepared to take the client risk on for nothing. I was not privy to the reason for their price, but one can assume that they had an internal or natural hedge against the terms of this currency VAT contract.

CASE STUDY SIX – PENSION FUND SOLUTIONS

I do not yet have a specific client for a pension fund case study; rather, I will discuss a number of pension fund scenarios that articulate the problems and market solutions, including, where applicable, VAT instruments and solutions.

The fundamental problem for a defined-benefit plan is not having enough money invested in appropriate assets which will ensure that future liabilities – promises made to the pensioner – are met. This problem will have to be solved by the corporate sponsor of the pension fund. However, there are a number of fundamental asset and liability problems. The assets of the pension fund scheme have been accumulating from corporate sponsor and pensioner cash flows going into the fund, which are then invested in the global capital markets to ensure that they provide a real rate of return to ensure that the pensioners receive their benefits, such as two-thirds of their final salary at retirement date. If interest rates fall during the investment cycle of the pension fund scheme, the value of the investments will generally rise in value; however, the cost of liabilities will rise because as interest rates fall, the company scheme must use more money to fund its pensioners' final benefits. And, of course, vice versa as interest rates rise. There are solutions to the pension fund problems. Thorne and Bektas's[1] outline of the traditional solutions to the stated pension scheme problems is given in Table 6.1.

The traditional solutions to the observations and problems in Table 6.1 are very good, but in the spirit of the VAT technology of easy-to-use and easy-to-understand instruments and solutions to the problems outlined, there are a few alternatives to the traditional solutions.

In observation 1 in Table 6.1, the pension scheme has a low proportion of its assets in bonds, resulting in a large sensitivity to interest rates and inflation as these impact liability values, and thus has an asset allocation which is not in line with its liability costs. In other words, it has an asset–liability relative volatility risk. There is a relative risk between the value of the pension fund asset return on investment and the liability costs; as the asset returns rise and fall, those return or portfolio values do not correlate or move in relation to the changes in liability costs.

I hope that you will recall from previous chapters that interest rate movements affect the assets and liabilities of the pension fund scheme. When interest rates rise, asset values fall while liability costs fall, and vice versa if interest rates fall. Think about the extreme movements in asset values and liability costs that will cause a catastrophic outcome in the scheme's asset–liability relationship. There is a break-even point as interest rates are moving up or down when the assets of the pension fund scheme are in balance or equal to the expected pension fund liabilities – determining this break-even and managing the relative volatility risks relative break-even point can be achieved.

Once this dynamic movement between asset values and liability costs is determined, a relative VAT can be put in place which lays off the outside extreme movements in asset values and liability costs (recall Figure 5.10). The VAT solution will allow the pension scheme to manage the relative volatility between the asset values and liability costs. If there is a concern that interest rates may move adversely, set the relative VAT at those levels.

In observation 2 in Table 6.1, the scheme is heavily reliant on equity returns and has no protection from declines in equity prices or from equities underperforming the liabilities. In this case, simply use an equity VAT to protect the downside, but do not forget that the client must set a downward adverse level in conjunction with the upward price volatility boundary. This equity VAT solution could also be used in conjunction with the relative solution discussed above. In isolation, the equity VAT is an absolute price volatility solution and instrument. Using an absolute VAT in isolation to the liability cost risks could cause greater risk for the scheme in its ability to meet its liability costs.

In observation 3 in Table 6.1, the scheme has large holdings of index-linked gilts but wishes to earn higher returns by taking a prudent level of credit risk. The traditional solution, to replace the index-linked gilt portfolio with corporate bonds (rating and risk profile decided by the trustees) and inflation swaps, may make sense for many, but the cost of the annual inflation

---

[1] Robert Thorne and Serkan Bektas, 'The Role of Investment Banks', *Pensions Week*, 29 November 2004.

Table 6.1   Examples of pension fund asset/liability issues and solutions

Observation	Perceived obstacles to solving the issue	Potential enhancements the pension scheme might consider
1. Pension scheme has a low proportion of its assets in bonds, resulting in a large sensitivity to interest rates and inflation as these impact liability values.	• Desire not to adversely impact the contribution requirements. • Concerns about lack of liquidity, high dealing costs, loss of exposure, loss of exposure to high return assets.	• Construct a bond portfolio with the desired return characteristics and utilize each cash flow timing swaps to address the liability matching requirements. • Consider matching liabilities with interest rate and inflation swaps (i.e., if desired, without modifying the physical investment portfolio). • Transition out of equities into bonds when the equity and fixed income market returns meet predefined relative value guidelines.
2. Scheme is heavily reliant on equity returns and does not have any protection from declines in equity prices or from equities underperforming the liabilities.	• Lack of appetite to divert part of the asset portfolio to fixed income, partly due to the issues listed above and partly due to a concern that this would lock in a low point in the equity markets.	• Utilize equity options to bound the range of potential returns. Mitigate or eliminate downward risk while keeping exposure to equity markets up to and beyond the funding valuation assumptions under a nil-premium combination of options. • Use products that combine liability and equity behaviour, permitting equity risk-taking relative to the liabilities.
3. Scheme has large holdings of index-linked gilts but wishes to earn higher returns by taking a prudent level of credit risk.	• Limited liquidity in the corporate index-linked bond market and overall concern that the supply of index-linked products is insufficient.	• Consider replacing the index-linked gilt portfolio with corporate bonds (rating and risk profile decided by the trustees) and inflation swaps.
4. Scheme considering implementing a large portfolio reallocation out of equities into bonds (right away or when equity, interest rates, inflation markets reach predefined target levels).	• Concern about implicit and explicit costs of transitioning. Lack of comfort with the prevailing market levels and desire to capture an improved market environment.	• Structure of transition mandate that leads to the portfolio reallocation being implemented over time according to the guidelines established by the scheme. • Utilize outperformance options to monetize the exposure and return the scheme decides to forgo by virtue of the trigger levels established for transitions.
5. Scheme considering investing in alternative assets such as hedge funds, emerging market funds or commodities.	• Lack of familiarity with the underlying asset classes and/or the investment approach. Concern that the investment comes with risks that are not well understood by the scheme. • Poor liability matching characteristics of these assets.	• Invest in alternative assets through liability-matched products or by putting a bond return floor on the investment returns. • Portable alpha products that translate excess performance generated by alternative assets to liability outperformance.

swap must not be greater than the additional coupon flows received by the fund by investing in corporate bonds. If this is the best course of action or solution for a pension scheme, perhaps think about using a VAT for extreme adverse movements in corporate debt, in the event that the value of the corporate bond portfolio falls dramatically in value. This can occur when interest rates are rising and the business cycle causes companies' profitability to fall, causing yields or values of the corporate bond portfolio to fall more than government bonds. If the event did occur, the yield spread between government bonds and corporate bonds would widen. The use of an extreme volatility VAT to manage the extreme valuation levels could be helpful to prevent this type of event. Once again, an upward band would have to be determined in conjunction with the adverse or lower band to the VAT solution. However, the object of the investment exercise is to enhance income flows from higher-yielding bonds versus government bonds, which means that the capital or principal price movements can be managed and contained from adverse absolute or relative value volatilities.

In observation 4 in Table 6.1, where a pension scheme is considering implementing a large portfolio reallocation out of equities into bonds (right away or when equities, interest rates, or inflation reach predefined target levels), the use of a risk budgeting VAT might provide the right solution.

> The goal of risk budgeting is to optimize risk by 'spending' each unit of risk efficiently; not to hold down any particular element of market risk at the expense of the overall risk profile of the portfolio. Allocating investment dollars is an important tool but it ignores the need to efficiently allocate risk appetite and to reflect the changing dynamics of risk. Asset allocation emphasizes return, out-performance, and P&L flows. Risk budgeting adds another dimension: it is a function of volatility and correlation as well as a function of dollars. Constant assets in a risk budgeting framework can result in widely fluctuating risk. Risk budgeting is an optimization exercise. All else being equal, an investor who maximizes risk-adjusted performance will perform better than one who does not.
>
> While risk budgeting and risk-adjusted return management need not necessarily go hand-in-hand, they usually do. Risk budgeting enables a plan sponsor to evaluate the portfolio contribution of various exposures to risk. The first step is to determine current risk exposures. Once a plan sponsor has developed the ability to measure the risk of each of its managers and strategies, using the risk measure as the denominator of the risk-adjusted return equation is a simple and powerful next step. The ultimate accomplishment in the process is to have risk as the basis of 'strategic risk management.'
>
> Risk budgeting alone – or any single approach for that matter – is not the answer. An organization needs a disciplined approach to risk, one that includes the quantitative aspect but does not rely exclusively on it. We believe strongly that only about one-third of the components of a good risk management approach are quantities.'[2]

The risk budget VAT solution is similar to the relative volatility solutions described earlier, but in this case the scheme would like to manage the relative performances between the equity portfolio and the ultimate preferred bond portfolio. In this case, the scheme must determine the overall pension fund asset allocation resulting from the final asset allocation from equities to bonds. Once the final portfolio allocation volatility has been determined, overlay a VAT solution on top of the present asset allocation, which is concentrated in equity investments. The overlay risk budget VAT will prevent the fund from hedging the potential adverse fund value movements during the time of the major asset reallocation. The VAT contract terms will settle on the date when the actual and final asset allocation from equities to bonds is completed.

---

[2] Capital Market Risk Advisors (CMRA), Leslie Rahl, http://www.cmra.com/html/risk_budgeting.html

In observation 5 in Table 6.1, the pension scheme is considering investing in alternative assets such as hedge funds, emerging market funds or commodities. I do not have a VAT solution for this type of allocation – an absolute VAT can be constructed around the returns of the alternative investment, but the point of an alternative investment such as hedge funds, emerging markets or commodities is to acquire the total return-on-investment that this specific asset class offers the pension fund scheme.

However, a pension scheme may want to consider an investment in a pool of capital that is participating in underwriting the pension fund relative or absolute VAT solutions and instruments. This is similar to a total return fund, and I described the investment discipline that arises from underwriting VAT contract risks in Chapter 5. Therefore, an investment in this type of pooled investment will offer an attractive return and does not correlate with other risks or assets held in an investment portfolio. By investing in a VAT investment pool, the pension scheme is also playing a part in creating greater pools of liquidity for the pension fund industry for those who seek to manage or lay off absolute and/or relative volatilities using VAT technology.

7

Conclusion

The objective of this book has been to describe the way in which the traditional capital market pipeline works, and the way in which corporates, insurance companies and pension funds presently manage their non-core global financial risks using the traditional risk management instruments known as derivatives. The regulatory environment is changing in generational proportions; the introduction of corporate governance laws and new accounting regulations, coupled with insurance and banking industry capital regulatory requirements, is moving us towards a risk-based capital structure.

In the midst of the traditional capital market derivatives for managing global financial risks, introducing a new and radically changed regulatory environment has opened the door for much needed financial risk management innovation. As quoted in the Introduction, Mr Greenspan suggested that there is a need for the private sector to come up with new ways of bundling or unbundling global financial risks and to invent a new business process in which to transfer those in a more hedge-efficient, cost-efficient, transparent and counterparty-diversified manner. The volatility assurance transaction technology is designed to address this need.

Recall the findings of the recent Fitch Ratings company survey cited in Chapter 3.[1] Each one of the survey conclusions demonstrates the difficulty of using traditional derivative instruments and their effect on the new reporting standards being implemented. The VAT technology addresses each one of the survey's four conclusions.

1. As discussed, the VAT instrument can be structured to manage both income statement and balance sheet global financial risks. I believe that the solutions described in this book do not affect the income statement, whether one is hedging the balance sheet or income statement. The set and forget budget assurance characteristics remove the uncertainty of any hedging payments from the client to the underwriter. The risks, along with the solution outcome, are quantified at the outset of the contract period, and the uncertainty of hedge deviation and risk mitigation outcomes is removed.
2. Globalization means doing more business around the world, but it also means that the company will have greater amounts of various global financial risks, such as interest rates, in the various countries, foreign exchange exposures with each country and, depending upon one's home country, hard commodity purchases for manufacturing the product plus the additional currency risks when purchasing the hard commodity in US dollars.
3. The disclosure problem can be remedied by means of a volatility assurance transaction, which is easy to understand, easy to use and easy to account.
4. A perfectly correlated hedging instrument in line with underlying cash assets or risks solves the problem of restatement risk. There is no restatement if the underlying cash assets are valued correctly because the VAT instrument will not move in value as it is in perfect correlation with the cash assets.

---

[1] 'Hedge Accounting and Derivatives Study for Corporates,' Fitch Ratings, 23 November 2004.

I have spent nearly four years developing the VAT technology and hope that my findings and ultimate conclusions are of value to the reader. I have attempted to demonstrate that global financial risks should be tackled only by professional capital markets risk managers, and that the VAT technology offers an effective way in which to outsource global financial risks and at the same time receive set and forget budget assurance against unforeseen price volatility arising from them. The alternative is the status quo and, as we can see from the daily financial press, the traditional derivative instruments fail to deliver the 'peace of mind' experience that many industry leaders outside of the global capital markets are desperately seeking.

References

CHAPTER 1

Peter L. Bernstein (1996) *Against the Gods*. New York: John Wiley & Sons, Inc., p. 1.

'HSBC chairman warns price war looms for world's banks,' *Financial Times*, 3 August 2004, p. 1.

Simon Kwan, 'Industry Risk – Mega banks Pose System Risks,' Global Association of Risk Professionals, *Risk News*, 18 June 2004.

'Largest banks by market capitalization, July 2004,' *The Banker*, 2 July 2004.

'The largest banks by assets, June 2004,' *The Banker*, 2 July 2004.

'Gentlemanly words as co-chief bows out,' Financial Times, 25 June 2004, p. 29.

'Deutsche Bank's Dilemma: Fight or Join U.S. Titans?' Wall Street Journal, 16 June 2004, p. 1.

'More banks are asking rivals to handle currency trading,' *Wall Street Journal* Online, 28 July 2004.

Tanya Azarchs, 'The dark side of bank consolidation,' Standard & Poor's Rating Direct Report, 27 May 2004.

'Seven US banks have lion's share of derivatives,' *Risk* Online, July 2003.

'The ultimate stress test: modelling the next liquidity crisis,' *Risk* Online, November 2003.

'Corporate Loan Demand Tumbles,' *Financial Times*, 21 June 2004, p. 21.

'Banks – the coming storm,' *The Economist*, 21 February 2004, p. 83.

'Trading wars,' *The Economist*, 28 August 2004, p. 13.

'Deutsche Bank: A giant hedge fund,' *The Economist*, 28 August 2004, p. 65.

'Capital markets arm of Citigroup in UK has accumulated losses of $960 million,' *Financial Times*, 16 August 2004, p. 1.

'VaR: Ready to Explode?,' *Risk* Online, July 2004.

'FSA issues stern warning to bank bosses over conflicts of interest,' *Financial Times*, 25 September 2004, p. 2.

'Basel II for Dummies,' Global Association for Risk Professionals, 28 June 2004.

'Impact of new BIS standards on Japanese banks,' in *Japan Markets Outlook and Strategy*, JP Morgan Securities Asia, 28 July 2004.

'Reality check on Basel II,' *The Banker*, 1 July 2004.

'World foreign exchange trading soars to peak of $1,900bn a day,' *Financial Times*, 29 September 2004, p. 1.

CHAPTER 2

Peter L. Bernstein (1996) *Against the Gods*. New York: John Wiley & Sons, Inc., p. 8.

Mary Pat McCarthy and Timothy Flynn (2004) *Risk from the CEO and Board Perspective*. McGraw-Hill, p. 113.

Philippe Jorion (2003) *Financial Risk Manager's Handbook*, 2nd edn, Chichester: John Wiley & Sons, Ltd, p. 265.

'International Capital Markets,' IMF, August 2001.

'How a Singapore Fuel Company Lost $550 Million in Oil Trading,' *Wall Street Journal* Online, 3 December 2004.

'Singapore hit by new $550m trading scandal,' *Financial Times*, 2 December 2004, pp. 1 and 26.

John Digenan, Dan Felson, Robert Kelly and Ann Wiemert, *Metallgesellschaft AG, A Case Study*, http://www.stuart.iit.edu/fmtreview/fmtrev3.htm

Gary Klopfenstein and Alex Koh (1997) *Foreign Exchange: Managing Global Currency Risk – The Definitive Handbook for Corporations and Financial Institutions*. Glenlake.

'Powerhouse currencies make waves in their homelands,' Market Insight, *Financial Times*, 24 June 2004, p. 48.

'Vicious circle of hedging continues to weigh on dollar,' Market Insight, *Financial Times*, 29 July 2004, p. 42.

'Corporate disclosures,' *Risk* Online, April 2002.

'Q1 scapegoats: Energy and weather,' *Risk* Online, July 2002.

'Real problems' *Risk* Online, January 2003.

Ford Motor, Inc., 2001 Annual Accounts, p. 42.

Doron Levin, 'Ford Motor Blows $1 Billion on Palladium Trading,' http://www.turtletrader.com/ford_palladium.html, 28 January 2002.

'US insurers lose $24 billion on bond investment,' *The Times* Online, 21 October 2003.

'Global Financial Stability Report, Market Developments and Issues,' IMF, April 2004, p. 77.

Michael Hyman (2004) *The Power of Global Capital: New International Rules – New Global Risks*, Thomson Publishing, pp. 81, 86, 94.

'Risk management for insurance companies, "A new regulatory world"' *Risk* Online, August 2004.

'Inquiry inflames Equitable row,' *Financial Times*, 9 March 2004, p. 1.

'Investors Face Lean Times as Payouts Fall,' *Financial Times*, 23 February 2004, p. 4.

'Life Assurers Face Tighter Rules on Fund Management,' *Financial Times*, 26 June 2004, p. M28.

'Standard Life Sells $7.5bn Shares,' *Financial Times*, 19 February 2004, p. 19.

'The Hunt for Yield Hots Up: Investors and Pension Funds Plunge Deeper into Illiquid and Riskier Assets,' Comment & Analysis, *Financial Times*, 22 July 2003, p. 15.

'Pensions black hole is threat to profits,' *Financial Times*, 28 July 2003, p. 1.

'Pensions crisis to cost $27 billion a year,' *The Times,* 11 November 2003, p. 1.

'Public sector pension deficit hits $580bn,' *Financial Times*, 11 August 2004.

'Share rises fail to fill pensions black hole,' *Financial Times*, 17 January 2004, p. 1.

'Weekly Review of the Investment Industry,' *Financial Times*, 26 January 2004, p. 1.

Martin Wolf, 'Through the demographic window of opportunity,' *Financial Times*, 29 September 2004.

'Work longer, have more babies: How to solve Europe's pension crisis,' *The Economist*, 27 September 2003, p. 13.

Martin Wolf, 'Europe must grow up if it wants to be taken seriously,' *Financial Times*, 10 November 2004, p. 17.

The Pension Puzzle, IMF, March 2002.

'Funds gamble pensioners' money,'*Financial Times,* Weekly Review Of The Investment Industry, 26 January 2004, p. 1.

'Companies double their payments to pensions,' *Financial Times*, 11 April 2004, p. M1.

'Companies failing to plug pension shortfall,' *Financial Times*, 22 July 2004, p. 2.

'US Pensions Agency Issues Warning,' *Wall Street Journal* Online, 7 October 2004.

'Benefits or Bailout,' *Financial Times*, 3 September 2004, p. 15.

'GM Nearly Closes Pension Gap,' Reuters Online, 12 December 2003.

'Funds may move £150bn from equities,' Financial Times, 27 May 2004, p. 3.

'Time to end a scandal,' *The Economist*, 30 October 2004, pp. 14 and 15.

CHAPTER 3

Mary Pat McCarthy and Timothy Flynn (2004) *Risk from the CEO and Board Perspective*. McGraw-Hill, p. 85.

Alan Greenspan, American Bankers Association Annual Convention, 5 October 2004.

'Global Financial Stability Report, Market Developments and Issues,' IMF, April 2004, pp. 90 and 92.

'Seven US banks have lion's share of derivatives,' *Risk* Online, July 2003.

'The ultimate stress test: modelling the next liquidity crisis,' *Risk* Online, November 2003.

'Derivative disclosure calls mount,' *Risk* Online, April 2003.

'The lunatic you work for,' *The Economist*, 8 May 2004, p. 80.

'Corporate [Mis]governance,' *CFA*, May/June 2004, front cover.

'Understanding Corporate Governance,' *Financial Times*, 5 September 2003, p. 11.

'Does Sarbanes–Oxley Hurt Shareholders and Hide Poor Management?' *Risk News*, The Global Association of Risk Professionals, 19 November 2004.

'Average US group Face $5m Compliance Bill,' *Financial Times*, 12 November 2004, p. 33.

'German Groups Rue US Listings,' *Financial Times*, 19 November 2004, p. 47.

'Understanding IFRS,' *Financial Times*, 29 September 2004, p. 2.

'ASB Tells UK Companies to Ignore EU Ruling on Accounting Standards,' *Financial Times*, 12 October 2004, p. 1.

'Corporate reporting shake-up faces delay,' *Financial Times*, 14 October 2004, p. 1.

'Thickening fog over accounting row,' Editorial, *Financial Times*, 14 October 2004, p. 18.

'Summary of Statement 133,' Financial Accounting Standards Board, June 1998.

'Corporate Risk Management In An IAS 39 Framework,' Guy Coughlan, JP Morgan & Risk, pp. 5 and 6.

'Hedge Accounting and Derivatives Study for Corporates,' Fitch Ratings, 23 November 2004.

'Corporate Governance,' Part 1, *Financial Times*, 5 September 2003, p. 11.

'Understanding Corporate Governance,' Part 3, *Financial Times*, 16 January 2004, p. 9.

Global Financial Stability Report, 'The Revised Basel Capital Framework for Banks (Basel II),' IMF, September 2004, pp. 70 and 71.

Philippe Jorion (2003) *Financial Risk Manager's Handbook*, 2nd edn, Chichester: John Wiley & Sons, Ltd, p. 339.

'Lufthansa Seeks a Clearer View,' *Risk* Online, 4 August 2004.

Rexam Annual Report & Accounts 2003, p. 3.

'Canny Hedging Gives Rexam 14% Profits Rise,' *Financial Times*, 26 August 2004, p. 19.

'Risk Management For Insurance Companies,' Special report, *Risk*, August 2004, p. 16.

Paul Clarke, paper presented to HSBC seminar on 'FSA compliance for insurers,' *Insurance Regulations Change – The Integrated Prudential Sourcebook*, London, 27 January 2004.

'A capital solution,' *Risk* Online, July 2004.

'After a year of US corporate clean-up, William Donaldson calls for a return to risk taking,' Interview in the *Financial Times*, 24 July 2003, p. 15.

CHAPTER 4

Benoit B. Mandelbrot (2004), *The (Mis)Behaviour of Markets*. Profile Books, pp. 3, 13, 208, 229, 234, 254–255.

B. Joseph Pine II and James H. Gilmore (1999) *The Experience Economy*. Boston: Harvard Business School Press.

John Nugee and Avinash Persaud, 'The dangers of being risk-averse,' *Financial Times*, 17 September 2004, p. 19.

Mary Pat McCarthy and Timothy Flynn (2004) *Risk from the CEO and Board Perspective*. McGraw-Hill, p. 113.

Richard G. Barlow, 'The Net upends tenets of loyalty marketing,' *Advertising Age*, 17 April 2000.

CHAPTER 5

Clayton Christensen (1997) *The Innovator's Dilemma*, Harvard Business School Press.

'International Capital Markets,' IMF, August 2001, p. 4.

CHAPTER 6

Robert Thorne and Serkan Bektas, 'The Role of Investment Banks,' *Pensions Week*, 29 November 2004.
Capital Market Risk Advisors (CMRA), Leslie Rahl, http://www.cmra.com/html/risk_budgeting.html

CHAPTER 7

'Hedge Accounting and Derivatives Study for Corporates,' Fitch Ratings, 23 November 2004.

Index